THE QUEEN'S
CHAMELEON

Figure 1: John Byrom in 1762

THE QUEEN'S CHAMELEON

The Life of John Byrom
A Study of Conflicting Loyalties

Joy Hancox

JONATHAN CAPE
LONDON

by the same author
THE BYROM COLLECTION

First published 1994

1 3 5 7 9 10 8 6 4 2

© Joy Hancox 1994

Joy Hancox has asserted her right
under the Copyright, Designs and Patents Act, 1988
to be identified as the author of this work

First published in the United Kingdom in 1994 by Jonathan Cape
Random House, 20 Vauxhall Bridge Road, London SW1V 2SA

Random House Australia (Pty) Limited
20 Alfred Street, Milsons Point, Sydney,
New South Wales 2061, Australia

Random House New Zealand Limited
18 Poland Road, Glenfield,
Auckland 10, New Zealand

Random House South Africa (Pty) Limited
PO Box 337, Bergvlei, South Africa

Random House UK Limited Reg. No. 954009

A CIP catalogue record for this book
is available from the British Library

ISBN 0-224-03047-7

Typeset by SX Composing Ltd, Rayleigh, Essex
Printed in Great Britain by
Mackays of Chatham PLC, Chatham, Kent

The web of our life is of a mingled yarn, good and ill together: our virtues would be proud if our faults whipped them not; and our crimes would despair if they were not cherished by our own virtues.

Shakespeare, *All's Well That Ends Well*

Contents

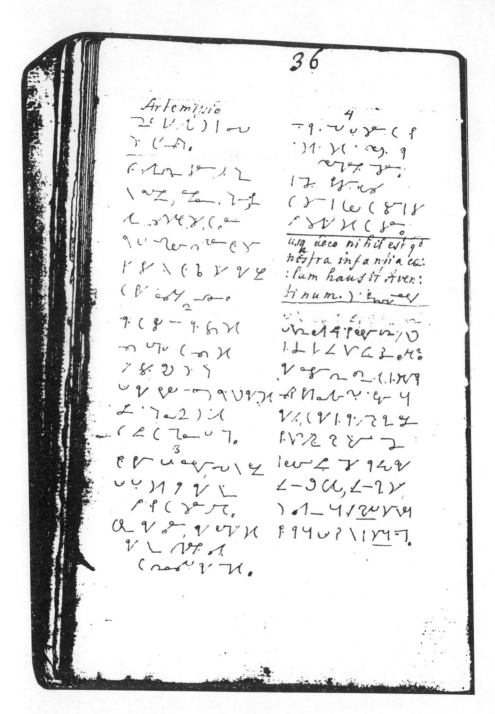

Figure 2: 'Artemissia' in shorthand

Illustrations

Acknowledgments

I would like to thank H.J.S. Clarke for making the Byrom short-hand manuscript book available for so many years. Without his generosity of spirit my book would not have been possible.

To the staff of Jonathan Cape I express my gratitude, in particular Tom Maschler and Pascale Hutton, but above all my editors, Tony Colwell and Pascal Cariss, for their perceptions and sensitivity. Special thanks are again due to my agent, Anne Dewe of Andrew Mann Ltd, for her characteristic energy, care and commitment.

I would like to acknowledge the Reverend Neville Barker Cryer, Past Grand Chaplain and Past Master of the Quatuor Coronati Lodge for his informed assistance with masonic material, and Charles Carter, Secretary of the Quatuor Coronati Correspondence Circle, for making the lodge's records and publications available to me.

I must also acknowledge my husband, Allan. Throughout this long quest I have had the benefit of his intellect and scholarship.

Many have contributed to this project in either a professional or private capacity since it began in 1971: Mark Ash, Allan Barlow, T.D. Bishop, William Clowes, Margaret and Michael Darlington, Ann Evans, Wing-Commander Gordon Haywood, Dr Neil Hopkinson, Miles Huntington-Whiteley, Brian Lawn, Mike Leber, Richard Leigh, Betty and Helen Macdonald, Sir Robin Mackworth-Young, Adam McLean, Dr Alan Moreton, Elaine Ogden, Malcolm C. Pittam, Dr Michael Powell, Ruth Robinson, John Robson, Ann Smith, Jackie Stanton, David Taylor and V.I. Tomlinson. A number of those who helped have since died, but I would like to honour their memory here: Major L.A. Clowes, Mary Marriott M.B.E., Bill and Muriel Millner, Alan Francis Philpotts, Sir James Pitman, Alan Smith and W.H. Thomson.

I owe a special debt to Byrom Studios, Salford, for their photographic help, Kall Kwik, Manchester, who prepared many of the illustrations, and Alison Swinnerton for her secretarial skills.

I am indebted to many institutions for their co-operation and help: the university libraries at Bath, Cambridge, Manchester, Oxford and Tübingen; the British Library and the specialist collections at Chetham's Library, Manchester, the Guildhall Library, the Grand Lodge Library, London, the Royal Library, Windsor, the Royal Society and the Science Museum Library, London; Manchester Central Library and Salford Local History Library; the Public Record Offices at Chancery Lane and Kew, and the Chetham Society for its invaluable series of scholarly publications.

I would also like to thank the following for permission to reproduce illustrations: the British Library, Schweighardt C.44.d.5. (pl. 10); © British Museum (pl. 12); H.J.S. Clarke (figs 2 and 5); the Controller of Her Majesty's Stationery Office, Adm.39.352 Naval Records 1727/8 (fig. 8); Manchester Central Library (pls 4 and 6; fig. 3); by courtesy of the National Portrait Gallery, London (pls 7 and 8); The Royal Collection of Her Majesty the Queen (pl. 13); City of Salford Museums and Art Gallery (pl. 11); Westminster City Archives (fig. 4). Figs 6, 7 and 9 are in private possession. (The remaining illustrations are owned by the author.)

To all the others who have contributed and are too numerous to mention I am also deeply grateful.

Unexpected Beginnings

EARLY IN 1969 I discovered that my house in Salford had once been a farm with a long history. In 1729 the tenant farmer had been Thomas Siddal, and his tenancy lasted until 1745, the year of the second Jacobite rising. Siddal turned out to be a Jacobite himself and the son of a Jacobite, also named Thomas. The father, a black-smith by trade, was executed for his part in the first Jacobite rebellion of 1715 on behalf of the Old Pretender, James Stuart. His head had been stuck up on a pike in Manchester as a warning to other likely rebels. Thomas junior was then a boy of seven, but not so young as to be terrified into submission. In 1745 he rallied to the cause of the Young Pretender, Prince Charles Edward Stuart, and served as his Ensign in the Manchester Regiment. Arrested in Carlisle and tried in London, he suffered the same fate as his father thirty years before: his head was also sent back to Manchester to be exhibited on a pike.

I wanted to know more about the two Siddals, father and son. What was it that made them readily face being hanged, drawn and quartered? Why did they remain loyal to a cause others abandoned or were prepared to betray?

While Siddal was in prison awaiting trial in 1746, an anonymous letter was sent from Manchester to the Secretary of State, the Duke of Newcastle, which said:

> If Tom Siddal was to be examined (tho I think he would prove very stiff) it wd not be amiss, for it's certain that fellow knows enough to save 20 such heads as his.[1]

Efforts to get this information from him failed and he took his knowledge with him to the grave. What was this secret?

I turned my attention to John Byrom, a fellow-townsman and contemporary who had kept a detailed journal. Byrom was reputed to have been a secret Jacobite, and in 1748 was denounced in a pamphlet by the Reverend Josiah Owen as the 'master-tool' of the Manchester faction. Perhaps his diary contained references to Siddal that might lead me to an answer.

The journal comprises four volumes. I found the first reference to Siddal in an entry for October 1736, when Byrom and he were sitting together in St Ann's coffee house in Manchester, sharing the latest copy of *The Grub Street Journal*. This, together with other entries, showed that the two men knew each other. If, then, the accusations about Byrom's Jacobite sympathies were correct, how had he managed to escape detection? Before I could find an answer to this question, another emerged. Repeated through the journal I found the word 'extract' before an entry or one of the many letters interspersed. Why had the papers been edited? If they were in some way 'indiscreet', then what was left was a distortion of the truth. *The Private Journal and Literary Remains* of John Byrom was first published in 1854, ninety-one years after his death. It was paid for by his great granddaughter, Eleanora Atherton, the last of his descendants, a spinster who had inherited the accumulated riches of one of Manchester's foremost families. Any omissions, therefore, must have been with her insistence or approval.

The Journal proper begins in October 1722 and ends in 1744. The rest of the four volumes is made up of a miscellany of letters dating from his childhood until just before his death, some scholastic papers and a few of Byrom's own poems. They deal with his days at school and Cambridge, his time in London and his final years in Manchester. All this material constitutes the first source for any biography, but the omissions render it unsatisfactory.

The editor, Richard Parkinson, an Anglican canon and antiquarian, described the journal as a 'simple narrative of the daily doings of an extraordinary man'. Was it really as simple as he would have us believe? The fact that it was edited belied this, a suspicion confirmed when I learnt that the original manuscripts were said to have been burned on the instruction of Miss Atherton.

Why would Miss Atherton, evidently so proud of John Byrom, insist on the destruction of his writings? The manuscripts, written in Byrom's own system of shorthand, had been transcribed by her personal companion, Sarah Bolger, over a period of thirty years. It seemed unlikely that she would have readily acquiesced in destroying the source of a life's work. Of course, if the manuscripts contained revelations Miss Atherton considered indelicate, then they might have to be destroyed. Surely only some such overriding reason could be behind the burning of this unique record.

Byrom's extensive collection of books had been left by Eleanora Atherton to Chetham's Library in Manchester. The Librarian, Dr Powell, showed me a letter quoting Canon F.R. Raines as the source of the tradition that the papers had been burned. Francis Robert Raines was a local worthy well known to Miss Atherton; the order, therefore, was probably genuine. But was it carried out? Eleanora died in 1870, leaving a number of charitable bequests, some of which were still in operation. She left her private papers to Sarah Bolger, who had worked for her for more than thirty-five years, becoming her indispensable companion and private secretary. With a handsome legacy from her former employer, Sarah duly retired to Bournemouth where she built a house called 'Atherton' and lived in some style until her death in 1889.

As an executor to her own will Sarah Bolger appointed Mary Anne Degge, who had been lady's maid to Eleanora Atherton. She had won the affection and trust of both women, for each left her legacies. Sarah instructed that 'the said Mary Anne Degge shall have all my letters and papers including those bequeathed to me by Miss Atherton'.[2] This shows that she made a conscious decision to ensure that certain papers inherited from Miss Atherton did not fall into the hands of the main inheritors of the Byrom estate.

After a prolonged search which took me from country churchyards to stately homes, I found that Mary Anne Degge had taken up service with the Macdonald family. At one time they had lived close to Miss Atherton's town house – Mary had no doubt entered the family simply by moving next door. One of their ancestors was the legendary Flora Macdonald who helped Bonnie Prince Charlie to escape after the failure of the 1745 uprising. Each trail I followed arrived at the '45 rebellion and advocacy of the Jacobite cause. Had Sarah Bolger entrusted certain papers to Mary Anne Degge because of the sympathies of the family for whom she was working?

Mary died in 1926, at the age of ninety-three. It was frustrating to discover that she had left no will and I have not been able to find evidence that any papers left to her by Sarah Bolger survived. All that remains are a family prayer book and a silver fruit knife engraved with her name, given to her by Eleanora Atherton.

The other beneficiaries of Sarah's will were her two sisters, who received legacies of money; a cousin, Simon Wall, who also received a gift of money, and finally another cousin, Richard Wall, to whom she bequeathed 'the residue and remainder of my property of every description'.[3] Among this was a collection of books and manuscripts, some of which had belonged to Byrom.

When I investigated these bequests, various Byrom relics came to light: a small diary kept by Byrom's sister, Sarah Brearcliffe, with an account of his last weeks; a sketch-book used by his granddaughter Ann; a wallet belonging to his son Edward and commemorating his father's death, and several pieces of shorthand written by Byrom himself, of which the most significant was a page from the Journal, the entry for John's birthday in 1728.[4] Why should this of all pages have survived? A third of the page had been omitted from the published version and this gave some indication of the probable scale of the total omissions.

None of the other main beneficiaries of Eleanora Atherton's estate produced the missing manuscripts of the Journals. Although fresh shorthand material emerged from different sources during these investigations, it looks as if manuscripts of the Journals were indeed destroyed.

Among Sarah's bequests I did find a number of leather-bound manuscript notebooks written by Byrom in shorthand. One in particular caught my attention. Roughly bound in book form, it was in fact several notebooks combined. The rough and ready appearance of the pages, with crossings-out and corrections, showed it was original source material. The book had been well used and carefully preserved. It bore the name of John Houghton, who was Byrom's literary editor and brother-in-law. Shortly before Byrom died, his daughters and friends started to collect some of his poems together for publication. Houghton took over the task and arranged the contents of the two-volume edition of 1773. The material their father had acquired was retained by Houghton's three spinster daughters until 1817, when it was returned to Eleanora Atherton.[5]

The first ten pages of this manuscript book are blank; pages 11 to 45 contain a sequence of poems deliberately separated off from the rest of the book (Group A). They are followed by 54 more blank sheets. Pages 101 to 210 contain poems known to have been written by Byrom (Group B). The rest of the book is blank except for an Index to Group B and two short poems on the final page. Group A was in fact written in a single notebook which has been sewn in with the others. The titles of poems often have personalised subheadings, and there are Latin quotations interspersed between the poems. These devices link the subject matter of the verses intimately together and show one man's overall view in the structure and planning of this section.

A number of manuscripts written in both shorthand and longhand by Byrom have survived apart from this notebook and help to establish its authenticity. The Index in longhand at the back included titles of poems in the 1773 edition, but it did not contain any reference to the pages of shorthand poems in the first part. These were a mystery waiting to be deciphered.

With a rare copy of Byrom's shorthand manual I was able to compare the poems in Group B in the notebook with the published versions. In this way I could see how Byrom applied the principles of his system and learn the idiosyncrasies of his own shorthand script. Since the new material is confined to one section in the volume (pages 11-45), it may be regarded as a self-contained sequence. When deciphered, they appear to tell the story of an encounter between the poet and a woman, the poet's deep love and his eventual disillusion as the affair turns sour. Interspersed are one or two short poems, mostly epigrams, dealing with public events. These may have been placed in the sequence as a reminder of the ways of the world, almost like a counterpoint to the personal ambitions and unhappiness of the poet.

Byrom's first published pieces appeared in *The Spectator*. The poem 'A Pastoral' (also known as 'My Time, O ye Muses') was published anonymously and essays on Dreaming under the name of John Shadow, a *nom de plume* he liked to use. In part Byrom was following a convention of his age, but he practised subterfuge in many guises, and evasiveness was an important element in his character. He appears to have enjoyed the success of his poems almost like a bystander, relishing the speculation about their authorship. However, this can cause problems for a biographer. Often his verses were attributed to other writers, including friends, for years after his death. In 1773 John Houghton found it necessary to reassure readers of the first edition that the poems were 'the genuine productions of Mr Byrom ... carefully transcribed from his own Manuscripts.'[6] The newly discovered notebook confirms his authorship of the poems in it.

Byrom collected an impressive library of 3,327 books and 41 manuscripts which reveal the breadth and depth of his learning and interests. It was housed at Kersall Cell, the country home in Salford which he enjoyed in his later years, and it remained there for more than a century. In 1848 Miss Atherton arranged for a catalogue to be privately printed as a record of its treasures. When she died she bequeathed it to Chetham's Library, stipulating that it should be 'set apart kept and distinguished as "The Byrom Library" ... unmixed with the other books of the Governors though open for public inspection'.[7]

However, the catalogue makes no mention of Byrom's Journal (the manuscripts of which Miss Atherton ordered to be destroyed), nor of the shorthand manuscripts of poems and Byrom's miscellaneous sheets of shorthand, nor even, curiously, of a copy of his shorthand manual. Clearly she considered all these to be a separate issue.

It is fortunate that some of this material has survived through the careful preservation by Sarah Bolger. No doubt the birthday page was kept as a reminder of the years she had spent transcribing the Journal, and as a proof of Byrom's shorthand writing. The notebook contained material which Sarah, for some reason, could not bear to see destroyed. Eventually it went by default to her main beneficiary, instead of Mary Anne Degge for whom it was intended but who, by then, could not be traced.

Byrom had an inborn facility for verse-making and, apart from a large output of devotional verse, produced many light poems of a purely autobiographical nature. It is not surprising, therefore, to find fresh autobiographical material in the unpublished notebook. What is unusual in the first section is the depth of the passion expressed and, at times, the tone of bitter disappointment. Apart from his role in a doomed relationship, the poems reveal Byrom's connection with a select group of men with Masonic and Templar associations and his own covert political ambitions.

If the extraordinary story these poems tell is true and is placed in the context of what is already known about Byrom, then for the first time the full horror of the tragedy of an idealist tempted into intrigue which destroyed all he held dear can be seen.

CHAPTER ONE

Early Years
1691/2–1718

JOHN BYROM was an enigma, a playboy, a philosopher, a poet and possibly a spy. The many facets of his character present a dazzling complexity, and his apparent aplomb soon reveals hidden depths which invite investigation. The power, influence and knowledge he acquired in so many areas during his shorthand career in London are constantly surprising. For example, in May 1725* he writes in his Journal:

> I went to Richard's at seven, where I found a note from Mr. Leycester to come immediately to Thompson's coffee-house, about something that would be of advantage to us both in particular and shorthand in general; when I came there the business was, they wanted to know what the secret was that I had mentioned to Clowes would fall the Stocks, which I was particularly loth to tell them, and thought much about it; at last I hinted to them that the congress at Cambray would break up upon the separate agreement between Spain and Germany; but they were not satisfied with my answers, nor I with their questions, so I came away.

Here he is, dancing a curiously evasive minuet with two of his closest friends, a Cheshire squire, Ralph Leycester, and his cousin, the lawyer Joseph Clowes. They have summoned him on the pretext of

---

* For the greater part of Byrom's life, the calendar in Great Britain was still based on the Julian Calendar or Old Style (O.S.) system. In 1752 Pope Gregory XIII's reformed calendar was finally adopted by both church and state. This is known as the New Style (N.S.) system. Eleven days had to be dropped from the calendar to bring it into line with the actual year, and New Year, which had previously been celebrated on 25 March, now began on 1 January.

This changeover sometimes leads to confusion in calculating dates. For example, Byrom was born on 29 February 1691 Old Style, but 1692 New Style.

wanting to help promote his shorthand, when what they really want is inside information about the state of the stock market. Byrom, unwilling to divulge what he knows, attempts to put them off with vague hints – and the party breaks up. How could he be in a position to foretell a crash in stocks? This is just one example of how the confidentiality surrounding his shorthand turned him into a privileged insider, confidant of the rich and powerful.

Byrom's life is full of paradoxes. He was successful and wielded great influence through his work and the friendships it brought, but he never owned his own house and died possessed of little material wealth. This must have been by choice. For a man who led a double life it was necessary to travel light. Yet he could ride out to a secret meeting in Derbyshire with the Duke of Devonshire and play the peacock when he chose. Like a chameleon, he adapted well to his surroundings.

He was cloaked in mystery. As well as his vast library, he owned a unique collection of drawings which can only be described as source material for serious purpose and prolonged investigation. He used them with some of the leading intellects of the day, including the President of the Royal Society, Sir Hans Sloane. Yet much of this work was done *sub rosa* in his aptly named Cabala Club. The material had a long and ancient pedigree containing such luminaries as Sir Robert Boyle and John Dee. How did Byrom come to be its guardian? And why was all his work buried in silence after his death? Why is there so little mention of it in the voluminous Journals? The formidable hoard of shorthand material, the collection of drawings and his experiments with codes were hidden from the world for generations. Despite, or perhaps because of, the presence of a literary executor, all this was suppressed. So much so that one is left wondering whether there was not a deliberate campaign to blot out certain areas of his life, to prevent posterity from reading between the lines of those heavily edited diaries in order to hide some grave truth – Siddal's truth – some event or series of events of which Byrom was part and which affected him deeply. Certainly the bitterness evident in some of the unpublished material that has recently come to light is so marked that it speaks of a profound shock to his psyche which cannot easily be accounted for simply by thwarted ambition or even an unhappy love affair.

The truth about John Byrom summons up Scott's lines in his poem 'Marmion':

> O what a tangled web we weave,
> When first we practise to deceive!

It is time to untangle that web.

The Byrom family coat of arms displays three hedgehogs and the motto 'Frustra per plura', an abbreviation of 'It is vain to use more means to achieve one's end when less effort will do', a rather laid-back sentiment which belied the energy the Byroms expended in gaining their wealth. They were typical of the industrious gentlefolk who spent their lives in business and trade. At the turn of the fifteenth century, Manchester was already important as a centre of commerce. As clothiers, fullers and woollen manufacturers, the Byroms were one of the great merchant families of the town. They became the chief dealers in wool in the north-west as well as importers of iron. In building their fortunes, they laid the cornerstone for Manchester's prosperity in the Industrial Revolution.

Edward Byrom, John's father, was a linen merchant, who ran his business from a property called the Shambles. Hard-working although not always strictly accurate in his measures (he was fined several times for using a clothyard too short), he extended the family business with a warehouse in London, and made sufficient money to buy Kersall Cell, a picturesque Tudor house by the side of the River Irwell, which became the family's country home when John was five months old. He overstretched himself, however, by further purchases of land, for when he died suddenly in August 1711 he left an estate burdened with debt.

Uncle Joseph was far more successful. Starting as an apprentice to a silk merchant, with fourpence in wages at Christmas 'if he demanded it', he amassed a large fortune, bought the ancestral home, Byrom Hall, and a chariot and two horses for his wife, Elizabeth. Other extensive purchases of land included some in Manchester which enabled him to join the undertaking to link the town by water to Liverpool and thus increase Manchester's outlet for trade. When his brother Edward died, Joseph bought the Shambles property to enable legacies to be met.

John was born into a family with one elder brother and four sisters; two more girls followed. He received his early education at home, and his love of learning developed rapidly. In his early teens he was sent to King's School, Chester, where his true potential soon showed itself, and he was transferred to Merchant Taylors' School in London, in preparation for Cambridge. Grateful to his father for the opportunity to study, but fearful of disappointing him, he was anxious to point out that he was a year behind his peers at the school and less likely to get into Cambridge. Always industrious, as his father demanded, he wrote home to reassure him that he was doing his best. He entered Trinity in July 1708 and the following year won a college scholarship worth £14. Sensitive and artistic, despite his success he admitted in a letter: 'I want sadly to hear from Lancashire'. But he soon settled into a life at Trinity where the Master, Richard Bentley, was already infusing the students with greater zeal for their studies than had been shown for generations. As an undergraduate John Byrom was dutiful and undoubtedly brilliant. He became a favourite of Bentley. His intellectual horizons widened and his aptitude for language soon showed itself. Apart from Classics, he was reading French, Spanish, and Italian; later he added Hebrew and Dutch. He also showed a mind of his own. When the university refused to license a sermon preached in Great St Mary's, Cambridge, he obtained a copy from the London publisher to see what the fuss was about. The large issues of the university life appealed to him more than expanding the family business.

For relaxation he turned to music and loved the sonatas of Corelli so much that he asked his father for a spinet. He was told to stick to algebra. He caused further displeasure by paying a guinea to have his wig altered in London. His father ordered him to have his wigs made up from his sisters' good hair in Manchester.

By his late teens Byrom appeared to be on course for a brilliant career in the Church, when his father died. His elder brother Edward, now twenty-four, took over the business and their father's debts and found himself obliged to pay a legacy of £300 to John in instalments. The death was a shattering blow to the whole family. Business kept Edward for much of his time in London looking after the warehouse. John had always been a favourite with his sisters. The young women doted on him when he returned from Cambridge during the vacations, and he learned the complexities of the female character from the long hours spent in their company. Sarah, his younger sister, gives one of the earliest pictures of Byrom as a young man. In a letter of October 1712, she tells how he spent part of the summer:

> Brother John is most at Kersall; he goes every night and morning to the waterside, and bawls out one of Tully's orations in Latin so loud they can hear him a mile off; so that all the neighbourhood

thinks he's mad, and you would think so too if you saw him. Sometimes he thrashes corn with John Rigby's men, and helps them. He is very good company, and we shall miss him when he is gone which will not be too long now; Christmas is very near.[1]

Sarah describes him as 'very good company' and undoubtedly his frank open nature won him many friends wherever he went. Despite the worries of the burdened estate and John's enviable freedom from the family business, Edward was on good terms with him. He even found time to send John more sheet music[2] and helped him with his college expenses. At times Edward's kindness must have been strained, as when John wrote lamenting that he had no black suit to wear in mourning for Queen Anne![3] The brothers were very different. John's talents seemed ideally suited for the life of a scholar in eighteenth-century Cambridge, leading perhaps to being head of a school or master of a college, but for all these positions he would have to take Holy Orders.

Unfortunately events outside the university put an end to such ambitions. Towards the end of 1713 Queen Anne fell dangerously ill and the matter of her succession raised an awkward question for some of her subjects. James II, the last Catholic King of England, had been deposed in the Glorious Revolution of 1688. After his death in 1701, the Oath of Abjuration required all clergy of the Church of England and holders of public office to renounce 'the Pretended Prince of Wales' (the son of James II) and his claims to the throne. When George I succeeded Anne in 1714, the Oath was re-introduced to strengthen his succession. For some the old idea of the divine right of kings was dead, but for others the Oath posed a serious moral dilemma. Could the hereditary right to rule and ties of personal allegiance be set aside at will? In 1714 Byrom was faced with these questions when (against severe competition) he was elected a Junior Fellow. Only a few months before the Queen died he was confiding his scruples to John Stansfield, the manager of the Byroms' London warehouse:

But this Oath – I am not satisfied so well as to take it, nor am I verily persuaded of its being unlawful; it has always been the custom of nations to set aside those whom it was found not for the good of the public to reign.

He repeatedly put off making a decision, for he could appreciate the argument of the new Establishment:

The Queen and Parliament have settled the succession in a Prot-
estant family, and made what provision they can for our religion
and liberties, and why must we not be content?[4]

John had felt the kindling of Jacobite sympathies when he was a
youth of seventeen in his first year at Cambridge. On 5 November
1709 – the anniversary of Guy Fawkes's attempt to blow up Parliament and also of the landing of William of Orange at Torbay – a
High Churchman, Dr Henry Sacheverell, preached a highly inflammatory sermon at St Paul's. It was seen as an attack on the principles
of the Glorious Revolution and Sacheverell was impeached in the
House of Commons. The following March he was suspended from
preaching for three years. Byrom was one of many who felt some
sympathy for him. He did not admire the manner in which Sacheverell expressed his views but admitted, 'I esteem his cause to be
good.' In fact Sacheverell remained something of a hero to him. In a
journal entry for 8 July 1714, Byrom describes his response when
Sacheverell visited Cambridge to receive a degree: 'he went by my
window just now; if he had not had too much company with him,
one might have asked him to come in.'[5]

Sacheverell's scruples in defence of his High Church principles reminded Byrom of his own forebears. Several had suffered for their
staunch support of the Royalist cause. His great-grandfather, the
Reverend Isaac Allen, had been a solid and devout servant of the
Church of England and his sovereign Charles I. After the defeat of
the king he refused to conform to the wishes of the Presbyterians
and alter the form of his church services. For this he was thrown out
of his living and imprisoned, not to be restored to his church until
the return of the monarchy. Isaac's son, Captain John Allen of
Redivales, Bury, made a considerable fortune and was nicknamed
'The Golden Tanner'. Zealous in the King's cause, he served the
Earl of Derby, and his loyalty cost him much of his property. For
Byrom himself, matters came to a head when, in 1715, he was sworn
into a Senior Fellowship. Within three months he had to take the
Oath of Abjuration or leave. In May he was still undecided. With no
father to turn to he chose to confide in John Stansfield: 'I am not
clearly convinced that it is lawful, nor that it is unlawful; sometimes
I think one thing, and sometimes another.'[6]

In the end the highly promising career was forfeited; true to his
background he joined the list of non-jurors who sacrificed personal
advancement for their principles, and left Cambridge.

Among the many friendships Byrom made at Trinity, one led to an interest he later turned to his own advantage. Tom Sharp, son of the Archbishop of York, had been dabbling with a problem which had intrigued people for centuries – the most efficient method of reducing the signs and sounds of the English language to a reliable set of symbols for the purpose of writing speedily and secretly. Recognising Byrom's linguistic brilliance, Sharp invited him to help, and the two men spent much time on the project. Byrom soon saw the faults in the system they were working on and it was abandoned. However, he saw the need for shorthand, and with characteristic energy set about learning all he could on the subject.

Byrom left Cambridge in July 1715 to return to his family, keenly aware of the expense and expectations invested in his education. He wrote to his brother in London: 'I shall be glad to see you in the country. I hope I may meet with opportunities of discharging the obligations I owe to you all in some measure equal to the sense I have of 'em.'[7]

However, there is no record of his activities until the following April, when he was touring Oxford with his sister Sarah Brearcliffe. The Journal is inconveniently silent, but in the intervening months the country had been disturbed by the abortive rising of 1715. The Earl of Mar had raised the Stuart standard in Scotland late that year. James landed at Peterhead on 22 December, but by the end of January the rebellion had failed. James and Mar fled to France in February. It was not the most opportune time for a non-juror to be seeking a career. Even before the uprising there had been unrest in Manchester. The three-year ban on Dr Sacheverell was over and he made further inflammatory utterances. In response Thomas Siddal senior led the demonstrations against the Presbyterian chapel in Cross Street which led to his execution.

It is impossible to be sure of Byrom's activities at this time, but in the spring of 1717 he decided to go to the Continent. In an undated letter from Deal to John Stansfield he wrote: 'There is no going to Calais without a pass, but to Ostend I am told one may; but the passage thither is uncertain. Now certain or uncertain, my present intention is for that place, if passage may be had in any time.'[8] His determination to leave is evident. He tells his sisters he intends to go to Bruges, but his arrival at Montpellier is announced in a letter to an unnamed addressee (probably his brother), signed Sa. Woolmer.[9] Circumstances were beginning to direct his steps towards a life of subterfuge.

Montpellier was the seat of an ancient French university and Byrom appears to have told his family that he was 'studying physic' there. He enrolled in a private course of anatomy with the idea of becoming a doctor. His name, however, has never been found among the registers of students for this time. No doubt he assumed a different one. He had been told by his brother that all persons who 'have gone beyond seas, or all who have been with the Pretender' have been 'excepted out of the act of Grace' – that is, had placed themselves beyond the king's pardon. Now that he was a non-juror, his activities rendered him suspect. As a precaution his family kept his movements secret and Edward, as head of the family, was prepared to encourage John to settle to medical studies in Montpellier: 'be not in too much haste to come home if you think you can benefit yourself by any studies at Montpellier'.[10] Edward was anxious to be able to say something respectable about his non-juring brother: 'we think now to let our friends know that you are studying physic at Montpellier'. That would make his absence abroad appear acceptable. John seemed happy with the idea, at least for a time. 'I am going into physic for this winter, which I shall continue or leave off as you think fit to advise me, though I cannot help being sorry that it has not always been my study.'[11] Edward continued to supply funds, and John enjoyed the milder weather, the local wine, and, despite his limited resources, dressed in the French fashion. He visited a convent to watch his landlady's niece take the veil, and went to Mass several times to compare services. But, most important of all, in the winter of 1717 he visited Avignon to meet the Old Pretender. There is no entry in the diary for the precise date, but in conversation with William Law much later in 1739 he admitted the encounter. 'I said that I saw him once; he said. Where? I said at A(vignon); he said, Did you kiss hands? I said Yes and parted.'[12] In retrospect it is clear that Byrom did not go to Montpellier with any burning ambition to be a doctor; the reputation of the university medical school was secondary to the proximity of Avignon and the exiled Pretender's court. At Avignon Byrom was unlucky enough to lose the seal of his watch, and was very much put out, for, if it fell into the hands of a government agent, the consequences might be serious. Even so, despite the fact that the seal could reveal his identity, family pride made him ask Edward for the correct heraldic description of their coat of arms so that he could have another seal engraved at Montpellier.

However much he claimed to be interested in medicine, Byrom

did not stay long enough to gain a degree, and never practised as a doctor. His sisters became anxious to have him home and settled, for in 1718 Phoebe wrote to tell him that the librarian at Chetham's Library was dying, and that the trustees were enquiring whether he was interested in the post. Chetham's was one of the first free public libraries in England. It was named after a wealthy landowner, Humphrey Chetham, who in 1651 endowed a school for forty boys and a library 'for the use of scholars and others well affected'.[13] £1,000 was specified for the purchase of 'godly English bokes' and it was not long before the post of Keeper became a valued appointment. To Byrom's family it seemed an ideal opportunity.

Byrom wrote to his brother that he could like the post very well provided he did not have to take the Oath, and asked whether it would be a hindrance to him if he did not. This was the stumbling block to many openings. Four days later he wrote to John Stansfield: 'pray let me know whether you would have me turn doctor', for in medicine no such Oath was required. In less than twelve months he returned to England and was writing from Trinity College in May 1718 to tell his brother:

> I should be very willing to have the Library, and am very much obliged to you for your pains in engaging the feoffees; if you can be sure of it let me know further; it will be better worthwhile than staying for a Fellowship, whose profit will be slow a coming: besides 'tis in Manchester, which place I love entirely.[14]

Some inner fickleness made John falter at this point. He knew full well what his brother wanted – serious dedication to a medical career – and what would make his sisters happy – John safely home in Manchester. Neither alternative appealed, and, with almost contemptuous indifference, Byrom remained in Cambridge. In July he wrote to his brother from London a letter full of apologies not only for his absence but also his silence (he had gone to Cambridge supposedly to collect £50 owed to him by his college). While his family made every effort to secure him a permanent post, Byrom involved himself in the troubled affairs of the Master of Trinity. Richard Bentley was not only one of the great scholars of the day, he was also one of the great Masters of the college. Unfortunately his intelligence and energy were matched with an arrogance which led him to rule the college in a dictatorial manner, and many of the Fellows rebelled against his authority. Eventually the matter was formally investigated by the College Visitor (the Bishop of Ely), and

Bentley would have been dismissed if the Bishop had not died in 1714 before he could give judgment. The death of Queen Anne the same year also helped to save Bentley's scholastic skin. Amid all the business of state concerned with the Hannoverian succession, his case was overlooked.

Undeterred by such a narrow escape, Bentley continued to rule in his old high-handed way. By now he was adept at making enemies and the university deprived him of all his degrees for flouting the authority of the Vice-Chancellor. Despite such outrageous behaviour, however, he retained the support of Byrom, who looked fondly on Trinity as a little kingdom, with Bentley as the King, the Fellows the House of Lords, while the students were the House of Commons. Not surprisingly he endeared himself to both Bentley and his family. Years later he recalls in the Journal their opinion of him. 'He said I had always been an honest lad, that his wife and daughter thought there was much honesty in this Byrom.' The daughter in question was the famous Joanna, or Jug as she was called, still a child when Byrom was at the college, but destined to grow into a beautiful woman who captivated the hearts of many of her father's students.

It has been said that she is the 'Phebe' in Byrom's first published poem, 'A Pastoral'. Light and playful, it appeared in *The Spectator* in October 1714, introduced by Addison himself, who felt that it had 'something in it so original that I do not much doubt but it will divert my readers'.[15] It continued to amuse for years to come, and was set to music several times. Growing up with his sisters, Byrom knew just how to tease and flatter the eleven-year-old girl – if she is indeed Phebe. In 1725 he sat up till one in the morning with her cousin recalling his 'courtship'.[16] Admittedly, the year he wrote 'A Pastoral' Byrom was a candidate for a college Fellowship. Was this his method of ingratiating himself with her father, as some have said? It was his evident innocence as a young man which endeared him to people, and which was remembered to his advantage when he came under suspicion later. The poem, once its authorship was known, began to open doors to him at all levels of society.

Byrom's support for Bentley in 1718 took the form of an anonymous pamphlet, 'Review of the Proceedings against Dr Bentley', written with such caustic wit that critics thought it was Bentley's own work. Byrom had joined battle with enthusiasm, ignoring family pressure to secure the post at Chetham's. Edward was angry that he was not more concerned for his future and regarded John's behaviour as self-indulgence. While Byrom dallied, another Trinity graduate, Francis Hooper, expressed interest and, when the Keeper died, hurried from Cambridge to ensure his appointment. Byrom remained behind, more interested in getting the pamphlet printed.

In fairness to Byrom, there was much to admire in Bentley. He was a man of exceptional learning, who founded a new tradition of scholarship based on comparative analysis of texts. He introduced important university reforms, improved teaching facilities and encouraged distinguished foreigners as lecturers. But he had made a name for himself long before he became Master. In 1692, the year Byrom was born, Bentley was invited to give the first Boyle lectures. He entitled them 'A Confutation of Atheism' and wanted to include Sir Isaac Newton's 'System of the World', as argued in his *Principia*, as evidence of Divine design in the world. Newton was delighted and the two men became friends. Later Newton allowed Bentley to see to the printing of the second edition of *Principia* in 1713. (Bentley pocketed the income and did not pay a penny to the editor.)

The controversy surrounding Bentley, his exacting standards of scholarship and his work on a new edition of the *Principia* fired Byrom's own ambitions. Even if he were only holding on to the coat-tails of greatness, it was preferable to being buried in provincial seclusion in what was still a country town. So it is not surprising that Byrom's protestations to his family were at odds with his actions. Evasiveness became increasingly necessary once he had refused the Oath of Abjuration and diplomacy led to deception. His youthful ventures in print had been either anonymous or masked by *noms de plume*. It was curiously appropriate that shorthand became the means of Byrom's survival, for it is language in disguise.

CHAPTER TWO

A Chance Encounter, etc

Not far from Cambridge one of the great commercial fairs of Europe, Sturbridge Fair, took place every year on the site of a lepers' hospital. It dated back to the reign of King John in the thirteenth century and was held annually from 24 August to 28 September. The amount of business transacted outstripped the great German fairs of Leipzig and Frankfurt. Daniel Defoe has left a vivid account of its size and vitality in Byrom's day. People travelled from all over the country to buy and sell.

> It is impossible to describe all the Parts and Circumstances of this fair exactly; the shops are placed in Rows like Streets, whereof one is call'd Cheapside; and here, as in several other Streets, are all sorts of Trades, who sell by Retale, and who come principally from London with their Goods; scarce any Trades are omitted, Goldsmiths, Toyshops, Brasiers, Turners, Milleners, Haberdashers, Hatters, Mercers, Drapers, Pewterers, China-Warehouses, and in a word all Trades that can be named in London; with Coffee-Houses, Taverns, Brandy-Shops, and Eating-houses, innumerable, and all in Tents, and Booths, as above . . .[1]

The staples of the fair were wool and hops but there was plenty of entertainment too. 'Towards the latter End of the Fair, and when the great Hurry of Wholesale Business begins to be over, the Gentry come in, from all Parts of the County round; and tho' they come for their Diversion; yet 'tis not a little Money they lay out.' They were drawn by 'the Puppet-Shows, Drolls, Rope-Dancers and such-like', and at times no less than fifty Hackney-coaches would come from London and 'ply Night and Morning to carry the People to and from Cambridge; for there the gross of the People lodge; nay, which is still more strange, there are Wherries brought from London on

Waggons to plye upon the little River Cam, and to row people up and down from the Town, and from the Fair as Occasion presents.'

On one of the last days of summer in 1719, Byrom left his pamphleteering on behalf of Bentley and visited the fair, where he claims he had an encounter which changed his life. He was evidently drawn to a booth where a musical performance was taking place. In the audience one person stood out above the rest, a woman who made a deep impression on him, and his powerful feelings are recorded in the first poem in the MS notebook. But even then Byrom could not have known how far this meeting would disrupt and distort his future, drawing him into royal intrigue and tearing his own firmly held principles apart.

To The Fair Unknown
After Seeing Her at the Musick Booth at Sturbridge Fair[2]

Could these faint numbers glow with equal fire
To that which in his breast their writer feels,
Could Phoebus, like the fair unknown, inspire,
And verse but emulate the flame it tells,
The lover some success had found, and she
Been known to fame, tho' lost to love and me.

Wound not that love with too severe a name
Which was not _____ but passion in excess,
Conceal'd the shaft from whence the arrow came,
My hopes may be, but not my anguish, less.
Strikes not the lightning with a fate as true
Should vanquished reason wonder whence it flew?

If not in pity to your lover's woes,
For your own sake at least, yourself reveal.
Lest when I die, and you the latent cause,
You lose a triumph you deserve so well.
Nay ev'n repaid must all my suffering be
And envied in my fall, – if known I fall by thee.

Nay, nay more a thousand loves may lurk behind
And half the course of glory yet to run.
A flowing wit, discreet and beauteous mind,
May crown the conquest which your eyes began:

Nor bid me dread the thousand deaths in store,
I looked, I sighed, I loved, sighs, and was undone before.

In vain the midnight anchorite may boast,
Of tedious knowledge and laborious rules.
For what use life, its best employment lost
In the dull mazes of insipid schools?
Love must retain what science scarce began,
And mould the lettered savage into man.

Let lazy hermits dream in College cells,
Severely great and indolently good;
Whose frozen breasts, such glimmering rapture swells
As lifeless dull platonics understood.
Go tell the doubting sage: Who looks on thee
With Plato's eyes may question if he see.

Judge now my passion by severest truth
And read what rigorous justice can blame,
If I have erred, inform a willing youth,
At best mistaken only was my flame:
Is love a crime? Then teach me to adore,
And zeal shall be what passion was before.

The poem was written in the full flood of emotion sometime after Byrom had realised, or been told, the identity of the 'fair unknown'. He begins by stating that his powers as a poet are not equal to the task of describing the depth of his feelings. If he could express his love adequately, then, by publishing it to the world, he would lose her. This shows an awareness, even in hindsight, of her need for secrecy and *that* implies that, if he had known her identity beforehand, he would not have become involved.

By the time he had found out it was too late; he was completely captivated and had given himself to her – but not through lust. (Some such word is required in the space deliberately left by Byrom in the second verse.) It was love at first sight – 'I looked, I sighed, I loved'. The effect was shattering. The world of the academic scholar now seemed sterile. Without love, Cambridge offered little more than 'the dull mazes of insipid schools'. The ideal of Platonic love is the vision of a blind man. So, in the end, Byrom asks the fair one, and posterity, to judge him in the light of the secrecy she main-

1 John Byrom in his youth, with the family coat of arms

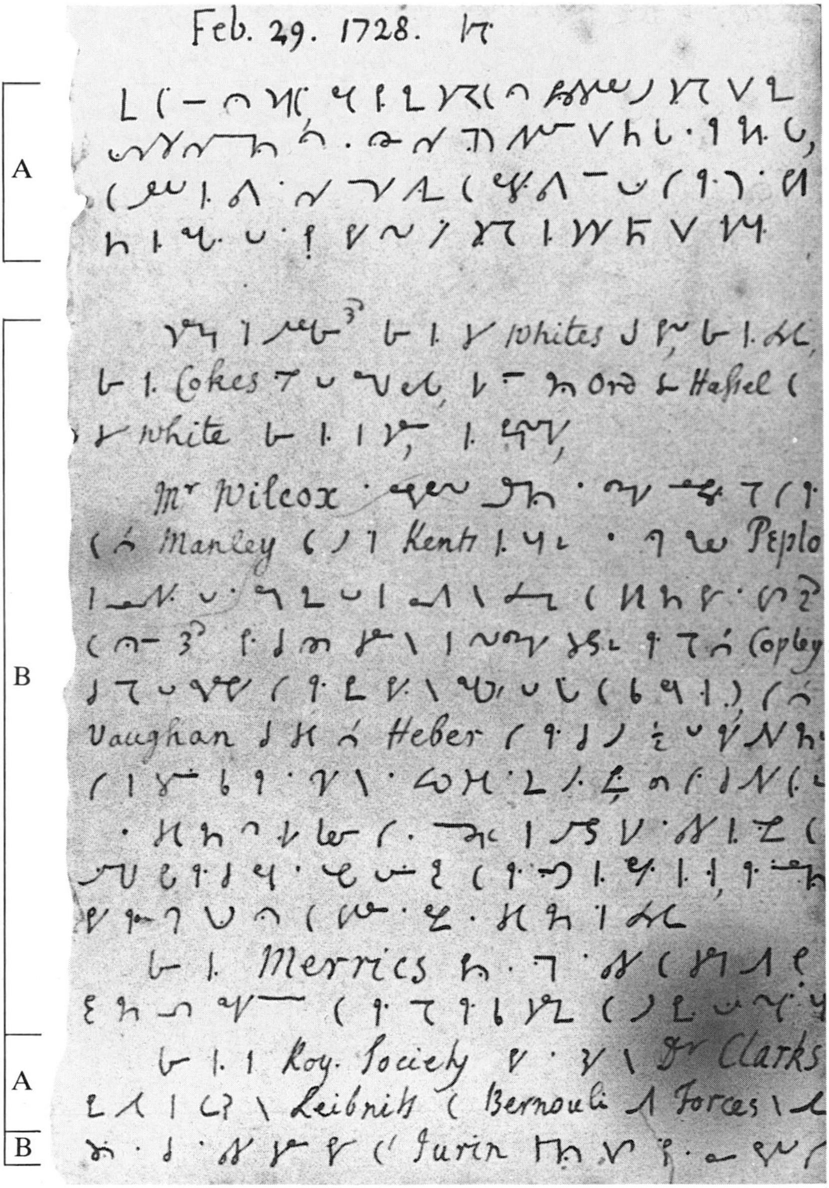
A
B
A
B
Feb. 29. 1728.
Mr Wilcox
Manley
Kent
Copley
Vaughan
Heber
Merrics
Roy. Society
Dr Clarks
Forces

2 The published portion of the first page begins with the announcement that this is Byrom's birthday, and continues with his pious determination to live a better life. However, the editors have omitted the passage where Byrom, writing about the election of a new Fellow to the Collegiate Church in Manchester, talks of bribery and criticises Bishop Peploe of Chester. The published version resumes with less contentious material: a visit to the Royal

Society. The editors then omit a suggestion from one of Byrom's friends that he publish his verses on the robbery at Epping Forest to make some money before a pirated version appeared. The last part of the entry, full of exemplary Christian thoughts ('it seems to be necessary to live so as to preserve our innocence'), has been included in full. A = published section; B = unpublished.

3 Eleanora Atherton (from the Sarah Bolger Collection)

tained. Having fallen in love, is he to be condemned? Is love *itself* a crime? If so, then only the beloved can teach him to control his passion and turn it into something more acceptable – adoration.

The poem expresses Byrom's genuine torment, and his dilemma deserves a certain sympathy. In a sense he was more sinned against than sinning, for the fair unknown was playing a dangerous game. If anyone were to blame, it was she, not the unsuspecting but all too willing youth.

Byrom got on well with his sisters, and he was at ease in the company of women throughout his life. This together with his charm and sense of humour made him popular with women wherever he went. The Master of Trinity's daughter, Joanna Bentley, was now a pretty young girl of sixteen. Despite the difference in their ages she had made an impression on him at the time he wrote 'A Pastoral'. For years after, Byrom's closest friends teased him about her, and his male vanity played up to the running joke, as this letter to his friend Stansfield shows:

> We were last night to hear the Famous Harper, Murphy, it was the first time I heard him, 'tis a glorious Instrument, we had ladies there, . . . but Jug! was not there. Heigh! Ho! ffare ye well Ile go take an Hatchet and hang myself.[3]

But there is no mistaking the difference in Byrom's feelings for the two women. For Jug it was playful flirtation, with the fair unknown it was complete infatuation.

This trait persisted throughout his life and gave rise to the satirical poem 'The Session of the Beauties or Cambridge Toasts'. It is the second poem in the sequence, immediately following 'To The Fair Unknown', and offers a catalogue of women who, on account of their physical allure, became the toast of the young bloods and university wits. Six of them vie with each other for pre-eminence and Byrom arranges a contest judged by Venus, to decide who is the fairest of the fair. Here he is in a jocular mood, but with a shrewd eye for female guile and vanity. As each parades before the Goddess, he appraises her like a true connoisseur. One whose best gift lay in her dancing is described cuttingly:

> Now smoothly gliding by the gazing throng,
> She falls, turns, bends, capers and swims along.
> Her Venus saw, and would have given the Prize
> Had but her wit been piercing as her eyes.

Or had her tongue with eloquence sweet
Moved with half the swiftness of her feet.

Years later, on a journey to London, his appreciative eye caused amused banter from his kinsman, William Chaddock. When the two men reached Daventry, Byrom wrote a short note to his wife and on the back of it Chaddock added a postscript:

My good cousin,
    I cannot forbear lending your husband a little help, because he says he has no more to say; but I have, and that is to inform you how happy 'tis for him that I gave him my company, because he seems to be rakish when he goes to London. He has followed a pretty lady for six miles together this very day. I did my endeavour to overtake them, and happily prevented his being carried off without me; in short I followed him so long that the lady thought fit to take another road, and left me my good companion, who is very hearty and well, and laughs much. Pray don't scold him upon this head till I give you information of other particulars. The post waits. My love to yourself and all cousins.[4]

Byrom's pleasure in female beauty never left him. In middle age he still noticed a pretty face. In 1737 he sees 'Miss Aston in the park, Dea Certe', and the instant comment 'truly a goddess' is in keeping with the man who set eyes on the mysterious beauty at Sturbridge and immediately fell in love.

Who was the fair unknown? The answer lies in a later poem, 'Artemissia', to which other poems are linked by word, phrase and imagery. To the title Byrom has added the words: 'supposed to be written upon the Queen by Dr. Slowfeet'. For this to have any topicality the queen in question must be Caroline of Anspach, Queen Consort to George II from 1727 to 1737. Another poem in this section is addressed 'To Amelia', and, while it may be a coincidence, Amelia is the name of one of Caroline's daughters. The sequence also contains an epigram on Sir Robert Walpole which can be safely assigned to 1726 while two other poems bear the dates 1730 and 1734, so the internal evidence points to the reign of George II and Caroline.

By the time Byrom came to write 'Artemissia', he had travelled emotionally a great distance from the infatuation declared in 'To The Fair Unknown'. The relationship had soured and in his bitterness he attributes to the woman certain qualities we know Caroline possessed. The beginning of the affair was surrounded by an aura of secrecy, which Byrom agreed to maintain. However, once he found himself rejected, his anger made him throw discretion to the winds and, in depicting her faults, he makes Artemissia easily identifiable.

Byrom's poem is closely modelled on some youthful verses attributed to Pope which describe a rather unprepossessing bluestocking. Pope, in turn, is said to have imitated a satirical poem by the Earl of Dorset about a mistress of James II. In the manuscript notebook Byrom mentions neither Pope nor Dorset, but he has done what countless poets have done before and since – taken a poem written by someone else and, with a few alterations, endowed it with a new life and meaning. The words which differ in Pope's version are shown to the right.

Tho' Artemissia talks by Fits
Of Councils, Classics, Fathers, Wits,
Reads Malebranche, Boyle and Locke,
Yet in some Things methinks she fails.
'Twere well if she would pare her Nails
And wear a cleaner Smock.

Haughty and huge as High Dutch Bride,
Such Nastiness and such Pride
Are oddly joined by Fate.
On her large Squab you find her *you* spread   you(added)
Like a *foot creeps up* a Bed,   [fat Corpse upon]
That lies and stinks in State.

She wears no Colours, (sign of Grace)
On any Part except her Face,
All white and black beside.
Dauntless her Looks, her Gesture proud,
Her Voice theatrically loud,
And masculine her Stride.

So have I *Son* in black and white,   [seen]
A prating *Bird* a Magpie height   [thing]
Majestically stalk.
The stately worthless *Admiral*   [Animal]
That *jars* the Tongue and Wags the Tail   [plies]
All Flutter, Pride, and Talk.

Byrom seized upon these lines because he saw how readily they could be adapted to tell a very different story. If he had simply wished to copy out Pope's poem as an anthology piece there would be no point in altering the lines and certainly he did not set himself up as an improver of other people's verses. Moreover, there are no known variants, either in manuscript or print, to the version of Pope's lines as here printed. The variants must, therefore, be Byrom's invention and raise the question of why he should take the trouble to amend the poem in this way. Pope's poem is one of a pair, companion pieces to each other. Byrom showed no interest in the second poem, so why did he alter 'Artemissia'?

The disagreeable subject of Pope's poem reminded Byrom of another lady, one who had been close to his heart – Caroline of Anspach. Support for this is to be found in the words appended by Byrom to the title. The queen referred to can only be Caroline, and 'Dr Slowfeet' is Byrom's self-mocking pseudonym. He had been too slow to get away. The Queen is easily identifiable from a number of clues. Artemissia is an intellectual whose talk ranges over a number of topics: politics (councils), classical literature (classics), religious writings (fathers) and the wits of the day. Queen Caroline herself was known for her intelligent interest in all these, and Malebranche was a particular favourite of hers as he was with Byrom. In fact Byrom so much admired Malebranche that he bought a portrait of him.

In the second stanza Artemissia is referred to as 'High Dutch Bride'. Originally High Dutch meant High German, but by the eighteenth century the Jacobites had used the phrase as a term of abuse against things and persons German. One meaning of the term is gibberish, rather like 'double dutch', and in this context refers to the Queen's poor mastery of English. Finally there is a clear reference to her stature in the lines: 'Dauntless her looks, her gesture proud,/Her Voice theatrically loud,/And masculine her stride.' These physical attributes apply to Caroline and they undoubtedly describe a woman given to command and fully expecting to be obeyed.

In each of the first three stanzas Byrom adds other, darker strands to the picture. In matters of hygiene the eighteenth century did not generally observe the same standards as we do today. Byrom, like Dean Swift, was an exception. He was aware of the connection between dirt and disease, and, in 1729, wrote to his wife about the health of their children, urging her to 'wash 'em often, health is keeping 'em clean inside and outside'.[5] Many men and women of quality preferred powder and paint to soap and water.

By the time Byrom wrote the poem, Caroline was suffering from an infected rupture of the womb which proved fatal. He picks up this same theme later in another poem in the group. Byrom's revulsion at her neglect of certain matters of personal cleanliness is unmistakable.

Nevertheless in the final stanza he makes the astounding claim that he has a son who, in the context, can only be Artemissia's son. The language used makes it clear that Byrom is no more proud of him than of his relationship with the mother. The son is full of his own importance: he is described as a 'prating Bird' and, like the magpie, fond of his own voice. The word 'Bird' replaces the word 'thing' from Pope's original. The shorthand symbols for these two words are quite distinct and in no way interchangeable. Byrom also alters the word animal in the same stanza. It now becomes 'admiral' and again the change from 'n' to 'd' in the manuscript is indisputable. Why this change? Prince William, Duke of Cumberland, was brought up with the intention that he should become Lord High Admiral. Admiral is also the name of a butterfly and this association links Caroline/William with the trap laid for the butterfly in another poem in the sequence, 'On a Spider' ('And that's a conquest little better,/Than thine o'er captive butterfly.'). A further clue to the Prince's identity is given by the word 'height' in the second line of the last stanza. Byrom was well aware of the layers of meanings in words, and here, as well as remembering his own height, he is playing on the different uses of 'height'. For Pope it was simply the stature of the 'prating thing', but Byrom's amendments – 'Bird' and 'admiral' – allow 'height' to carry fresh allusion, albeit satirically, to the high birth of his son – the consequence of his behaviour with the 'High Dutch Bride'. In the same way 'majestically' gains added point in Byrom's version. Cleverly, almost maliciously, he kept nearly all his alterations to the last stanza for dramatic effect. There is one other, however, in the second stanza which is critical. To make explicit his conduct with the Queen, Byrom amended one line to the point of it being ungrammatical. 'Her spread' becomes 'her you spread', an inelegant expression, but the inclusion in the shorthand of a separate dot for the vowel-sound 'u' is obvious, leaving the reader in absolutely no doubt as to its meaning.

The son in question could only be Prince William, Duke of Cumberland (the only son to survive apart from Frederick). He was born in 1721, two months after Byrom's sudden marriage to his cousin.

'Artemissia' is immediately followed by a quotation in Latin, two lines taken from the Third Satire of the Roman poet Juvenal:

> usq' adeo nihil est, quod nostra infantia caelum
> hausit Aventini?

> [Does it count for nothing that as a child I
> breathed the air of Aventine?]

With less emphasis now on Latin and Greek in education, it is difficult to realise that, in Byrom's day, Juvenal's lines would be readily recognised and, moreover, that the general drift of the complete poem would be familiar to the educated. The satire is a biting denunciation of the evils in Hadrian's Rome since the influx of foreigners, particularly Greeks, whom Juvenal seems to hold responsible for every vice imaginable. The two lines of the quotation sum up Juvenal's complaint – he is native born and can get nowhere in his own city. Clearly the lines have been placed between 'Artemissia' and the poem that follows in order to evoke certain associations and act as a link. There is, of course, an allusion to the 'foreigners' who now rule the country. George I never bothered to learn English at all and brought his German-speaking household with him. Caroline and George II did speak English, but not as natives and Caroline was happier with French. But Byrom is concerned with subtler points. He sees others getting on where he has been not only ignored but rejected. Juvenal rails at the fickleness of the goddess Fortuna, 'Lady Luck', and at the people she now favours:

> They are the sort that Lady Luck will take from
> the gutter and raise to the summit of worldly
> success, whenever she feels like having a joke.[6]

These lines would have a special significance for Byrom who, as he fell out of favour with Caroline, saw her waste her patronage on such nonentities as Stephen Duck, a farm-labourer turned poet, while he himself was spurned. Byrom understandably felt that he merited special consideration from the Queen, but the opposite happened. Moreover, if there were any doubt that in 'Artemissia' Byrom is referring to a 'son', the Latin quotation persuades us that this was his intention. The Aventine was one of the seven hills of

Rome, Caroline had seven surviving children, of whom William was her favourite – the summit (caelum) of her happiness. The heads of these children can be seen in the bottom right hand corner of her portrait by Amigoni. Byrom could claim that at the beginning of their relationship (nostra infantia) they had enjoyed that happiness together. Ironically, what should have made their heaven complete became the instrument of his final rejection.

The quotation from Juvenal leads the reader on to the next poem with the words, in shorthand, 'Upon a Westminster Scholar'. This, the title, is written immediately next to the Latin and above the verse, thus showing the close connection between both poems.

> In Fame's great list what glorious names are found
> That take their rise from this poetic ground?
> Here Cowley's muse which soared to Pindar's height
> Slept with the Cretans many a winter's night.
> Here Rowe, and here, too, he received his Greek
> Who from Euripides made Phaedrus [sic] speak.
> This genius, also, still had risen here,
> Ours is John Dryden, ours is Matthew Prior.
> But let us not our modern prize forget,
> We have not one poet for the present state.

The four English poets mentioned were products of Westminster School. Abraham Cowley (1618-1687) was considered in his own day a greater poet than Milton. By Byrom's time his reputation had declined but he was still admired for the ingenuity of his wit. An intellectual, a founder member of the Royal Society and interested in science, it is easy to see his appeal for Byrom. John Dryden (1631-1700) was not only the greatest poet of the Restoration, but is regarded as one of the creators of modern English prose. Matthew Prior (1664-1721), like Cowley now hardly read, was at the height of his powers the 'official' poet of Queen Anne. All three men were buried in Westminster Abbey, so the reference to 'this poetic ground' can be taken to mean both the school which nurtured them and the Abbey which received their bones. The point of the poem comes in the last two lines. Byrom sees himself as the poet excluded from acceptance. He, too, might have been the modern prize – the official poet of the Establishment – if he had not been dropped by Caroline.

The clues uncovered so far concern the identity of the fair unknown. 'Artemissia' is dominated by the presence of the Queen

who in the last stanza has a son. 'The Session of the Critics', however, is motivated by the son's inquiry into the supposed identity of
his father. Whereas in 'Artemissia' Byrom had adapted a poem by
Pope, here he is the sole author. The result is cruel in different ways
to mother, father and son. Its dates can be fixed with some certainty
and that in turn helps to place the 'Artemissia' sequence, which, as
its tone indicates, must have been written near the same time.

Behind the first and obvious level of 'The Session of the Critics'
lies another, more important one in which Byrom hints, through an
ingenious piece of double-bluff, that he was the father of William,
Duke of Cumberland. The poem was published anonymously as a
pamphlet and advertised in the *London Magazine* for March 1737.
The date is important, for the following month William was sixteen,
and Byrom had been manoeuvring for some time to become the
Prince's shorthand tutor. He had carefully cultivated the chief
tutors, won their approval and, just for a moment, thought he was
going to be appointed to their number, and, thus, gain access to
William. However, his appointment was turned down. On 26 April
he noted in his Journal: 'Dr. Hartley said he believed he knew where
it stuck, that it was the pence, but I suspected within myself something else . . .'[7] In the refusal Byrom suspected the hand of the
Queen herself, who by now was determined to exclude him completely from her life and William's. He must have heard early
enough of her decision to retaliate with the satire of 'The Session of
the Critics'.

Under the guise of an unseemly wrangling over personal reputa-
tions among scholars at Cambridge, Byrom writes about his own
reputation and his paternity of William. He had always been a frequent visitor to his old university, gathering new pupils, enjoying
the company of friends and, in the course of his stay, regaling them
with news from London and his own success, just like any old boy
returning to the hallowed haunts of his youth. It was a natural setting against which he could place an imaginary inquiry into who
should be awarded the prize of the Nettle – who should be deemed
the man with the most sting in his Tale or Tail. The poem is rooted
in the real context of Cambridge at that time and is full of in-jokes
which Byrom's contemporaries would have readily appreciated. In-
geniously, Byrom appears as 'John' and as 'The Master of Queen's,
with his coach full of Tully', an allusion to his relationship with
Caroline, and also a reminder of his habit as an undergraduate of
bawling Tully's orations on the banks of the Irwell.

1 Old Zoilus, the sourest Dame Critice forbore,
2 The pedantic dull Spawn of a Billingsgate Whore,
3 Was now by his Mother deputed to settle,
4 Who should wear the long scolded for Chaplet, of Nettle.

5 Down he flew to Trin. Col. and the Library sought,
6 To be near his own Bentley was ever his Thought;
7 With a Snarl of Disdain left the Chapel behind him;
8 For that was a Place, where he ne'er hop'd to find him.
9 With his Chaps full of Wormwood he mounted his Throne,
10 A Worm-eaten Parchment's illegible grown,
11 A tough Crab Cudgel for a Sceptre he waves,
12 And hollows, Heus! horsum, adeste, ye Slaves.

13 Bentley first was expected, but did not appear;
14 For he order'd his Delegate, Frog, to declare,
15 That to work up Down Here was his present Employ,
16 And he vow'd he would ne'er mix with the Scrub οἱ πολλοί
     [hoi polloi].

17 From the Garret, where long he had rusted, came down
18 Toby Thirlby cock-sure, that the Prize was his own,
19 Crying, Zounds! where's this Bentley? I'll give him no
     Quarter;
20 And hall'd out the Preface of his fam'd Justin Martyr.

21 His Disciples came next; Caleb scar'd at the Sight,
22 As he thought of Tom Tristram, ran away in a Fright.
23 An Embrio Claudian was Jordan's Pretence,
24 But alas proved abortive for Want of the Pence.
25 The Censor view'd Toby with a Smile of Applause,
26 And was almost inclin'd to have granted his Cause;
27 But bade him retire to his snarling Vocation,
28 And He'd ensure him the Nettle for the next Dedication:
29 But as for Friend Jordan, he only was fit
30 To coax his Preceptor, and cry up his wit;
31 And, since Caleb to publish was not very forward,
32 Let him drink his Subscriptions with Rustat and Norwood.

33 With Guts and his Rustics in roll'd Jerry Needham,
34 And roar'd for the Prize, but the Judge wou'd not heed him;
35 With dry Thinking, old Fumbler, ne'er trouble thy Brains,

36   Go spunge with thy Ninnies at Bene't and Queen's.
37   The Master of Queen's, with his Coach full of Tully,
38   Came into the Court, and endeavour'd to bully,
39   Crying, I've no Occasion to preach up my Merit,
40   I'm a hopeful young Lad, you have Bentley's Word for it.
41   Friend John, quoth the Judge, Thou had no Share in the
       Matter,
42   To much Dullness a Critic shou'd add some Ill-Nature;
43   In thy Tail and thy Notes We like Impotence find,
44   For a Husband and Critic Thou ne'er were design'd.
45   Tom Bentley next bustled to prefer his Petition,
46   But was jostled aside by the Stamford Physician
47   In his Hand he the Text of Euripides brought,
48   Piping-hot from the Press, but the Notes were forgot.

49   The Court humbly begged he would not trouble their
       Patience,
50   Paracelsus and Zoilus ne'er were Relations;
51   So off brush'd the Quack to his Pills and his Boxes,
52   From patching of Authors to curing of Poxes.

53   Up Honibert starts, and cries, Look ye here
54   Une Nouvelle Traduction, that cuts down Dacier;
55   For the Metre let Bentley and Her fight and Quarrel,
56   De Frenchman, begar, Sirs must shew ye the Morale.

57   What Morals you Dog, cry'd the Court, in a Pet?
58   Did ever a Critic turn Moralist yet?
59   O'er vanquish'd Librarians we challenge our Praise;
60   Let Lyly write Morals, or the Master of Caius.
61   With that they untruss'd the bold Critic of Paris,
62   And gave him the Nettle, but over his bare Arse;
63   The Smart of the Discipline damp'd his Pretensions
64   So he scour'd off to Whist with his Cully Pretensions.
65   At last the Vice Can, with his three Pseudo Squires,
66   Walks in, and the Cause of the Tumult requires;
67   For Men of the Gown such Deportment's not fitting;
68   Nor found I a Statute for any such Meeting.
69   The Judge smil'd at the Joke, and the Squabble to settle,
70   Said, Faith, let's decree this stern Cato the Nettle;
71   He alone the true critical Notions hath hit;
72   For his Edicts declare much Spite, and no Wit.

The contentious groves of Academe were an appropriate setting in which Byrom could drop his dangerous hints. Had he not met the fair one nearby? He knew of the rivalry and backbiting among university dons, and it provided him with sufficient material to satirise the scholarship which had made them so jealous of each other and which he came to see as arid compared with the passion she had inspired. After the encounter at Sturbridge he had been compelled to look afresh at university life: 'For what use is life, its best employments lost/In the dull mazes of insipid schools?'. It was precisely the 'tedious knowledge and labourious rules' rejected in that poem which had produced the pack of bickering scholars into which he carefully inserts himself and William in 'The Session of the Critics'.

He asks the reader to imagine that William has come down to Cambridge to sort out a dispute, sent by his mother, the Billingsgate Whore, an allusion to the Hannoverian coarseness in which Caroline sometimes indulged. Apparently he has heard rumours about his paternity and, urged by the fury of his mother (with whom Byrom was now at odds), he intends to rebut these stories. Zoilus is filled with 'wormwood' – bitterness – like Artemissia. Although Byrom inherited the title with the poem, the mythological associations of Artemis, with which he would be fully acquainted, make it doubly apt. Artemis was worshipped in ancient Greece as the mother-goddess, but in her more barbaric aspects she was also the fierce goddess to whom strangers were sacrificed and before whose altars youths were scourged until they bled. Byrom considered he had suffered cruelly at Caroline's hands. Furthermore, Artemis gave her name to the common English shrub Wormwood which blooms in July. By his reference to Zoilus with his chaps (cheeks) full of wormwood, Byrom links Zoilus intimately to Artemissia as her son, and we know Caroline/Artemissia's youngest son was William, Duke of Cumberland. The complex web of allusions makes it clear that Zoilus stands for William.

Byrom peoples the poem with figures he knew and, on the most superficial level, hits at their failings and vices neatly. The Fellows paraded in imaginary review before the Prince include the timid and the boastful, the drunkard and the idler. But Byrom is not simply concerned with denouncing who is the most vitriolic of these pedants. He also shows that he is so unlike the rest of them, so lacking in their spite, that he is the only one who could be considered the likely candidate as William's father.

He does this in a number of ways. When he first appears at line 23 Jordan's (John's) pretence or excuse is that he was fully occupied with 'an embrio Claudian', an edition of the works of a Roman grammarian Claudian which he has been compelled to abandon 'for want of the pence'. But he is also pretending (claiming) that he is responsible for a budding member of the house of Claudius, a potential king. Byrom knew that Caroline doted on William, and that for a time she and George II seriously wanted to make it possible for William to take precedence over his brother Frederick, Prince of Wales, to become the Heir Apparent. Despite his responsibility for him (i.e. his parenthood), Byrom, as he recorded in the Journal, was excluded from any involvement with William, because 'it was the pence'. The allusion to the shorthand project is clearly echoed in the words.

It is the chief irony of the poem that William decides John was *not* his father. His loyalty to the much-loathed Master of Trinity, his optimistic nature (which Bentley will vouch for), his ingenuousness displayed in his flirting with young Joanna Bentley, lead to the conclusion that John is too ineffectual, even impotent, to be capable of such an act. There was no sting in his Tail (as a lover) or in his Tale (as a scholar).

Byrom continues the mock inquiry to further heights of absurdity, introducing finally the Vice-Chancellor like a *deus ex machina* to resolve the dispute. By his denunciation of the bad behaviour of the squabbling dons, he earns the prize himself as the most spiteful man in the University. Byrom deliberately returns to the first level of the poem at the end, so that the dangerous taunts he makes against Caroline for keeping him from William are safely embedded inside an apparently 'academic' satire.

In the printed version of the poem in the pamphlet the references to John are consistently written as J-N, but in the shorthand notebook Byrom deliberately altered the first two of these to Jordan. The reasons for this may be found in other clues in the poem. Jordan is connected with his preceptor (line 30). Preceptor means not only tutor, but also the person in charge of a Preceptory or Commandery of the Knights of the Order of St John.

One of the characters in the same section is Tom Tristram, and the Tristram family had a long association with the Knights of St John in England. The land on which the headquarters of the Order was built at St John's Gate, Clerkenwell, was given some time in the middle of the twelfth century to the Order by one Jordan of Bricet.

Thus carefully placed near each other in the poem are at least three allusions to the Order of the Knights of St John. By deliberately altering the signs for his name from John to Jordan, Byrom apparently wished to associate himself with that Order.

The total number of lines in the poem, 72, would also have symbolic resonances to some readers. According to the tradition of the Cabala, each letter in a word had a numerical equivalent, and the sum of the numbers in a word could stand for or equate with the word itself. In *The Dimensions of Paradise* John Michell points out that 'η αληθεια – the truth, has the value by gematria of 72'.[8] This number has had a symbolic weight for mystics and hermeticists for many centuries. One of the founders of Christian Cabala, Pico della Mirandola, drew up his account of the system in 72 *Conclusions*. Byrom made a study of the Cabala and became so interested that in 1725 he formed his own Cabala Club. It is therefore no accident that 'The Session of the Critics' contains 72 lines, for he has hidden in it an important truth and the adepts close to him would understand.

The associations with the Knights of St John evoked by the use of Jordan's name and by the term 'preceptor' are equally intentional and reflect the interest in this order and the Knights Templar at the beginning of the eighteenth century, shared in part by certain Freemasons. Already in France in 1705 new links in the chain of tradition were forged with the formation of a new Ordre du Temple. The three senior grades of the Order were Companion, Commander and Grand Cross and comprised all consecrated Knights with their 'Esquires' (Byrom's 'pseudo squires' carry an echo of this).[9]

The once all-powerful Templars had been dissolved in 1312 and their property had been handed over to the Knights of St John. Although they in turn were suppressed in England in the Reformation, they continued to flourish elsewhere in Europe and their headquarters were still at Malta in Byrom's day. Between them the Templars and Knights of St John exercised a magnetic attraction because of the knowledge and power they had acquired across the centuries. The longing for access to that power and knowledge can be seen in the various groups – some masonic, some not – which sprouted up around this time. (In order to enter the French Ordre du Temple a postulant had to prove his suitability by being either a Knight of Christ, a Teutonic Knight, or the descendant of a Templar. To become a Novice Esquire, the rank below Knighthood, he had to prove his nobility in the fourth generation. The risks Byrom undertook in France in 1717, when, as a result of losing his seal he was compelled to send to England for the details of his family's coat of arms, become much more understandable if he needed the arms as proof of his own gentility, so that he could pursue a quest for knowledge.)

Further references in both Byrom's Journal and his poetry testify to his preoccupation with the freemasons and similar groups. In the Journal entry on 15 April 1737 he records in part a conversation with his fellow non-juror William Law about Chevalier Ramsey and the Masonic symbolism of the Dove. Both topics are so different from the rest of the entry that they must have held some special significance for him. Michael Ramsey was a Jacobite and for a while had been a tutor in France to Bonnie Prince Charlie. According to Masonic historians he was in London around 1728 setting up 'The Order of the Temple'.[10] Coincidentally, in 1737 – the year of 'The Session of the Critics' – Ramsey delivered his *Oration*, a lengthy account of the origins of Freemasonry, which he associated with the Crusades.

In another poem, 'The Grand Epidemic. To a Person Who Had Got the Itch.', Byrom makes reference to 'round table knights' and 'the nine' (the tongues or 'languages' into which the Templars had once divided their dominions). The atmosphere around him at this time was steeped in Masonic and Templar thought which became enmeshed with his own personal intrigue. Taken together all these facts point to Byrom's involvement in a group modelled on the lines of the Templars and the Order of St John.

Having advertised 'The Session of the Critics' in the *London Magazine* in March, Byrom continued his own personal campaign by publishing anonymously another poem from the sequence in the July issue of *The Gentleman's Magazine* – 'The Spider and Poet'. It was accompanied by a translation of the poem into Latin by 'R.Luck'. There is also a version in Byrom's original MS, with a slightly different title: 'On a Spider'. The poem was written earlier in the relationship than 'The Session of the Critics' and describes a happier state between the two lovers. It helps us to understand how the relationship was maintained for so long in secrecy.

On a Spider

1 Artist who underneath my table
2 Thy curious texture hath displayed,
3 Who, if we may believe the fable,
4 Was once a pretty blooming maid.

5 Insidious, restless, watchful spider,
6 Fear no officious damsel's broom.
7 Extend thy artful fabric wider,
8 And spread thy banners round my room.

9   Swept from the rich man's costly ceiling,
10 Thou art welcome to my dirty roof.
11 Here thou may'st find a peaceful dwelling.
12 Here undisturbed attend thy woof.

13 Whilst I thy wond'rous fabric stare at
14 And think on hapless poet's fate,
15 Like thou confined in lonely garret,
16 And rudely banished rooms of state.

17 And as from out thy tortured body
18 Thou draw'st thy slender strings with pain,
19 So does he labour like a noddy,
∴ 20 To spin materials from his brain.

21 He for some flattering tawdry creature
22 That spreads her charms before his eye,
23 And that's a conquest little better,
24 Than thine o'er captive butterfly.

25 Thus far it's plain you both agree.
26 Pity our deaths may better show it.
27 'Tis ten to one but penury
28 Ends both the spider and the poet.

The poem draws a parallel between the spider and the poet. The spider weaves a web to catch its prey, and the poet writes verses to win the affections of his beloved. But again there is a deeper level of meaning. The butterfly was a Jacobite symbol for the fully fledged Jacobite sympathiser, in this case Byrom; and Caroline is the spider who has caught him. She, like the spider, has been 'swept from the rich man's costly ceiling' and 'rudely banished rooms of state', a reference to the famous quarrel of 1717. Caroline had been forced to vacate her royal quarters at Hampton Court where there was an elaborately painted ceiling by Sir James Thornhill which contained in the cornices portraits of George I, Caroline, her husband and their son Frederick. (The symbol of the spider is doubly appropriate as it carries allusions to Caroline's love of silks and silk-spinning. She accepted the gift of some Irish silk from Dean Swift, and used to visit a Mrs Gale who kept mulberry gardens and silk worms in Chelsea.)

In the left hand margin against line 20 in the notebook there appear the three mysterious dots which can be found on particular diagrams in the extraordinary collection of geometric drawings which Byrom acquired over the years in pursuit of his scientific and cabalistic studies. The dots were a special signal to the initiates of a 'truth'. The image of the spider spinning evidently appealed to Byrom. In a letter to a friend in August 1723 he applied the metaphor with mock modesty to his shorthand: 'I wish I had other goods to send you than those spun out of my own brain.' The setting of the poem is the modest house Byrom rented in a discreet quarter not too far from the Princess's residence in Leicester Fields. Compared to the grandeur of Hampton Court, it might well be termed a 'garret'. The conclusion of the poem is not optimistic, and the strain of the subterfuge involved in keeping their relationship secret may be the reason.

At the bottom of the page in *The Gentleman's Magazine* in which both versions of 'The Spider and Poet' appear, and directly beneath the Latin, is a very revealing note which is obviously associated with the poem.

N.B. It would not be agreeable on several counts to oblige Claudian 17 publickly. Lines may answer the End another Way.

In 'The Session of the Critics', Byrom uses the phrase an 'embrio Claudian' for William. In this instance he appears to be using the columns of *The Gentleman's Magazine* to 'leak' some public acknowledgment of the relationship. Claudian/William was now in his seventeenth year, hence 'Claudian 17'. Byrom seems to be saying, 'If William wishes to know something of my relationship with his mother – let him read this poem.' Was its publication an act of desperation or defiance on Byrom's part, still smarting from being rejected as a tutor?

There are some minor differences between the published version of 'The Spider and Poet' and that in the original manuscript. The shorthand version is more personalised since the last stanza has 'our deaths' rather than 'your deaths'. At the time the magazine was being prepared for the press, Byrom was in lodgings with his cousin Jo Clowes at Gray's Inn and dining at Abingdon's, within convenient distance of the editor's office at St John's Gate and certainly near enough to keep an eye on the printing of his verses in that particular issue. From the content of 'On a Spider' we can tell that it had been written when he was well into the relationship, but before 'The Session of the Critics'. This, although composed later, did not anticipate the end. Caroline herself died in November that same year.

Between the end of 1736 and June 1737 the columns of *The Gentleman's Magazine* had been used to publish a series of poems recounting a relationship between a Carolina and an admirer. Byrom appears to have used the same journal as a means to leak poetical confessions to the public. The first edition of his poems (1773) contains a set of verses addressed to 'Sylvanus Urban', the editor of *The Gentleman's Magazine* (in reality Edward Cave), in which Byrom implores him to correct points of grammar in the journal. The jocular tone indicates the good-humoured relationship Byrom had developed with Cave. Cave had started the magazine by purchasing a small printing office in St John's Gate, Clerkenwell, in part of what was left of the Hospitaller's original foundation. The gate house itself became the frontispiece to the periodical, and today houses the library of the Order. Books are still published from this address by the Knights of St John.

The reader who follows the story of 'Carolina' like a paper-chase through the pages of *The Gentleman's Magazine* is left with two conclusions. After the death of the Queen any proof of Byrom's involvement with her becomes circumstantial. There were no blood-tests available to prove paternity. In the early years Byrom and Caroline had been extremely discreet, and Caroline had carefully distanced herself and William from Byrom long before her death. If there were any rumours they would have been dismissed as baseless; no court would have listened to them. With the Queen's death what point was there in even contemplating such a course of action? It would have been needlessly damaging, inflicting wounds on a monarch still not fully accepted. When the young Duke William became the 'darling of the nation' it was better to ignore any reflections on his legitimacy. If William himself did hear of them, his notoriously excessive brutality in crushing the Jacobite rebellion may have, in part, been motivated by the anger they would have

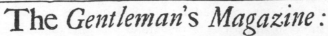

The *Gentleman's Magazine:*

St JOHN's GATE.

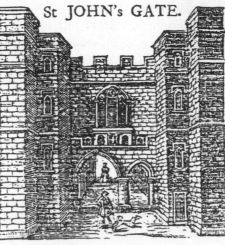

Lond.Gazette
Lond.Journ
Fog'sJourn.
Applebee's : :
Read'g : : : :
Craftsman
D.Spectator
GrubstreetJ
Wpy.Doctor
Daily.Post
D.Advertiser
StJames'sCh.
WhitehallCh
Lond.Ev.Sg
Weekly.Misc
General.Ev.
Old Whig
D.Gazetteer
Lon.Ev.Post
com. Sense.

York.News
Dublin 5 : :
Edinburgh 2
Bristol : : : :
Norwich 2
Exeter 2 : : :
Worcester
Northampton
Gloucester : :
Stamford : :
Nottingham
Bury.Journ.
Chester ditto
Derby ditto
Ipswich do.
Reading do.
Leeds.Merc.
Newcastle.C.
Canterbury
Durham
Kendal
Boston
Jamaica &c
Barbados :

For M A Y, 1737.

C O N T A I N I N G,

/more in Quantity, and greater Variety, than any Book of the kind and Price.

I. Original Miscellaneous L E T T E R S.
(1.) Country Curate's Objections against the Liturgy vindicated. (2.)
Remarks on *R. Y.*'s Account of Peopling the Earth, with a curious Computation. (3,) Inconsistency of Prescience and Liberty defended. (4.)
Mathematical Problems solved, and a new one proposed by Mr *Perryam*.

II. QUERIES in Theology, Philology, Morality, &c. (viz.) What was the first Offence of the apostate Angels? Why the Picture of the Bride in the *Aldobrandine* Marriage represents a *Black* ? Whether the same Reasons that give the Magistrate a Power over the Lives of the Subjects, will not justify Suicide? Challenge to Mr *Chubb*.

III. E S S A Y S Critical. Case of *Ornan's* Threshing-Floor, and the K. of *Rabbah*'s Crown. Critique on *Leonidas*. On a Passage in *Catullus*. *Tillotson*

mistaken about Revenge. *Old Whig* a Droller on Words. Apocrypha contains idle Fables.

IV. Political. Reflections on the *Scotish* Riot-Bill. The fatal Consequences of lowering Interest. Rat in the Statue. Snake in the Grass. Acquisitions on the Continent dangerous to *England*. Liberties of the People are the Ornament of the Crown. *English* deliberate Suicides.

V. Poetical. Ambition and Content. On Suicide. *Fulvia*, by *Richard Savage*, Esq; Description of *June*. The invalid's Story.

VI. Historical CHRONICLE.

VII. LISTS of Deaths, Marriages, Promotions, Preferments, Bankrupts, &c.

VIII. Foreign AFFAIRS.

IX. Price of Stocks. Bill of Mortality.

X. REGISTER of BOOKS.

XI. TABLE of CONTENTS.

By *S Y L V A N U S U R B A N*, Gent.

L O N D O N: Printed by E. CAVE at St JOHN's GATE, and Sold by the Booksellers of Town and Country; of whom may be had any former Month.

Figure 3: St John's Gate

caused. Byrom was contained by the Establishment and continued his subversive role. The sequence of poems in the notebook is concerned with important moments in the relationship which he chose to record in verse and preserve privately.

Because he sensed this policy of containment, even before Caroline's death, he used the columns of *The Gentleman's Magazine*. It was an ideal means to disseminate information – its sub-heading was *The Monthly Intelligencer* and, according to one editor (John Nichols), by its very nature its preparation depended on a 'sort of masonic secrecy'.[11]

Byrom's claims in these poems are so bizarre that one is bound to question their validity. Was he being serious? Are they the products of an over-active imagination, a fantasy produced by a besotted admirer of Caroline? Could they even be deliberate misinformation to discredit her? Byrom's everyday life shows that he was very much respected, but it also reveals that, in his political activities alone, he was capable of great duplicity. He suffered a serious breakdown in health between 1732 and 1733. This may well have been the result of the end of the affair. It could equally be seen as the cause of this fantasy. However, the publication of his epigram 'On a Lady Stung by a Bee' in the very first issue of *The Gentleman's Magazine* in 1731 is evidence of a *real* affair pre-dating any illness, and its presence in the MS notebook *as part of the Caroline sequence* must be seen as supporting his claims. Complex and allusive as some of the poems undoubtedly are, their layered texture is in keeping with Byrom's learning, linguistic sophistication, cabalistic studies and love of codes.

Corroborative evidence must be found from other sources. One body of material undeniably written by Byrom is his Journal. In the entry for 9 June 1729, he recorded a series of seemingly innocent meetings with friends at the King's Arms, Tom's Coffee House and Common Garden Inn. First, at the King's Arms, he met 'Mr Radcliffe', the exiled Earl of Derwentwater and a powerful masonic figure in France, one of the foremost Jacobite leaders. That day he had been given a copy of Byrom's youthful verses 'My Time, O ye muses'. At Tom's, Byrom conversed with Mr Taylor 'my disciple' and Tom Bentley, nephew of his old tutor, the Master of Trinity. Later he was joined by 'Mr Lounds', a Jacobite companion from his days in Montpellier, with whom he 'drank a bottle of wine and had much merry talk about Carolina [sic] madness'.

All these men had specific roles in Byrom's life. While the

Caroline poems are peopled with figures bearing conventional names drawn from classical mythology and history, they also contain real characters, as this Journal entry makes clear. Tom Bentley appears in 'The Session of The Critics'. Taylor appears in 'Trinitonians', a later poem in the sequence, and was so closely associated with Byrom that his name became attached to two of the poems. Moreover, Byrom is joking with Lounds about 'Carolina madness', of all things! Radclyffe was a kinsman of the Duke of Berwick, who first instructed the Young Pretender to the Throne, Prince Charles Edward, in the arts of war at the tender age of fourteen. (Two of his sons, Lord Peter Fitzjames and Lord Anthony Bonaventure Fitzjames, nephews of the Old Pretender James Stuart, were each in turn Grand Priors of the Knights of St John, so the allusions to the Order in the poems cannot be ignored either. Especially since Lord Anthony was in office when 'The Session of the Critics' was written.) To see this group, representative of so much in the poems, parade before us in the space of one day in Byrom's life reveals how closely Byrom's life and art were linked.

CHAPTER THREE

First Years in London

1719–24

Pᴿɪɴᴄᴇss Cᴀʀᴏʟɪɴᴇ of Anspach was the daughter-in-law of George I, who had come from Hannover to be crowned King of England in 1714. He had divorced his wife, Sophia Dorothea, in 1694, imprisoning her in a castle in Germany for her alleged adultery. Consequently, as Princess of Wales, Caroline acted for a time in place of George I's own wife at official functions. By 1719 she had been married to the Prince of Wales for fourteen years. Already they had four children: one son, Frederick, and three daughters. The two Georges cordially loathed each other and quarrelled violently after the birth of Caroline's second son, George William, in 1717. The dispute had arisen over the King's choice of godfather. The Prince and Princess were banished from the Royal court and deprived of their children. They set up their own establishment at Leicester House, where a separate and almost rival court grew up around them. The Prince amused himself with a succession of mistresses. The infant boy died after only three months. The three young princesses remained in the custody of the King, and the elder son, 'Poor Fred' as he became known, stayed behind in Germany. Caroline was thus very much isolated from her children, though, admittedly, she hated Frederick intensely for some unknown reason. An intelligent woman, one of the most intelligent consorts of any English king, she turned her attention to men of wit and learning, cultivating a coterie of writers and exhibiting a shrewd and diplomatic tolerance of her husband's mistresses. But she must have been a lonely woman. From time to time she was able to escape from the routine of Leicester House and in the company of one trusted companion made private excursions around London undetected. It follows that, should a convenient opportunity present itself, the Princess would grasp at a secret visit to such a celebrated event as Sturbridge Fair. The novelty would provide amusing relief.

No doubt the Princess decided to travel in disguise to enable her to move about easily. Such a disguise once adopted would have to be carried through until such time as it became safe or convenient to drop it. Byrom was the sort of man who would appeal to Caroline simply on the level of intellectual companionship. His alert, intelligent mind was interested in the same literary and philosophical topics as hers. After all, Caroline had been tutored by Leibniz, one of the great minds of the century and a man Byrom admired. Eight years older than Byrom, she was undoubtedly far more fascinating than any woman he had ever met.

The first encounter happened by chance, but Caroline must have felt some spark of sympathy for the love-struck stranger. They were both unusually tall and that in itself was a start. For the moment, the Princess kept her identity to herself simply to keep her presence in Cambridge secret, and it was probably arranged for Byrom to meet her again in London on neutral territory, still unaware of who she was. However, at some time early in the relationship the secret was disclosed. His intellectual merit was sufficient for the Princess to command him to attend on her. He would be able to do so publicly at one of her literary gatherings at Leicester House. But it could not have been long before they both sensed a growing attraction. It was then for Caroline to decide whether she wanted to continue the relationship, although in doing so she would be placing her reputation and life in Byrom's hands. His discretion was assured, for discovery could have led to his execution.

The life of the Princess when she first met Byrom did not make such an affair impossible. In their early days at Leicester House the Prince and Princess of Wales kept a brilliant court. Balls and masquerades enlivened the evenings and every morning there was a 'drawing room'. Although the Prince, like his father, had no great love for literature or men of letters, the receptions were frequented by the most accomplished of wits and fashionable society. There were times during the day when the duties of the royal pair converged and others when their activities were separate and distinct. The Princess held court over her literary salon and the Prince busied himself with affairs of state or his mistresses. They came together for the stately luncheons, which continued long into the afternoon, and then retired, in the German fashion, to sleep them off. But Caroline rose earlier than her husband to attend to her own interests. In the evening the Prince and Princess often amused themselves with different sets of friends in different apartments of their house, or even in different houses. For example the *Weekly Journal* for 12 August 1719 reports: 'On Wednesday night Her Royal Highness the Princess supp'd with the Duchess of Shrewsbury, at her Grace's house in Hammersmith.'

The Princess was very fond of dining out. It helped, too, that the Prince was a man who lived by the clock. By the time he was middle-aged his insistence on the punctual observation of routine for its own sake made many of his courtiers envy the more liberal gaiety of Caroline's court. So strict was the Prince's adherence to the clock that his whereabouts at any time were easily predictable. There were, therefore, occasions when it would be possible for the Princess to meet Byrom and many more when it was quite proper for her to receive him in her literary and philosophical gatherings without attracting undue attention. The accessibility of the high-spirited Princess was one of her greatest assets in enabling her to conduct a clandestine affair. A more retiring nature would have found it difficult to cover the traces.

The Princess could also take advantage of the Prince's absences from home, when he went back to Hannover or was enjoying himself in amorous pursuit of yet another female. In these escapades he was helped by members of his household, courtiers, and even politicians. One such affair was conducted in the country house of Robert Walpole. In the latter half of 1723 a physician's daughter, Mary by name, was at Houghton acting as a kind of companion to Lady Walpole. The girl was seduced by the Prince and became pregnant. Lady Walpole discovered what had happened and arranged for the girl to be married to a Mr Dunckerley who was in the service of the Duke of Devonshire.[1] After the birth of a baby boy, Thomas, the couple separated. Mrs Dunckerley was granted a grace and favour apartment at Somerset House where she lived until her death forty years later. The apartment then passed on to her son. Thomas Dunckerley was thus the natural son of George II but did not know this until his mother died. He himself had a successful career in the navy and became a Senior Grand Warden of the freemasons as well as a leader among them in 28 Provinces. George III thought fit to grant him a pension of £100.

Caroline was not by nature a libertine and there is no suggestion that she took a series of lovers in the way her husband did. She was an extremely clever woman and, despite George's repeated infidelities, remained to the end the woman he loved most. All the evidence suggests, however, that she never felt as deeply about her husband as he did about her. Her tolerance of his mistresses and clever political manoeuvring typify her careful and considered control of their relationship.

George and Caroline held court at Leicester House in the winter. In summer they would move to Richmond Lodge, and the great levée which the Prince held daily would bring the nobility and 'quality' out to the country. In 1719 George and Caroline moved out of Richmond earlier than usual to spend summer at Greenwich while alterations were carried out at Richmond Lodge. George sent a member of the household over to Holland to take the model of a house there as a basis for the alterations at Richmond. He seems to have interested himself much in the project. Apparently the Prince moved back sometime that summer, for the *Weekly Journal* for Saturday 19 September, announced that

> The same day some part of the Prince's Baggage was brought to his Royal Highness's House in Leicester Fields from Richmond where their Royal Highnesses are shortly expected. On Monday night last the Prince and the Lord Herbert went to Kensington to visit the young Princesses.

The Prince and Princess were not always together that summer. Somewhere between the end of August and early September the Princess went to Sturbridge Fair. That year the side shows did better business than the tradesmen. A report in the *Weekly Journal* announced news from the Fair.

> That Mr. Mills the Drollman's commodities sell better than the Tradesmen; some of whom are in a manner ruined by bringing their goods to the worst market that has been known there.

There is a noticeable gap in Byrom's Journal between July 1718, when he was in London, and 17 April 1721, three months after his marriage. This gap was partially filled by twenty letters to John Stansfield, discovered by Dr W.E.A. Axon and published in 1912.[2] These show that Byrom spent the time between 1718 and 1721 mainly in Cambridge or in London. A brief extract in the Journal from a letter, written by his sister-in-law Ann Byrom to Stansfield, abruptly announces his marriage to her sister Elizabeth. The first entry of the Journal proper, which follows soon after, does not read like the first entry to be written. The reader is plunged into the middle of something, the sequence is not continuous and the previous history has been deliberately omitted. It cannot be said with certainty when Byrom started his diaries, but it was as a bachelor. Whatever those early entries contained, they were not included and, with the rest of the manuscripts, were destroyed. Some may have been considered unsuitable for publication since they covered his early independence as a graduate. Care was taken, however, to publish that part of a letter announcing his marriage 'with the consent of father and mother'.

It is surprising how few of Caroline's personal papers have survived in this country. Among those still in the Royal Archives at Windsor is a series of letters written in French to Mrs Clayton (a confidante of the Princess and at one time a member of her household). Perhaps these might contain clues to a connection between Byrom and Caroline.

Among Caroline's letters to Mrs Clayton is one dated December 1719, in which she comments on the passing of the Peerage Bill in the House of Commons:

> Our majority had been considerable, 93, or more as we reckon'd it was so certain, that Mr Freeman assur'd me yesterday the minister had tempted the tories extremely so far as to promise them and their friends the employments, He said the same proposal was made to him.[3]

According to the archives at Windsor, the only Freemans known to have been employed in the Royal Household at that time were a waterman to Princess Caroline and a gentleman chorister of the Chapel Royal. Neither of these seemed likely political reporters, and that was the function which Byrom fulfilled for several people apart from the Royal Family. It is entirely possible that the Freeman referred to is Byrom. He varied his pseudonyms to suit the person or occasion. For example, at the time his brother, Edward, was worried by his decision to be a non-juror, John wrote to his sisters from Dover as John Edwards. To Stansfield, he was Sam Woolmer. With the press he hid behind John Shadow. In 1727 he used the name Francis Freeman when writing to his wife about a famous dispute in which he was involved at the Royal Society, concerning the proper mode of address to be adopted towards George I. Freeman was also the name he chose to use earlier with the Princess. (In doing so he was recalling the famous friendship between Sarah, Duchess of Marlborough, wife of the first Duke, and Queen Anne. The Queen had wished to remove any insistence on rank in their correspondence and signed herself Mrs Morley, Sarah replied as Mrs

Freeman.) If his chance encounter with Caroline was to be repeated then a reason was needed to justify his visits, should these ever be questioned. He was not an automatic member of the Establishment by birth, so he employed the one means he had to gain an entrée and serve the Princess. It looks as if in December 1719 Byrom was using his shorthand to keep the Princess of Wales privately informed about the business of the House of Commons. Byrom's system of shorthand was by no means the first, but it was certainly the finest of his day. One leading authority, E.H. Butler, describes it as 'so superior to all others that it earned him the enmity of his fellow authors'.[4] Byrom worked hard to achieve that superiority. After his initial dabbling with Tom Sharp in Cambridge, he continued to strive for a smooth-flowing script without any awkward joins between the signs and as close to the spoken word as possible. His work as Caroline's shorthand reporter was a welcome opportunity to test its speed and accuracy. By 1721 Byrom felt ready to teach his system personally as a confidential service to individual pupils for a fee of five guineas.

The Peerage Bill had been introduced in 1719 by opponents of the Prince of Wales. Its purpose was to limit the Prince's powers of patronage as Regent in his father's absence from the country and on his succession. It would enable the present ministry to create new Peers from their own supporters and limit the Prince in making further creations, thus depriving him of one of the principal means of asserting his power. The Prince fully realised the implications of the manoeuvre and was furious. Support from Sir Richard Steele with a new journal, *The Plebeian*, helped to defeat the Bill. It was this defeat which Byrom/Freeman reported to Caroline. His verbatim reports were highly prized for their accuracy. When the Lord Chancellor, Lord Macclesfield, stood trial in 1725 for misdemeanours in office, both prosecution and defence approached Byrom for the use of his shorthand skills. The Journal contains many references to him attending Parliament as a political reporter.

> I went on foot to Westminster, asked for Mr. Kenn, who was attending the secret committee about the late Chancellor above stairs; the man told me he was not to be spoke with, but Mr. Staples coming by got me upstairs and Kenn came to me, gave me one of the City Bills which I took down in shorthand in a little room there.[5]

Byrom's shorthand skills were an invaluable aid to the Princess and must have brought them closer together. At the same time, as a Jacobite it served his purposes to support the Prince and Princess in their quarrel with George I. Caroline was known to be sympathetic to certain Jacobite lords and had pleaded for them after the 1715 rebellion. Jacobites should have welcomed the passing of the Peerage Bill since it would have limited the powers of the Prince of Wales and embittered further his quarrel with the King. With the House of Hannover divided against itself, the Stuart cause might gain ground. Surprise was expressed when some members of the Commons, together with Jacobite sympathisers, voted against the Bill, and Byrom reported this back to Caroline: 'One said to a Jacobite, you are mad if this Bill fails there may be a reconciliation in the Royal Family and then where is your hope?'[6]

Close upon the campaign against the Prince's power came the great financial scandal of the South Sea Bubble. It was a period of wild speculation and the South Sea Company had expanded with staggering speed in the previous three years. The King himself had been asked to be a Governor of the company, and everyone involved in the enterprise thought there were stupendous fortunes to be made. The Prince and Princess of Wales had shares worth £30,000 and the climate of financial speculation was almost hysterical in its rashness. Eventually the inevitable happened and the inflated credit of so many companies which had shot up from nothing – including the South Sea Company itself – collapsed. Great families and fortunes were undone overnight. The centre of commerce was split wide open. Many people were driven to suicide. The Chancellor of the Exchequer was sent to the Tower.

It was at this time, when surrounded by so many disasters, that the Princess found she was once more pregnant. In July 1720 she writes to Mrs Clayton: 'I fear I am with child, the accidents which have lately happened give me no encouragement.'[7] The pregnancy ended with the birth of Prince William, Duke of Cumberland, on 15 April 1721.

On Saturday 15th instant, a little after Seven o'Clock in the Evening, her Royal Highness the Princess of Wales was happily delivered of a Prince at Leicester House, ... Her Royal Highness's safe delivery being soon made publick by the firing of the cannon in St James's Park, an universal Joy was seen that Evening among all sorts of people throughout London and Westminster of which the usual Demonstrations were shown by Ringing of Bells, Illuminations and Bonfires.

The date of the birth became a private joke for Byrom. When a prospective pupil apologised for not being able to pay his fees, Byrom brushed his embarrassment aside wittily by saying that it did not matter, and that if he (Byrom) died before his pupil could pay, then he could pay his 'fifteenth son',[8] both the son he did not have and the son born on the fifteenth. Byrom enjoyed puns even when only he realised their full meaning.

Two months before that birth, on St Valentine's day, John Byrom married his cousin Elizabeth Byrom in Manchester. The marriage is an odd, rash act on the part of Byrom. He had no profession, but was in effect living off his wits by gambling on the success of his shorthand. He had no regular address but moved between London, Cambridge and Manchester. What is more, after his marriage he made no attempt to settle, but left his wife in Manchester while he returned to London. He had no inherited wealth with which to support a family, and there are signs in a letter written by his sister-in-law Ann Byrom that his wife's family were opposed to the match.

> Mr. Stansfield: I received yours last week, and designed answering it by first post, but could not have an opportunity, we having been pretty much engaged this week for on Tuesday last sister Elizabeth was married to Dr. Byrom, with the consent of her father and mother, and the wedding kept here, and we having had a deal of company.[9]

Stansfield seems to have had no idea Byrom was intending to get married. Ann's announcement is not made with any great enthusiasm, but more as an apology for not replying earlier. The letter is surprisingly brief considering its news and the person to whom it is addressed. Stansfield had been employed by Byrom's father as early as 1709. He had thus worked for the family for more than eleven years, and became a close friend to John when he was still at school. He was sympathetic to the Jacobites, and Byrom consulted him over the Oath of Abjuration. He stayed with Stansfield in London, calling him affectionately 'dear landlord', for he was genuinely fond of him and his wife, and was godfather to one of their children. In normal circumstances Byrom would have written personally to break the news. Instead there is only a cursory note, which might lead to a suspicion that the marriage was a sudden one, hastened by necessity. But Elizabeth's first child was born eleven months after the wedding day. Was it simply that the marriage was arranged with a suddenness that deprived the Byrom ladies of the usual pleasures involved in preparing for such an event? If so, what reason could Byrom have for getting married, when he had no house of his own to which he could take his bride? They appear to have lived for a while with Elizabeth's parents. It was there that their first child was born. In October 1722 they moved to a house near to the town centre which they rented from a Mr Hunter, and which became their home for the rest of their married life. John was either never able to afford a house of his own or simply chose not to buy one. Elizabeth's father, Joseph, was faced with a son-in-law who had done little or nothing to establish himself, and had even thrown opportunities away. Such recklessness must have made him appear most undesirable. Joseph's opinion of Byrom does not seem to have improved with time. When he made his final will in 1733 he had seen enough to prompt him to ensure that Elizabeth was protected financially until she died. He left £500 in trust 'for her sole and separate use' and after her death the endowment went to her children and was not 'liable or subject to the control debts forfeitures or engagements of the said Byrom her husband'. Joseph left a further £1,000 for Elizabeth and her children, but in the event of their deaths it was to revert to his own sons. John was not completely excluded; with Elizabeth he enjoyed income from property in Cheshire, but Joseph was careful to ensure he could never dispose of any capital.[10]

The speed of the marriage and the unfavourable circumstances surrounding it suggest expediency rather than romance. Byrom had met the Princess only a year or so earlier, in late August or early September 1719. It seems that, once he had moved to London and started shorthand reporting on political matters for the Princess, he also became her lover. Could Byrom's marriage have been part of an elaborate plan to divert attention from his political and social ambitions?

Caroline's activities and whereabouts in the spring of 1720 can be established easily. The newspapers of the day carried regular bulletins of the movements of the Royal Family. Since Prince William was born in April 1721 his conception must have taken place around the previous summer. On 5 June she was still in London attending church at the Chapel Royal. Four days later the Prince went to the Haymarket Theatre without her. By 18 June they had moved to Richmond where they held a large reception to which their own daughters were allowed to come. The following day, the Prince and Princess held a great court. The *Weekly Journal* stated that the

Royal couple were intending to go to Bath 'next month'. On Saturday 2 July the Prince held a great levy which brought the aristocracy flocking from London to Richmond. A week later members of the royal household set out for Bath 'to make preparations for their Royal Highnesses coming'. The following Saturday they were still at Richmond, for their daughter Anne visited them there. After the middle of July Caroline and George must have left for Bath, which had by then become highly fashionable. Beau Nash, self-appointed arbiter of taste and style, held court there. The visit of the Prince and Princess gave the royal seal of approval to those parading in the Pump Room. Considering all these activities, therefore, the most likely time for the conception was before Caroline left London for Richmond, between the latter end of June and the beginning of July 1720.

Marriage did not alter Byrom's intention to preserve as far as possible his independence in order to pursue his own aims. It cannot be said that he ever made a serious attempt to support his wife. In this respect one of Elizabeth's attractions was her father's wealth. Not that John wanted the money for himself; on the contrary, he saw that Elizabeth's father could keep her far better than he could, and this enabled him to go off to London each year. If to provide for Elizabeth had been the prime motive in seeking a career John could have quashed his scruples and taken the Oath of Abjuration. Or he could have followed a career in medicine without taking the Oath. He did neither. Instead he chose to use his shorthand as a tool to shape his future along paths he wanted to follow. There was, of course, only one possible place to teach on a large enough scale to make it a success – London. There he would find men and women who needed a system of confidential communication. Surely his family could see that, and accept his frequent absences from home. Byrom entered upon a double life. He would go to London and Cambridge for the winter months and, if he had no other engagements to prevent him, then return to Manchester and his family. So intent was he in pursuing his aims that he was not always at home for Christmas or birthdays or funerals. On the one hand, he appeared to be an ambitious husband aspiring to make his living, on the other, his mode of life and career allowed him maximum freedom of movement, convenient access to the houses of the great and, by emphasis on confidentiality, provided him with an acceptable air of mystery which he could use to cloak any activity he wished to hide.

Byrom set about teaching his shorthand in earnest. One might have expected him to stay, if only initially, with some of his relatives in London. He did not. Nor did he lodge with the Stansfields. Yet he had little capital and did not take rooms of his own. Instead he borrowed those of his friends when they did not need them. Otherwise he lived at inns and dined at coffee houses. This rather nomadic mode of life suited his purposes. It left him accountable to no-one but himself.

He would have cut a striking figure in the streets of London. The portrait painted of him in his youth shows him to have been good-looking with fine features, a high forehead, striking eyes and a rather full almost petulant mouth. According to the Reverend Mr Hoole: 'He was one of the tallest men in England, so that in the course of 50 years he appears to have met only two men taller than himself.'[11] In fact: 'he stood 6 feet 4 inches in his stockings'.[12] While never wealthy he was conscious of his dress. It was an age of elegance and within the limits of the means at his disposal he showed a flair for style with his capes, cravats and ribboned canes. He did not affect the extremes of fashion or show any interest in them. The circles he moved in demanded a good standard of dress for him to cut a convincing figure. With a new suit of grave brown clothes and a horse-hair tie-wig, he made sure he was right from top to toe. His sisters provided him with cravats, the local washerwoman laundered his set of fourteen shirts, the barber called to shave him and the shoemaker came to keep him well-shod. Finally he added a few accessories to finish off the effect – a silver snuff-box, a ribbon for his cane and a silk handkerchief. His was a manly elegance in which he paid scrupulous attention to personal cleanliness. Pride in his appearance would make him stop to have his stockings darned en route to visit a friend or pupil. And he would carry his sword, as all gentlemen did, although at times he was likely to forget it. He was so keen on this point that he sometimes borrowed swords from his friends and lost those as well! His much vaunted piety did not prevent him from playing and enjoying games of cards and billiards. He took snuff and enjoyed a pipe of tobacco. He showed an interest in all the variety of life around him in London and on his travels. He frequented the Opera, the boxing ring, exhibitions of paintings, and was always rummaging in bookshops. Indeed, he became an avid collector of books and often in his Journal recounts with glee his latest purchases. Above all he was convivial by nature. He loved company and conversation and, like many men of similar disposition, enjoyed good food and wine. These did not always agree with him. On occasions he would drink three pints of wine and pay the penalty next day.

Byrom never rose to riding in a coach of his own, but he was able to earn a reasonable living and make his way in good society. He was helped by his Cambridge connections and those members of the landed gentry of Lancashire and Cheshire whom he knew and were resident in London. So it was possible for the relationship with Caroline to continue. It was extraordinary enough that Byrom should become involved with the Princess of Wales in the first place. It was even more extraordinary that the relationship continued for several years. Because of her rank the affair must have been initiated by the Princess. For the same reason, and despite all the difficulties and dangers of such an enterprise, it would be for her to decide that it was to continue. Having been a faithful wife to an unfaithful and singularly unattractive husband, she found qualities in Byrom which made her love him and persist in that love. Caroline's intelligence never allowed her heart to rule her head, and she was supremely skilled in manipulating people to serve her own ends without them realising it. It would be no different with Byrom. She found him useful and his usefulness endeared him to her. For his part he was completely captivated.

Given the need for subterfuge in their relationship, it was fortunate for both John and Caroline that masquerades and masked balls were very much in fashion. The Prince and Princess frequently went to public balls, liked to wear masks and to mingle with the crowd. On one occasion George I, in disguise, was accosted by a woman who made a Jacobite toast: 'A bumper to King James'. Without revealing his identity, the King replied, 'I drink with all my heart to any unfortunate Prince.' In one of his letters home in 1726 Byrom recounts his own visit to a masked ball. (Better to write himself than let gossip reach his wife's ears.)

> I have not time to tell you what fine folk I saw at the masquerade on Monday night! The eldest of the Mr. Ords would present me with a ticket, and having dressed me up in his black clothes, bar gown etc., I went to that famous assembly. When I have leisure I'll tell you as well as I can what kind of place it is.[13]

However, no relationship could be maintained, let alone develop, at public receptions or dances. At some stage it must have become essential for the Princess and Byrom to have somewhere they could

4 The Old Wellington Inn, formerly a shop selling
Manchester wares and John Byrom's birthplace

5 Kersall Cell, the Byrom country home

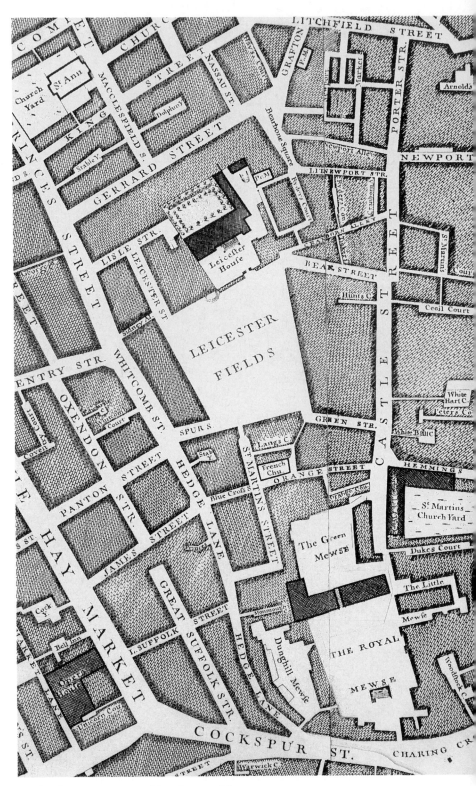

6 Rocque's map of London, 1746

7 Queen Caroline of Anspach, consort of George II (from a portrait by
Jacopo Amigoni)

meet in secret. Where could such a place be found? The total population of London in Caroline's day could not have been more than 700,000. Then as now the City, with the centre of business spreading from St Paul's to the Exchange, was at its heart. Another centre of activity had grown up around the Houses of Parliament in Westminster. Fashionable society gathered at St James's and the Mall. In fine weather St James's Park was thronged with people from the highest level of society and by others anxious to ape their betters. To escape detection they would have to avoid houses in the more fashionable squares or streets. On the other hand they could not meet too far from Leicester House because of the demands of the Princess's duties. The shorter the distance, the less likely she was to be seen. Byrom was in the habit of borrowing or taking chambers near Gray's Inn. This was east of Leicester House and remote from fashionable St James's.

The most suitable place for their meeting would seem to lie somewhere between Leicester House and Gray's Inn. The Journal does not render up any obvious address, but if Byrom did rent a property then tenant rolls might still exist which record it. The archives for the area concerned are kept at Westminster City Reference Library, and although they do not contain the relevant tenant rolls, the library does have the Rate Books for the Parish of St Martin in the Fields which included the area around Leicester Fields. The books contain the Overseer's Accounts, which record, street by street, the rates paid by tenants in the various wards of the parish. Though some of the books have been damaged with the passage of time, the entries for many of the streets remain clearly legible. In one street, New Round Court, a property was listed as being rented in the name of 'Thomas Siddall'.[14] The first entry in Siddal's name was in 1720. This was followed by others, up to and including 1725. It looked like another example of Byrom's use of an alias to cover his tracks. In renting a house for his clandestine meetings with Caroline he used the name of a real person for whom he had a genuine regard.

The choice of Thomas Siddal was a clever one: his father Thomas had been executed and the boy himself was still only twelve, living in the family home at Manchester. To Byrom, a High Churchman and a Jacobite, the name was rich in resonances. It belonged to a fellow Jacobite whose courage he admired and whose allegiances he shared. There can be no doubt about Byrom's sympathy and respect for the Siddals. After the execution of Thomas junior in 1746, Byrom carefully preserved the tailored cloth in which his head was wrapped and sent from London to Manchester. This was not simply a gesture of piety; but also a sign of his remorse. Was the relationship the secret Siddal took to his grave? The tailored cloth remained with Byrom until he died.

Although New Round Court no longer exists, a similar court off the Strand has survived frequent redevelopments of the neighbourhood to give some idea of the kind of house Byrom tenanted. Heathcock Court is still accessible from the Strand, with its narrow covered alleyway leading straight from the street to a warren of modest Georgian buildings of three storeys. It is possible to check the exact location of New Round Court from Rocque's map of London for 1746 and Horwood's map of 1799. It lay only a few streets away from Leicester House, tucked away between Chandos Street and the Strand. The house was linked by a network of back streets to St Martin's Churchyard. From there it was only a short

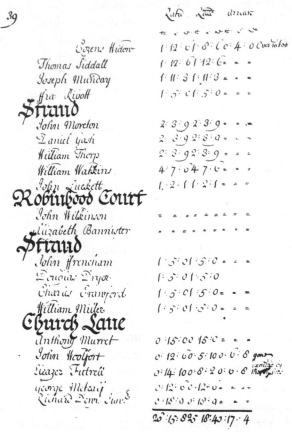

Figure 4: Rate book for New Round Court, 1723

distance to the Royal Mews or Leicester Fields and Caroline's residence. By means of any one of several routes the Princess could
reach New Round Court with little fear of being noticed. One
advantage of the site was the narrow alley to the Strand. Anyone
going to and from the house could do so without being noticed from
the public highway. The back courtyard meant that the properties
were not overlooked. It was a site ideally suited to Byrom's purposes, chosen with great care. The property then formed part of the
London estates of the Dukes of Bedford. The head of the family at
the time was Rachel, Lady Russell. The Duke, her grandson, was
still only a child, and the estates were managed by a steward called
Hoskins, who would be responsible for letting individual properties. Byrom would continue to reside near Gray's Inn and conduct
his public life from there. The house in New Round Court was used
solely for the relationship and is the setting of the poem 'On A
Spider'.

With New Round Court as a central point of reference, Byrom's
movements at this time can be seen in an altogether different light.
For example, the fact that his Journal records that he dined in March
1724 at the One Tun Tavern in the Strand gains interest from its
position virtually facing New Round Court. One Tun Alley in fact
took its name from the tavern. A news item for 6 December 1718 in
the *Weekly Journal* tells us something about the colourful clientele:

> Last Thursday four highwaymen drinking at One Tun Tavern
> near Hungerford Market in the Strand, and falling about dividing
> their booty, the Drawer overheard them, sent for a Constable and
> secured them, and next day they were committed to Newgate.

By 1724 the inn had obviously become more fashionable for we find
Byrom complaining of the expense of the food: 'five shillings apiece
– a good dinner but very extravagant!'

Byrom had returned to Manchester from London earlier to move
house from his parents-in-law on 5 October 1722. This meant he
had a settled address in Lancashire. A few pages of diary survive for
the first part of this month, recounting his visits to relatives and
friends. The next record of his actions is in July 1723, when he
visited Cambridge and Oxford to begin to collect important academic figures as subscribers to a proposed edition of his shorthand
manual. In Cambridge he gained the support of Dr Robert Smith,
a Fellow of Trinity and, later, Bentley's successor as Master. He
taught both George II and the Duke of Cumberland, so he was a

good catch. At Oxford Byrom was not so lucky. The Vice-Chancellor and one or two Fellows from Brasenose agreed to subscribe, but Oxford was, generally speaking, slower to show interest in the shorthand. He then returned to London to look for new pupils and continued cultivating important people. In a letter to Elizabeth he makes this quite plain: 'To-night I have been with Mr. Kelsall; he may be of great service, being a favourite of Walpole and acquainted much with the great folk.'[15] In pursuit of the great folk he went to Tunbridge Wells for two weeks in August. One person he was anxious to see there was James Jurin, an old friend from Cambridge who had taken up medicine rather late, but, nevertheless, became a doctor of genuine repute, and was one of the first advocates of vaccination for smallpox. Already Secretary to the Royal Society and therefore 'acquainted much with the great folk', he agreed to subscribe. In a letter home Byrom explained his visit as solely one of business, but he managed to combine business with pleasure. The poem 'Tunbridgiale', intended for his friend Ralph Leycester, describes Tunbridge and the society there. The tone of letter and poem differ noticeably. To his wife he wrote:

> My dear love.
>
> I came from Tunbridge last night along with the gentleman I went with on Friday morning: 'tis a very pleasant place, and a world of company there. I saw Dr. Jurin, showed him my method, he liked it mightily, and has promised to do me service; my four companions subscribed on his recommendation and Mr. Ord and five or six more promised they would.[16]

The poem concentrated on the more pleasurable aspects of the 'world of company':

> If with Things here below we compare Things on high,
> The *Walks* are like yonder bright Path in the Sky,
> Where heavenly Bodies in such Clusters mingle,
> Tis impossible, Sir, to describe 'em all single:
> But if ever you saw that sweet Creature Miss *K---y*,
> If ever you saw her, I say, – let me tell ye,
> Descriptions are needless: for surely to you,
> No Beauty, no Graces, can ever be new.[17]

There is reason to believe that Byrom is alluding to Princess Caroline here, for in the shorthand version of the poem in the manuscript book the symbols are not K---y but C-l-n.[18]

Figure 5

The letter is a matter-of-fact statement reassuring Elizabeth about his subscribers and his intention to return home. The poem is frivolous and jocular, written by a man who enjoyed dalliance. The letter and poem represent the two faces of Byrom – one turned towards Elizabeth, the other towards Caroline.

Byrom wrote innumerable letters to his wife. Ostensibly these were to keep her informed of his whereabouts and activities. But they tell much more. Strangely enough, he wanted his wife to destroy his letters. In one, written over 10-12 November 1723, he recounts some very trivial incidents. He twice asks her to burn it: 'I am weary with writing all this nonsense, which be sure to burn when thou hast read it', and later: 'Well, farewell my Bets both; burn this and write to thy affectionate husband, J.B.' The letter appears to be harmless, why should he be so insistent? He may well have been afraid that, because of the nature of his involvement with the Court, his apparently trivial jottings might later prove incriminating. However, unknown to Byrom, Elizabeth kept his letters, and no doubt found comfort in them during his long absences. By their survival, they help to give the lie to his appearance of concern and loving care.

John protests his affection with every letter home, but sometimes the entries are surprising. He was born in a leap year on 29 February and it may well be that because his birthday was a movable feast, dates and anniversaries came to have an unusual importance. Faced with a birthday which could be celebrated on either 28 February or 1 March, he may have felt some special significance in the fact that the birthday of the Princess fell on 1 March. Did this coincidence encourage a lover's superstitious belief in destiny? He chose to marry on St Valentine's Day, almost as if the occasion of the feast day would be auspicious for a marriage which appears to have begun almost as a matter of convenience. In his Journal he does not remember the anniversary any more than his wife's birthday.

References to the birthday are not regular and, when they occur, are expressed almost as afterthoughts. In 1724 he writes:

My dear Love!

How do you do? Is not this your birthday? Just as I took my pen here to write it comes into my mind that it is. I wish you joy of it and a great many of 'em, and that you may long live to enjoy all the good things I can wish for you.[19]

Byrom's admission that he has remembered her birthday at the last moment is so open, one can only conclude that, either the anniversary meant nothing to him, or he did not care to disguise his forgetfulness. He makes all the right noises once he has remembered, but they come a little too late and too dutifully.

This perfunctory manner becomes worse. In a Journal entry of 30 January 1726, there is no mention that it is his wife's birthday at all, and in a letter from Cambridge three days before her birthday in 1728, he forgets to mention it. Two years later he only remembers as he is walking along the street in Cambridge. In this instance absence does not seem to have made the heart grow fonder:

As I am going to Emmanuel College to breakfast with one of my scholars (Mr. Abbott) it comes into my head that this is thy birthday and so I have stept into the coffee house to wish thee much joy on it, and a happy succession of them . . . [20]

In contrast he often manages to drag in some sort of reference to Caroline's birthday up until 1730. By 30 January 1737 a great change had come over Byrom towards Elizabeth and the tone was very sober, almost too pious:

Sunday. Mrs. Byrom's Birthday. God send her many happy returns of it; that she may live, if it be His good pleasure, in this world to see her children brought up in His fear and love, her husband a true penitent, and herself well prepared to depart to a heavenly eternity; and this it is in the power and will of God to grant for the sake of our saviour Jesus Christ, who came into the world to save sinners. Amen.[21]

Even allowing for differences in social customs between the eighteenth and twentieth centuries there is a clear distinction between Byrom's remembrance of his own anniversary and his wife's. To the rest of his family birthdays were occasions for visits and celebrations, and John had not been brought up to ignore them. Although he recalled Elizabeth's birthday only as he sat down to write to her, when his own birthday came round in 1724 he celebrated it with a pre-arranged dinner party and a visit to the Opera. Just as he presented one view of Tunbridge Wells to his friend Leycester and another to his wife, so, too, he gives one account of his birthday to his wife and writes another in his Journal. The entry in the Journal states:

> Feb. 29th 1724: this day I am years old thirty-two ... I went to Mrs. de Vlieger's in Leicester Fields, where I dined; and from thence we went to the opera, where we found Mr. Leycester waiting at the door; we went to the first row in the gallery; I did not much like this diversion. After I had waited on the ladies to the coach we took coach and came to Wilson's, Mr. L. and I, and thence to bed.[22]

Mrs de Vlieger lived in Leicester Fields. She was, therefore, a close neighbour of Princess Caroline, who was celebrating her birthday the same weekend. Byrom wrote to Elizabeth three days later.

> March 3, 1724
>
> My dear love; I have been prevented from writing to thee these two posts. I was engaged to dine at Mrs. de Vlieger's on Saturday, whence they all went to the opera of Julius Caesar, and I for one. Mr Leycester sat by me in the front row of the gallery, for we both were there to get good places betimes; it was the first entertainment of this nature that I ever saw, and will I hope be the last, for of all the diversions of the town I least of all enter into this ... [23]

The Journal makes it clear that the dinner was arranged in honour of his birthday and the visit to the Opera was a continuation of the celebrations. The inference from the letter is different. Byrom does not begin by mentioning his birthday, rather he uses the dinner engagement as his excuse for not writing to Elizabeth earlier. He makes sure she knows that he did not like the opera, and would have her believe that it was this visit alone which prevented his writing sooner. But in the Journal he mentions going to the theatre again on 2 March, to see a play, *The Merry Wives of Windsor*. He does not tell Elizabeth this, nor that he 'waited on the ladies to the coach'. In fact Elizabeth could be forgiven for believing that he and Leycester sat on their own in the gallery. These are small points but, taken

together, they present a very different picture of the occasion to
Elizabeth. The deliberate omission of a second visit to the theatre in
three days further indicates his uneasiness.

Byrom was beginning to evolve a special technique in writing to
Elizabeth about his life away from home. He separates the different
levels of pleasure, and presents to Elizabeth those he knew would be
acceptable. A birthday dinner is described as a duty engagement.
Any detail which would have given Elizabeth some idea of the fla-
vour of the evening is missing, particularly women. Why write such
a flat account? The Journal shows up the brevity of the letter and
Byrom's growing deviousness, or was he simply being tactful?

However, even in the Journal, Byrom was circumspect. The mention of Leicester Fields is very matter of fact. It sounds like any
other London street, whereas, since the arrival of the Prince and
Princess of Wales, Leicester Fields had become the focus of much
social activity for the aristocracy and quality.

The coincidence of Byrom's and Caroline's birthdays, the proximity of Mrs de Vlieger's house to Leicester House, the nature of the
celebrations – including a visit to the theatre, and Byrom's careful
account of the event to Elizabeth – lend weight to the possibility
that Caroline and he may have shared part of these celebrations
together. The following year, too, Byrom spent the Princess's birthday in the company of people with close connections to her. He
called at the house of the Duke of Richmond, Lord of the Bedchamber to George I, and later George II. His wife was a Lady of
the Bedchamber to Princess Caroline.

In 1726 there was no 29 February, so Byrom's birthday fell on
the same day as Caroline's. He marked the occasion by a double
celebration. The day before, he founded his Shorthand Society,
gathering together eight of his closest supporters at the King's
Arms. He was at his convivial best, acting as host as well as chair-
man, happy to foot the bill for supper and wine. From now on he
was the Grand Master and began the proceedings with a light-
hearted but knowledgeable review of the history of shorthand,
pointing out how it had always been valued in every civilisation by
'men of true taste and learning'. Before the gathering broke up the
friends agreed to meet every Monday afternoon in Byrom's lodgings
to practise. The following morning, the birthday itself, he sent a gift
of Paradise stocks to an anonymous friend, whose identity has
always been a mystery, but who in all probability was Caroline. The
Paradise stock is an apple tree of French origin once widely used to

produce miniature trees and prized as a curiosity rather than for its fruit. Byrom visited a gardener, Fairchild, who 'at first said he had no Paradise stocks to spare but after we talked he said my friend might have half a dozen'. Byrom, evidently, was interested in purchasing this particular shrub and no other, and would not take no for an answer. Because of its French origin, the gift would have been an elaborate, cryptic compliment (the sort that appealed to Byrom). Caroline often spoke and wrote in French, and the flattering suggestions in the word 'paradise' would be obvious to her. However the gift was not simply a compliment, it was also a private joke between Byrom and the Princess, which went back to the year they first met.

Seven years earlier, when the Prince's position had been threatened by the proposed Peerage Bill, Sir Richard Steele helped campaign against the measure, and won the admiration of the Princess. In seeking election to Parliament, Steele concocted a witty stratagem to divert votes from the opposition. He scooped out the core of an apple and put ten guineas inside. This, he said, would be given to the wife of any of the voters who should be the first to be brought to bed with child nine months from the election day. Several opponents fell for the trick and hurried home to enable their wives to qualify for the apple. Byrom and the Princess would have enjoyed the joke, which became well known, and so the gift of the Paradise stock carried with it sexual overtones which the Princess could not fail to appreciate. (Byrom and his friends revelled in this kind of multi-layered obscurity. Ralph Leycester's family seat was the Manor of Toft, and after the ridiculous scandal of Mary Toft, the 'rabbit woman', the name of Toft became a standing joke between Ralph and John, the more so because several mutual friends had been involved in the investigation. Byrom celebrated Mary Toft's farcical claim to have been delivered of a litter of rabbits in a letter written in verse. Ralph Leycester commemorated it by sending a yearly gift of a hare for him to dine off. The joke was maintained for many years, almost to the end of Byrom's long life.)

By 1728 Caroline was no longer Princess of Wales but Queen. As such her birthday became more of a public occasion, so Byrom might well be expected to take note of it. Yet he continues to notice the Queen's birthday while ignoring the King's. In 1728 he writes to his wife: 'Major Hamilton of the Guards killed himself last night at the King's Arms Tavern by drinking Queen Caroline's health as they say.' The following year he noted in his Journal: 'The bells ringing for Queen Caroline; at home by the Alderman's fireside

writing this diurnal nonsense.' On 3 March 1730 he wrote: 'Yesterday (Monday) was an exceeding day for Queen Caroline.' (An
exceeding day was a term used for a celebration more than usual, yet
not quite a feast day.)

After 1730 Byrom makes no mention of the Queen's birthday.
This coincides with the appearance of a new favourite in Caroline's
life, the courtier and wit Lord Hervey, who became her closest male
confidant. Hervey's rise saw the end of Byrom's relationship with
Caroline, which had lasted from 1719 to 1730. During this time
Caroline continued to manage George II with her customary skill.
Other writers have noticed the element of calculation in her attitude
to her husband, which accounts for her willingness to bear George
two more daughters. During this same period Elizabeth Byrom presented John with five children. This in no way detracts from the
depth of feeling Byrom and Caroline had for each other. Indeed, if
there had been no other children in the two marriages it would have
aroused comment in their respective circles. Furthermore, according
to the fashionable morals of the day, it was quite possible for Caroline and Byrom to be good partners to their spouses and at the same
time fond of each other.

John's first child was a daughter, Elizabeth. She was born in
January 1721/2 and is better known as Beppy, the author of a diary
of the 1745 rebellion in Manchester. The second child was a boy,
Edward, born on 13 June 1724. In addition to a general interest in
the welfare of his own children he does show an unexpected interest
in Prince William throughout the Journal. Byrom is leading a
double life which must have imposed great stresses upon him, and,
now and again, through the public mask signs of strain can be seen
gradually developing. Byrom laid great store on the significance of
dreams, believing they contained elements of truth it would be foolish to ignore. As early as 1714 he wrote in *The Spectator*: 'Dreams
are certainly the results of our waking thoughts', and 'the ideas
which strike the fancy arise in us without our choice, either from
the occurrences of the day past, the temper we lie down in, or it
may be the direction of some superior being.'[24] Therefore, when,
in the privacy of his Journal, Byrom takes the trouble to record
his dreams, they may well correspond accurately to his state of
mind. On 20 March 1725, he writes:

> Dreamt this last night, that is, about six this morning, that my
> wife was dead, which threw me into some reflections on the
> miseries and shortness of human life.[25]

So far as is known, Elizabeth was in perfect health at the time. The reason for the dream may have been simply his absence, but, if that absence was compounded by infidelity, guilt could have produced his sombre observation on the shortness of life. But worse was to come. Three weeks later Byrom went by coach with some friends to Hampstead:

> Monday April 12th
> Sister Ann Byrom called on me to go to Hampstead with her to see the Miss Morts, so I dressed and went with her to the Black Swan in Holborn, and we ate a mutton chop at the Castle Tavern, went in the coach to Hampstead with a Dutch lady and another woman; the Misses Morts were not come from the country, so we took a turn by the wells and came back again after drinking a dish of coffee apiece at the coffeehouse, where we took coach, the Dutch lady being disposed to come back with us and another old woman, and we took up an old gentleman, a footman; I paid 4s. for the coach there and back again.[26]

The trip to Hampstead was arranged with his sister Ann. Its overt purpose was to visit the Miss Morts who were Quakers: their religious views interested the Byroms. But this was only a cover. In the coach to Hampstead, as though by chance, were a 'Dutch lady and another woman'. Byrom's friends included a lady with a Dutch name – Mrs de Vlieger, who had arranged his party the previous year. Byrom's entries in the Journal are often coded to look deceptively innocuous: the other woman in the Hampstead party may well have been the Princess herself.

The trip was an audacious piece of self-indulgence on Byrom's part which he was to pay for later that day. On his return to London he received news that his son Ned was ill, was in fact 'going to die'. In a panic he dashed round his acquaintances in town trying to find his brother-in-law Josiah for fuller details. In the end he caught up with a letter from his brother, Edward, to his sister Ann: 'Tell the doctor that his son Neddy is out of order, and my sister thinks he will have the measles or smallpox, but which she cannot tell yet. . .' At first Byrom thought of returning to Manchester the next day. Despite his concern, however, he changed his mind and decided to stay in London.

He contented himself with writing a letter to his wife. The following day, 14 April, his friend Joseph Clowes invited him to a boxing match at Figg's Amphitheatre. Byrom thought at first Clowes had called with news of his son, but he had not, so John declined to go. A letter arrived from his wife the same day saying that Ned had improved and that she thought his condition was due to teething, 'But he was hot and breathed short, that she wished I was there; by her account I thought he must be better.' Byrom felt sufficiently relieved now to go to the boxing match and enjoy the rest of the day with friends. That night, however, he dreamt Edward was dead: 'Thursday (April 15th) – rose at ten, had slept very well, had dreamt that my child was dead . . .' The dream upset him sufficiently for him to seek solace in saying prayers out of the *Book of Common Prayer*. It was an ominous night for such a dream, since it heralded the 4th birthday of Prince William. This anniversary reminded him of his duplicity, and disturbed his conscience at a time when he was needed at home. The inner turmoil caused by the coincidence of these two events erupted in the dream of Edward's death. On both occasions when he dreamed of death it was people totally innocent of any deceit who 'died'. Was their innocence such a burden to him?

Edward was Byrom's second child and only surviving son. One would have expected Byrom to have felt particularly warm towards his son and heir. But there is no doubt that the tender-hearted Dolly was his favourite child, and that in the quick wit of Beppy he found a special pleasure which he does not display to the same extent with Edward. Although often away from home for months at a time, Byrom was prepared to play the heavy-handed father when the occasion arose, at times too much so.

> Our son, Edward, who bled his nose into the milk, and coming upstairs with Beppy, who told us of it, he making no other defence but by saying he could not help it, which was adding a lie to his crime, – I told him he forced me to whip him; so I took him downstairs, and in the Great Parlour gave him some correction, and reasoned with him about the matter, he promised amendment.[27]

At the time the boy was a mere six years old.

The Journal, like Byrom, presents two faces to the public. The minutiae of everyday living, eating, drinking and dressing are recorded in a perfectly straightforward manner. 'This morning I saw a mouse jump off the chair where my candle was.' On the other hand, when he wishes to record some event whose full significance he does not want to reveal, he does so obliquely. There was no particular reason why Byrom should record entries concerning Prince

William. It might be argued that, while resident in London, Byrom would naturally record any national event he observed. But the Journal is not a record of public events; it is a very personal document. However, just as his sense of guilt burst into his dreams, so too his curiosity over the welfare of the young prince breaks out in a number of entries.

In 1725 Prince William undertook one of his first public engagements – his installation as a Knight of the Bath at the tender age of four. Byrom showed great interest in this. On 5 June, after a visit to Westminster Abbey, he went into Westminster Hall to watch the preparations for the forthcoming ceremony. Ten days later, at a meeting with some shorthand friends at the Sun Club, conversation came round to the Investiture which was to be the following Thursday. Byrom records his visit to watch the ceremony on that day:

> We went near one o'clock with Daniel Bramston and another gentleman by water to the Parliament Stairs, 4d., to see the Knights of the Bath; we all sat at last on the scaffold by St Margaret's Church; I paid 2s for my seat, and very well too for just as I went on it began raining, and most of the people were wet to the skin. About four the Knights came from the Abbey, the Princess and Prince William in a chair, and the Prince in another, they were too much crowded together.[28]

The event and the preparations for it evidently caught Byrom's imagination. Normally hard up, he did not hesitate on this occasion to pay for a seat under cover and waited for three hours. What seemed to strike him most was the sight of the little prince on his mother's lap in one chair and the Prince of Wales in another. Did the separation of the couple in this way have a special meaning? Did recording it give Byrom some special satisfaction? In the light of his claim that William was his son, it is not too fanciful to think this was so.

As to his wedding anniversary – a revealing fact emerges. The Journal contains no reference to it until 1738. That year on their wedding day Byrom wrote to Elizabeth as 'My dear Valentine' and the following year he did the same, signing himself

> Dear Valentine
> Entirely thine, J.B.[29]

Significantly, the delicacy of these endearments comes only after Caroline had died.

CHAPTER FOUR

Societies and Clubs
1724–7

BYROM HAD TO EARN his living in a way which would allow both his personal feelings and political beliefs freedom of expression. The first essential was to find a reason for his prolonged absences from Manchester and that was provided by his shorthand. He promoted this with remarkable speed and, although his system has long since been superseded, the success he met with testifies to its efficiency and his own charm. Some of his pupils were pre-eminent in the professions, others were leading figures in society. Among them were several Members of Parliament, Masters of Cambridge Colleges and Justices of the King's Bench. The charge of five guineas was the same regardless of how long it might take for pupils to become adept. It obviously paid to teach intelligent people, although there were occasions when some patrons had trouble with the finer points of the system. Despite this, Byrom earned enough money to continue this way of life for several years. He taught his pupils in their own homes and, because of his shorthand and his abilities as a man of learning, his reputation soon grew. So much so that he and other nominees were 'severally put to ballot and elected Fellows' of the Royal Society on 12 March 1724 and admitted the following week.[1]

Founded in 1660, the Royal Society is the oldest scientific society in Great Britain and one of the oldest in Europe. In 1724 Sir Isaac Newton was still President and remained in office until his death in 1727, when he was succeeded by Sir Hans Sloane. Any man with pretensions to academic distinction, particularly in science and philosophy, would be flattered to be a member. Through it several important scientific innovations were discussed and promoted. At its weekly meetings Byrom consorted with Newton himself (now an old man), the philosopher David Hartley, the physician Dr James Jurin, John Freke, a well-known surgeon, and John Theophilus

Desaguliers, a scientific engineer much admired by Newton. All these men became friends, together with such leading intellectual aristocrats as the Duke of Richmond, then a young man of twenty-four but already a member of Court. The warm advocacy of his friends did much to promote Byrom socially and professionally.

During Byrom's membership the Royal Society met in Crane Court off Fleet Street every Thursday afternoon, starting at four o'clock, with a long break in the summer. His Journal records the wide variety of topics discussed. He was present at the initial debates over the advantages of vaccination against smallpox, still a dreaded scourge. There were experiments to demonstrate laws of physics, medical papers on 'suppuration', correspondence from other European countries, even the examination of oddities presented to the Society such as a tooth with four fangs and, by courtesy of a London cook, 'a chicken's liver with two hearts!'. Occasionally Byrom admitted to being bored. Papers on theoretical science were happily balanced with others of a more practical nature – the invention of a new type of sash window or a machine for extracting foul air from a mine. He himself delivered two lectures on his shorthand which were duly printed in the Society's *Philosophical Transactions*. The meetings provided a very useful platform for promoting the system among the most learned men in London, but there was a social side to these activities as well. Byrom would frequently dine and drink with his particular cronies either before or after the meetings. Pontac's tavern was a favourite rendezvous. Run by a Frenchman, whom, it was said, much learning had made mad, it offered the choicest Bordeaux wines and superb food. Byrom records the meal there when he was introduced to the Duke of Richmond, in March 1725. They dined off salmon, neck of veal, pigeon pie, chicken and asparagus, all washed down with French wine.

Byrom had been hoping for some time to meet the Duke, who, in his capacities as A.D.C. and Lord of the Bedchamber to George I, was an influential figure. He was also Grand Master of the Free-masons. Byrom had in fact hoped to meet him through a pupil called Hill, who lived at Richmond's London house. Between March 1 and 16 Byrom made repeated attempts to call on Hill, for, as with other pupils, Byrom would have taught him at his home, and that would have given him an entrée into Richmond's house. In the end it was Ralph Leycester who arranged for him to meet the Duke. He invited Byrom to join them for the meal at Pontac's where he introduced him to Richmond who was 'very merry and good company'. Considering the meal they ate this is not surprising! Another guest, Martin Folkes, destined to succeed Hans Sloane as President of the Royal Society in 1741 and himself a mason, made a point of mentioning Byrom's shorthand to the Duke almost in passing: 'Mr Folkes just mentioned my having found out shorthand, but nothing more was said of it then.' However, after the meal Byrom travelled to the Royal Society in a coach with Folkes, Sloane and the Duke, and on the journey 'we talked about masonry and shorthand'. Byrom, in turn, made a point of asking the Duke if Mr Hill lived with him, knowing full well that he did. It looks as if Hill was mentioned as a mutual acquaintance to ingratiate Byrom further with the Duke. That Richmond was the catch Byrom was angling for seems confirmed by the fact that shortly after his meeting Byrom lost all interest in Hill. But he remained in touch with the Duke for more than twenty years.

By now Byrom's friends and pupils were expecting him to publish his shorthand method and many had subscribed towards the book. However, he would not be rushed. To one impatient subscriber he said he 'would not promise it should be out in twenty years', and some took their money back because of this attitude. In truth it did not suit Byrom to publish the system yet. Despite the success he was enjoying, he remained reluctant to rent rooms for himself on a permanent basis. He much preferred to use the legal chambers of his two Manchester friends, Edward Chetham and his cousin Joseph Clowes. Frequently he would let Elizabeth know that 'I am removed to 'Squire Joseph's'. His excuse was that he could not plan more than a week ahead. Evidently he wanted his family and friends to believe his existence in London was essentially rootless and that the uncertainty of his prospects prevented him from making any proper arrangements. However, he had been prepared to commit himself to the house in New Round Court, probably employing the services of Edward Ferrand, an apothecary in the City whom he had known for some years and who owned houses in this court. But by the end of 1725 Byrom gave up renting the house. After five years of tenancy the risk of detection must have grown greater and discretion may have dictated that it was time to leave.

Although infatuated with a Hannoverian princess, Byrom remained true to his non-juring principles. He managed some kind of accommodation between the two areas of his life for a time, although in the end it had devastating consequences. In one of the unpublished poems, 'On a Lady Who Exposes Herself Too Much to View', we get a glimpse of his resentment at having to share Caroline with the world at large, for the public is blind to her real worth. Here he addresses her as Stella – the bright star in his firmament.

> Young Stella bright in beauty's royal dawn
> Displays to constant view her radiant eyes,
> But unregarding like the daily sun
> Her glaring charms are seen without surprise.
>
> I would the fair one win with well-timed care,
> Like seldom comets in a gloomy sky.
> Then would the nymph be vital as the star,
> Then princes would expire and monarchs die.

He wishes to win the 'fair one' in suitably fulsome terms, but, in doing so, does he betray a longing to reconcile personal desire with political ambition? A resolution of the conflict is hinted at in the ominous last line. Meanwhile his dilemma had to be paid for on a personal level.

Byrom was ever a complex man, capable of deceit yet also exhibiting the finest scruples, an adulterer with a conscience. His conscience contained the seeds of torment that were to grow during his relationship with Caroline. This period in the Journal is scattered with evidence of the effects of this inner conflict: an oversensitive stomach forever reacting to his various moods, hypochondria, depressions, and excessive drinking which he fought hard to conquer.

In April 1725 he expresses concern about 'my hands trembling'.[2] The following month he chides himself: 'It seems wrong in me to drink so much Dorset and stay up so late.'[3] A few weeks later he is still regretting his self-indulgence: 'I came home sorry that I had gone there, having had wine enough and meat before. I must resolve not to do this in the future.'[4] There are other signs of the deterioration in Byrom's health. He grew noticeably thinner. 'Dined at Mr. Pimlot's, loin of veal, I ate sparingly; Mr . . . he had lately had the smallpox, called there after dinner, he said I looked thinner than I did when he saw me last about a year ago.'[5] His predisposition to absent-mindedness developed into increasing carelessness and he was frequently losing things, a tell-tale sign of his preoccupied mind. Constantly on the move from place to place, and always anxious to cover up his tracks, the loss of any item must at times have alarmed him, lest it should be the cause of his discovery, as with the loss of his seal on his visit to the Old Pretender. His carelessness became so well known to his friends that they played tricks to tease him out of it. Once he managed to lose his luggage on the way to London. This may have been not entirely his own fault, but it certainly threw him into a panic. His relief on its recovery is noticeable, as a letter to his wife shows: 'I don't know what's in 'em but was afraid of some papers etc.' In London it was perhaps inevitable that he had his pockets picked and was disturbed by the ease with which it was done: 'Had my handkerchief picked out of my pocket very strangely about Ludgate Hill, for I had my hand in my pocket most part of the way and was resolved it should not go.'[6]

Evidently he had lost other things that way. As he was continually losing his sword, it is a pity that it was considered such an essential item of dress: 'I called at Mr. Hassel's chamber for my sword which I had left there.' (25 May 1725.) Not long afterwards (6 July 1725) he writes: 'I left my sword at Mr. Clark's this morning.' The loss of a book in February 1726 in Manchester disturbed him greatly. Admittedly, it was one of his shorthand books 'with the white parchment cover'. The contents are not known, but they were sufficiently important to Byrom to make him advertise for the book – a little too hastily, for he later found it in his box in London. Its value had thrown him into such a state of confusion that he could not find it in his luggage. On another occasion he got so fussed about losing 'my gloves etc' he rode out into the country to find them – without success. Which bothered him more – the gloves or the 'etc'? One of the most devastating losses occurred in 1727: a very valuable watch. Once more Byrom was driven to advertise.

> Lost at New Market, on Thursday 13th April 1727, a gold repeating watch, in a Black Shagreen outside case, the name Freeman with a steel chain, and a lady's picture in water colours, plain set in gold, viz: a red Cornelian engrav'd with a Devil carrying away Cupid, and the other a white aggot[sic] engrav'd with a Head; whoever brings it to the Cocoa Tree House in Pall Mall or to Mr. Hoops at the Ram Inn in New Market, shall have ten guineas Reward for the whole or a proportionable for the Picture, or any other part, and no questions asked.[7]

The quality and opulence of the object are striking. The name Freeman makes it look like a present from Caroline and the picture is possibly a portrait of the Princess herself. The reward, ten

guineas, was very handsome and shows both the value of the article
and its worth to the owner. Byrom singled out for particular mention the return of the picture, suggesting that he was more interested
in that than either the watch or seals. If indeed it was a portrait of
Caroline his anxiety is understandable. Byrom names two places to
which the objects could be returned. One was in London, the Cocoa
Tree, a well-known Jacobite chocolate house which he often frequented. The second was in Newmarket, where the watch had been
lost. A week after the loss Byrom wrote to his wife after returning
from Cambridge later than he had intended. He excused himself by
saying he had lent his horse to a friend to attend a funeral. If he had
lost his watch at Newmarket during his visit to Cambridge, he may
well have stayed on longer to search for it.

He ate out every day for breakfast, dinner and supper. Fortunately
there was a great variety of coffee houses and taverns both in the
City and near St James's. One favourite was Richard's. It was popular and respectable, used by businessmen in the City and 'good
honest country gentlemen', and at one time Byrom could be seen
there every night at six o'clock. When staying at Gray's Inn he
would breakfast at Squires, which was patronised by the benchers
and students of law. Most fashionable of all was White's Chocolate
House in St James's Street, where it was possible to buy tickets for
balls at the King's Theatre in Haymarket, one of which we know
Caroline attended in masquerade. Widow White, the proprietress of
White's, hired and sold masquerade habits.

Like other visitors, Byrom had his mail delivered to one or other
of the coffee houses, and it was not unusual for him to visit three or
four taverns in one day. At one extreme he would indulge at Pontac's, at the other he is patronising the Fleece in Covent Garden, a
notorious resort of bullies, famed for its brawls and immorality.

Byrom enjoyed the social and intellectual stimulus provided by a
number of the clubs proliferating in London. From 1723 he was a
regular in attendance at the Sun Club, which met in Paul's Churchyard. Members included Sir Hans Sloane, Dr James Jurin, his old
friend Ralph Leycester, and George Graham, the distinguished
clockmaker. Some of them belonged to the Royal Society, whose
members, not surprisingly, found their way into every group
engaged in the pursuit of knowledge. Some were also members
of the newly emerging lodges constituting The Grand Lodge of
Freemasonry in England. In 1725 The Lodge of Antiquity gathered

above the room where the Sun Club met, and Sloane suggested Byrom should go upstairs to see it in session for himself.

Discussions at the Sun Club ranged over every imaginable subject: metaphysics, the notion of infinity, shorthand and ciphers, hydraulics, mechanics and the art of memory. The Sun Club usually met on a Tuesday, the Royal Society on a Thursday, and Byrom's Shorthand Society on a Monday. In addition he set up a very special group, open only to a chosen few, his Cabala Club, whose meetings remained a secret from its inception in 1725 until at least 1735.

On 9 March he writes:

> Thence to the Club in Paul's Church Yard, where we had two barrells of oysters, one before and another after supper. Mr Leycester, Glover, White, Bob Ord, Graham, Folkes, Sloane, Derham, Heathcote, a talking gentleman I had never seen before; paid 2s 6d. apiece . . . I told them I was going to establish a Cabala Club . . . [8]

Some of these men were or became distinguished figures in society. In addition to Sloane and Graham, there were Martin Folkes, a leading mathematician who was elected to the Royal Academy of Sciences in Paris, and William Derham, who became President of St John's College, Oxford (where he had once been Whyte's Professor of Moral Philosophy). These were the men to whom Byrom chose to make his announcement about the Club. Apart from one other brief reference it is not mentioned again in the Journals, though there may, of course, have been other entries concerning the meetings which were omitted by the editors for prudential reasons. That it met regularly for years is certain, but its activities remained wholly unknown until the extraordinary cache of mathematical and geometrical drawings explored in *The Byrom Collection* came to light.

The Club takes its name from the Jewish Cabala – a mystical system within Jewish tradition originating with the ancient religious fraternity, the Essenes. It developed into a highly complex body of spiritual teaching which attempts to unite the initiate directly with God. The ideas were borrowed in part by Christians who evolved a version of their own. Because the teachings were concerned with such sacred mysteries, they were kept a closely guarded secret and the terms 'cabal' and 'cabala' came to be associated with secret societies and occult sciences. From there it became debased even further almost as a term of abuse for mumbo-jumbo, but for Byrom it was associated with the revered tradition of learning and spiritual guidance.

Since it had such a long tradition there is, of course, a large and ancient body of literature about its beliefs, but what makes Byrom's fascination with the Cabala interesting and important is that it is connected to original drawings of which he was, for part of his life, custodian.

These cover other subjects apart from the Cabala and are linked with freemasonry, architecture, the beginnings of technology and the emergence of science from alchemical thought. Similar and complementary drawings have since been found in the collections of Sir Hans Sloane and Sir Robert Boyle. There is no doubt that Byrom obtained some of his material for the Cabala Club from one Jonathan Falkoner in Bartholomew Close in 1735. He describes Falkoner's strange 'collection of nine figures and papers of Rose about the cabalistic alchemy'.[9] However, they surfaced ten years after the Club was formed. Before then his material came from several sources. One was Jacques Christophe Le Blon (1667-1741), a Huguenot engraver and artist who had come to work in this country in about 1718 and stayed here until 1732/34.

Le Blon invented a process for printing colour reproductions of oil paintings which was in effect the beginning of colour reproduction in print as we know it today. It was so successful that George I ordered one of the rooms at Hampton Court to be entirely furnished with them, and in 1725, the year the Cabala Club was founded, Le Blon's process was published under the title of *Coloritto or the Harmony of Colouring reduced to Mechanical Practice and Infallible Rules*. Le Blon was a highly inventive artist but a disastrous businessman. He went on to invent a second procedure, the art of weaving tapestry, for which he was granted a Patent by George I in 1727 and which enabled him to reproduce colour copies in tapestry. The King was so impressed by Le Blon's work that he commissioned him to copy the series of great cartoons by Raphael (they now hang in the Victoria and Albert Museum but were then housed in the Cartoon Gallery built at Hampton Court by Sir Christopher Wren). George I died later the same year, but Le Blon was allowed to work in rooms set aside at the palace by George II in 1728, and he lived there during the undertaking. A special factory was built at Chelsea, where the copies were to be transferred to tapestry. In the course of his work at Hampton Court Le Blon would have met Queen Caroline, whose enlightened interests extended from science and mysticism to literature and art. No doubt Le Blon would have discussed his work and those geometrical drawings he owned which later became part of Byrom's collection. These had been drawn in the early seventeenth century by an ancestor, Michel Le Blon (1587-1656) a distinguished engraver who had worked for a time in England as an agent for Charles I, and had been very interested in the ideas of the Christian Cabala and their representation in graphic form. Caroline would thus be renewing a royal interest shown in this country by the Stuarts.

From the times of the ancient Egyptians geometry has been associated with discovering truths about the observable world, and it has been used to open the way into profound areas of speculative thought. Mathematical order and progression, and the harmony and proportion inherent in geometry, were symbolic of the order, harmony and proportion believed to be present in the universe. Certain shapes, such as the triangle, square and circle, became endowed with moral properties. Among the drawings in Byrom's custody are a number concerned with building, and architecture is the supreme example of geometry and proportion in the man-made world. A recurring pattern in some of Byrom's drawings is one which is also found as the background design of the Great Pavement in the Sanctuary at Westminster Abbey, which in its own ordered structure is a statement about the nature of the world. Placed in the Abbey in the thirteenth century, the pavement is so valuable that for most of the year it is now protected by a floor covering, and is only revealed to the public at certain times in the year. But the philosophical tradition which created it is related to ideas expressed in some of Byrom's drawings. Both have elements in common with the Cabala.

Byrom's library contained a number of standard texts on cabalistic thought, and, in an undated letter to Ralph Leycester from 1730, which belongs to the small group of MSS preserved by Joseph Clowes, he wrote derisively about the lengths to which some philosophers went to demonstrate that numbers had symbolic and spiritual attributes – for example, seven was considered the measure 'not of mortal, but of immortal and blessed things', as could be seen in the seven planets, seven days of the week, seven ages of man, seven movements of his body, seven notes in music, etc.

Byrom at this stage was not very impressed by such arguments. Later he goes on to give his opinion about the Cabala.

If thou consultest the Rosicrucian and the Freemasons, thou wilt find in them certain remains of the ancient Cabbala, of which they have retained the secret without the understanding, and which is the true reason why these latter do (and justly enough) boast that their secret cannot be found out; although I do believe that more might be known of it than the preternatural ... if it were worth while to make it necessary, which it will hardly be, unless some number of gentlemen would be as unanimous in making it a point of open criticism as they are in making it a piece of secret nonsense ... [10]

Byrom is not attempting to discredit the Cabala but attacking those groups or individuals whom he considered were guilty of deliberate mystification about its ideas. The Freemasons had 'retained the secret without the understanding'. Byrom evidently believed there was something of real value here that deserved to be unravelled and made known so that it could be 'a point of open criticism' instead of 'a piece of secret nonsense'. He wanted the Cabala to be studied openly, not clouded by secrecy. This was his motive in founding the Cabala Club and the reason for his excitement, years later, when he heard about Mr Falkoner and his strange papers. New material might mean new evidence – new proof for a tradition of knowledge ignored, forgotten and, when rediscovered, all too easily misunderstood.

Byrom was evidently sensitive to the pain of others, as many entries show. For example, he was distressed by the current practice of putting blisters on patients to relieve illness. His study of 'physic' in Montpellier, admittedly short-lived, did not harden him professionally, for in 1730, when he was invited to attend a medical dissection, he declined 'for fear of the smell'. The elegant Augustan world of order contained within it filth and disease on an alarming scale. Chamber pots were still being emptied into insanitary streets, and, when the fashionable world took its cures at Bath, people stood up to their necks in waters flowing with each other's germs. Byrom was so particular he could not bear to eat bread which had been buttered with a knife tasting of onion: 'Thence to the Fountain, where I had half a pint of wine and bread and cheese 7d; the boy brought me a knife that had cut onions, which I spread some bread and butter with, and it like to have made me sick.'[11]

Despite the scantiness of his medical training, Byrom allowed people to call him 'Dr' Byrom when he found it convenient. He also presumed to offer medical advice and even treatment on occasion. In an age when so many quacks flourished, Byrom's rudimentary knowledge might well have seemed to some the wisdom of an expert. No doubt whatever advice he gave was motivated by compassion. But the fact remains he was never fully trained in medicine. Yet in 1725 he is recommending a preparation of 'Benedictine Pills' to a friend. This may seem a minor fault when a dancing master could pass himself off as a doctor to the King,[12] but the slenderness of Byrom's medical knowledge was a dangerous flaw in that, at times, it encouraged him to appear to be what he was not.

At Montpellier he had made the acquaintance of a man called Lounds, who appears several times in the Journal and is usually referred to by Byrom as 'my fellow traveller'. Lounds was in fact an ardent Jacobite. He had gone to France to be with the Stuart malcontents and on his return he joined a club of Stuart supporters in Rochdale. Yet when they met again years later, in the Court of Requests in London, Byrom, aware of the clandestine circumstances of their first encounter, had been prepared to be ignored, but 'my fellow traveller in France surprised me by speaking to me'. The uncertainty of Byrom's reaction is revealing, for Lounds would know about his own political sympathies with the Stuarts, which found expression in his meeting with the Old Pretender. Also, Lounds would be aware that John's medical studies had been cursory, merely an excuse for his sojourn in France. The paths of the two men crossed from time to time and, in 1736, it was Lounds who defended Byrom's medical competence when it was called in doubt by a relative. Whenever he was cast in the role of doctor, Byrom was not completely at ease. He seemed conscious of the fact that, whatever knowledge of 'physic' he had, he was still playing a part. Sometimes this was to his advantage, at others his pretensions were best forgotten. On the one hand, by allowing his family, friends and acquaintances to call him 'Doctor' Byrom, the epithet stuck sufficiently for people to think of him as 'Doctor' Byrom even after his death. An index to the *Philosophical Transactions* of the Royal Society lists him as 'John Byrom M.D.' as late as 1787. On the other hand, he was very eager to warn his wife not to address him as Doctor when she wrote to him at Cambridge. The assumption of a medical degree, if he did not possess one, might prove very embarrassing in university circles. Of course, if he had gained a qualification at Montpellier under an assumed name, then that would account for his reluctance to use it in this country consistently and with confidence. Byrom grew accustomed to adopting a role suitable to the company and circumstances in which he found himself, but for him it became a lie he had to live, not just with regard to his medicine but with his political sympathies and the promotion of his shorthand.

For several months in 1726, Princess Caroline was in a state of constant anxiety over the health of her second daughter, Amelia. Now a young girl of sixteen, her illness seems to have begun with a severe cold which developed complications. Amelia was still separated from her mother and living in the King's household because of the long-standing family feud. The King's doctors were unable to treat the symptoms successfully and Caroline in desperation sought help from another physician, Dr Friend. In doing so she used her confidante Mrs Clayton as the intermediary to ensure that Amelia received the treatment Dr Friend prescribed despite the fact that he was a strong Jacobite and had been committed to the Tower for his beliefs.

Byrom first met Dr Friend in 1725. His Jacobite travelling companion, Lounds, discussed him with Byrom, who was fully aware of Friend's excellent reputation as a physician. In her distress over Amelia, Caroline turned for spiritual comfort to Dr Samuel Clark, Rector of St James, who came to see her so often that she arranged to pay '100 guineas per annum for his chair hire'. Byrom had been acquainted with Clark's writings since his days at Cambridge and met him in May 1727.

Byrom's life began to go adrift when he fell foul of the President of the Royal Society. The origin of this dispute is referred to in a Journal entry for 18 May 1727. Byrom had been unwise enough to criticise 'the form and manner' in which the Society was to address the King and Prince of Wales. While this was being debated, Dr Ahlers, although not a member, was present and seen to 'use such an extraordinary exactness in acquainting himself with Mr Byrom's name'.[13] At the next meeting, Sir Hans Sloane had the statutes read out and Byrom took them down in shorthand, paying particular attention to the rules for the admission of strangers, and then spoke on his own behalf, questioning the behaviour of Ahlers – 'whether this might not reasonably give occasion to suspect some other design than a gentleman's bare curiosity'.[14] He called for Ahlers to explain why he 'did take down my name in such manner'. Sir Hans, a convinced Whig, wanted to put the matter aside, but two friends of Byrom, Ord and White, joined in, since to them it looked like a form of intimidation, an impingement on the liberty of members to speak their minds freely and especially unwelcome from 'strangers'.

Sir Hans did not want the matter to proceed and commented sarcastically on Byrom's own note-taking: 'Who knows what he writes?' Whereupon Byrom explained he was taking down the statutes. Sloane interrupted to shut him up – the complaint was insignificant. Byrom, however, persisted, not only for his own sake, but also for all members who would want to feel free to speak without giving offence or being misunderstood. White joined in, saying that the original debate that had given rise to this dispute had led to accusations 'that there were Jacobites in the Society'. The matter was now the gossip of coffee-houses and Byrom's name and that of Dr Nesbit, another member, had been bandied around as 'enemies to the government'.[15]

The debate continued, arousing the concern of many; Sloane still tried to brush it aside as of no importance, but was forced in the end to prompt Ahlers to say that he had meant no harm. Sloane's partiality became more obvious when he brought up again Byrom's proposal to have the wording of the loyal address deferred for a week. Folkes saw this as a devious ploy by the President, since that matter was closed and not under debate. Nobody took Sir Hans's side and the meeting ended with many members suspicious of Sir Hans and the President very suspicious of Byrom. According to Dr Nesbit, it was Sir Hans who had spread the accusation of Jacobitism. Byrom wrote to Elizabeth about the dispute, 'they say there have not been so many speeches this hundred years as there have been this month past'.[16] However, despite his light-hearted tone, he was sufficiently disturbed to delay returning to Manchester until the matter was resolved to his satisfaction. Byrom signed his letter 'Fran Freeman', a reminder that he was a free man who became a Freemason. Ironically, it was, too, the name he used privately with Princess Caroline.

Byrom's quarrel with the President continued throughout May. The reading of the minutes recording the complaint caused further argument which remained unresolved that summer. At one level he was defending the rights of the Society to speak freely, at another he was concerned that the accusation of Jacobitism might stick, and leave him for ever an object of suspicion. He had no wish to be spied on by members of the Royal Household, particularly those holding medical appointments. His reaction indicated that he did indeed have something to hide. On 3 June he wrote to Elizabeth that the dispute was, he thought, over:

We had more disputation at the Society last Thursday, warm work, at the reading of the minutes of my complaint. I'll send thee the minutes and the reason of the contentions thereupon shortly; I believe there is an end of 'em now, for I am going out of town, and King George is a going, and Mr. Ahlers is a going, and so sure the nation will be quiet. It was one word that the president would have had inserted in the minutes, which caused all the debates, which ended in rejecting the word, and letting the minutes be as the secretary had taken 'em.[17]

He knew where the King was going. On 27 May he had taken the trouble to tell his wife of His Majesty's intended movements:

My tailor, who brought home my new clothes (I asked your advice about them but you said nothing, so I followed my own fancy), grave Duroy, this morning told me that King George would take a journey into the north instead of going to Hannover.[18]

Byrom's behaviour in the dispute in the Royal Society was that of a highly sophisticated provocateur. His intervention had caused unrest among the members and was in keeping with his other subversive political activities. The entries in the Journal for May and June 1727 are erratic and disjointed in style. The pages of the diary are brief extracts and indicate that at this point the Journal presented a problem for Sarah Bolger and the editors. The gaps leave the reader curious and perplexed, but fortunately another group of shorthand books has come to light which contain diary entries not used in the published *Literary Remains*, nor any of the later volumes of Byrom's work – prose or poetry. At some time these notebooks became separated from the material used for the Journal, although Sarah Bolger made sure they were despatched to Miss Atherton's main heir after her death. They have never been seen since, and their neglect may be because some were used by Byrom's sister, Phebe, and his wife, and were thought to be general notebooks for family use. Others, however, were certainly used by Byrom. One of these covers the period from 1727 to 1731, and contains work on codes, their practice and application.[19] It lists names of people who are known to have been Jacobite spies in the rebellion of 1745. Their presence shows Byrom's involvement in a network of espionage. Among the names are Deacon, R. Jackson, Falconer and Salkeld.

Jackson was a Jacobite working secretly as part of an espionage network between Manchester and Scotland. Thomas Deacon was a

Figure 6: Composite of three pages from Byrom's shorthand notebook

non-juring Bishop running his own church in Manchester who lost three sons in the 1745 uprising. In 1727 he wrote to Byrom on 14 May addressing him as 'Dear Grand Master' and adding a mysterious postscript.

As to Mr Salkeld, give my service to him, but I have nothing to say about that matter at present, only you are to get the box and everything in it to him, and he is to take care of it till I send him further directions.[20]

Whatever the box contained, Byrom was most reluctant to have it in his care, he was alarmed at the danger he was running, and replied to Deacon:

Dear Doctor, I had yours last post, in which you tell me I shall perhaps be frightened because of your box; now I tell you that there is no *perhaps* in the case, for I am frightened out of my wits quite and clear, and shall not be my own man again these seven years. But to be serious, you did not do well to alter your mind and send this packet to me, for it is the only way to discover one of the triumvirate, that is to say, myself ... [21]

The other member of the triumvirate was Henry Salkeld. His name occurs in an unpublished diary entry for 1 April 1730 found in the new notebooks. In it Byrom talks of calling 'at Salkeld's where Jackson the town clerk was', and adds the strange comment 'Surprise I went, surprise I would.' Henry Salkeld, like Deacon, was a doctor, and hailed from Northumberland. He was a descendant of an earlier Henry who had married Ellen Byrom, daughter of Adam Byrom of Salford. So he and John were kinsmen. The Salkelds were devout Catholics and as such loyal to the Stuarts. In 1625 Thomas Salkeld was described as a 'very dangerous Popish Recusant'.[22] On the restoration of Charles II in 1660, Francis Salkeld was knighted and two years later made High Sheriff of Cumberland.

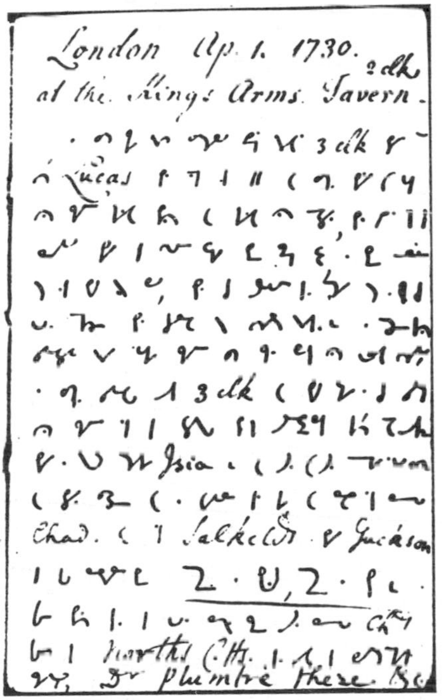

Figure 7
Shorthand transcription

I came here from Cambridge last Friday 3 o'clock with Mr Lucas. We set out 11 and came to Ware that night. My horse tired with me and tired me severely. We lay at the Crown where the man's daughter has just died. I was sick but it were of God. We had beginners to supper, but I had no stomach. We talked of moral fortitude. I spoke to my landlord for another horse which he got me next morning. I came to London about 3 o'clock and went after I had left my horse at the Dolphin. Went to Bishopsgate. Timing sad betimes, where I found brother Josiah and by the bye sister Anne came Willy Chaddock and I drank tea there and called at cousin Chad. And at Salkeld's where Jackson the town clerk was. Surprise I went, surprise I would. I thence home to the new coffee house by cousin Chaddock's. Thence to North's coffee hse, to read the Grub street journal. Dr Plumtre there etc.

Byrom knew not only Henry, the last of the line, but his brother Thomas. No less loyal to the Jacobite cause, they were related to Colonel Francis Strickland of Westmoreland, one of the 'seven men of Moidart', that motley band of companions who landed with Charles Edward Stuart on Eriskay in July 1745. These included Sir Thomas Sheridan, the Prince's former tutor and then over seventy; a non-juring parson named George Kelly; a young Scots banker from

Paris, Aeneas Macdonald; the Marquis of Tullibardine, a veteran of 1715 and so gouty he could hardly walk; an Irishman in the Spanish service, Sir John Macdonald, whom Charles made instructor of cavalry; and Captain John O'Sullivan, whom he appointed quarter-master general and whose disastrous tactics at Culloden made certain the Scots were defeated.

Together Byrom, Deacon and Salkeld were preparing for the restoration of the Pretender. Jackson was a reliable courier. Another significant name on Byrom's list of agents was Falconer, the descendant of the author of an early treatise on codes, *Cryptomensis Patefacta*, published in 1685. It is against this background that the death of George I should be examined.

George I made his last journey home to Hannover in June 1727. The *London Gazette* carried the customary notices announcing the stages of the King's departure:

> This morning [June 3rd] His Majesty set out from St. James's and imbarked at Greenwich on the Carolina Yacht for Holland; The Squadron of Men at War appointed to attend His Majesty is commanded by Salmon Morrice Esq., Rear Admiral of the White.

The King boarded the Carolina at nine o'clock. Later, dinner was served and sail was set to go with the tide to Gravesend, where bad weather delayed the fleet.

> Whitehall June 6th. The wind being contrary when His Majesty imbarked at Greenwich last Saturday Morning on the Carolina Yacht, that and the other Yachts could proceed no further than Gravesend, till Yesterday Morning, when the wind coming fair they got under sail at Ten o'Clock, and at Twelve passed by the Nore towards the Gunfleet; where they were to be joined by the Squadron commanded by Rear Admiral Morrice, appointed to attend His Majesty.

Off the coast of Holland the King transferred to a Dutch yacht sent in his honour to bring him ashore. In the early evening of 7 June he landed at Schoonhoven. He was accompanied in his carriage by Hardernberg, his Court Marshal, and Fabrice, his Hannoverian Gentleman of the Chamber. Close behind came his body of servants, including his Turkish valet, Mustapha. That night the King halted at a small place called Varth, not far from Utrecht. He had a light meal of a single carp and rose early next morning to continue on his way. During that day's progress King George stopped to eat dinner at Apeldoorn and reached Delden at eight in the evening. Here he is said to have received his wife Sophia's last letter, protesting to the end her innocence of adultery, for which she had been confined in the castle at Ahlden. To his entourage he seemed to be in both good health and humour and at supper consumed a large amount of fruit. He set out again at seven o'clock next morning.

The King told Hardernberg and Fabrice he had spent a bad night, suffering with stomach ache which he put down to having eaten too many strawberries and oranges at supper. The two courtiers suggested he should break his journey and rest at Delden, but he wished to press on. After about an hour and a half, however, the King ordered the carriage to stop so that he might answer a call of nature. He had always been a voracious eater, and his companions felt that the fruit was the cause of his trouble. His Turkish servant said later that the King had been forced to leave his bed several times during the previous night. There was concern, therefore, when he returned to the carriage; his face seemed distorted and he appeared to have lost control of his right hand. Suddenly he fainted. By sheer good luck the valet's carriage was close behind and in it was a surgeon hired by Hardernberg and Fabrice to attend to their needs. He diagnosed a stroke and ordered the King to be bled immediately. George recovered consciousness and indicated that he wished to continue the journey. He then fell into an unnatural sleep which alarmed the courtiers. Anxious efforts were made to find more doctors, but none was near at hand. Eventually the party reached Osnabrück some time between eleven and twelve at night. George recovered consciousness briefly, but, once he was in bed, sank back into a coma. He died at about one o'clock in the morning of 11 June.

Only one hour separated the death of George I from the birthday of the Old Pretender, 10 June, a day Byrom and his Jacobite friends celebrated. Was this a coincidence? Years later, in March 1736, Byrom encountered an old acquaintance, one of the Wards from Stafford, later first Viscount Dudley and Ward. They adjourned to a coffee house where Ward told Byrom of the curious death of his family's accountant, Cotham. 'He fasted on Friday and then ate pickled fish heartily, and did not drink anything to digest it and was taken ill and died the Tuesday after.'[23] Byrom was sufficiently struck by this incident to record it in his diary. Did it remind him of the death of King George? In his *Memoirs* Fabrice recorded that the King's meal of a single fish was a miserable one. This seems to imply an ungarnished dish and indicate that George may already have been

suffering from a queasy stomach. His first minister, Sir Robert Walpole, should have accompanied him, but had been prevented by an
upset stomach. Cotham had fasted before his meal; George possibly
had been unwell. The interval between eating the fish and death was
approximately the same for both men – four days. This coincidence
would have struck Byrom, hence the entry in the Journal.

Could something harmful have been added deliberately in the
carp? George had stipulated that his body should not be opened or
embalmed. Thus an autopsy to decide the cause of death was impossible. He died in his native land, and was buried at Leineschloss
church in Hannover near the grave of his mother, the Electress
Sophia. His aged mistress, the Duchess of Kendal, his entourage
and members of his family witnessed his burial. To all intents and
purposes it was a neat and tidy end.

Byrom's own movements at the time of the King's last voyage are
well documented. He made certain of this in his letters to his wife. It
is clear he himself was not on the royal yacht. If there were anything
untoward in the King's death, it would have been effected by an
intermediary, either in the royal entourage or among the ship's
crew.

One of the rough notebooks which Byrom used to practise his
shorthand has by some miracle survived. The pages are full of scrib-
ble, doodling and isolated phrases. Dates on two pages fix it to July
and August 1727, soon after the death of George I. On one left-hand
page is written a sentence which leaves an uncomfortable feeling:
'The K.G.B. died at Osn', which must mean 'The King of Great
Britain died at Osnabrück'. On the opposite page two unusual
words stand out: 'antimony' and 'Anodyne'. Antimony is an element used mainly in lead and tin alloys, but it can also be made into
a lethal and tasteless poison; anodyne is a pain-killing drug. The jux-
taposition of these two words with the abbreviated sentence raises
uneasy questions. It is as if Byrom at the time was so preoccupied by
the death of the King that his subconscious was playing tricks and
dictating the direction of the pen among all the scribbles. On the
right-hand page 'antimony' also appears in shorthand: ⟨shorthand symbol⟩ He
may well have been writing to someone when his mind began to
wander, for he writes out in shorthand at the top of the page:
⟨shorthand symbols⟩ (it is as you see I desire you should
take care for ~~the~~ your future our way).

In addition to newspaper accounts of the King's departure, there
are naval records in the Library at the Royal Naval Museum Green-

wich, and the Record Office at Kew. Kew holds the Captain's log book and the ship's muster rolls, which give an accurate account of every sailor on board and his duties. They also record illnesses, deaths and absences. In one of the registers folded and loose between the pages with other papers is the following letter:

Mr Beverly,

Mr Beale, Surgeon of the Yacht under my command having several checques upon him within the last seven months, this is to satisfie you, that when he was absent, it was with my leave, to attend some affairs he acquainted me he had in town to look after; given under my hand the 27th January 1727/8.

J. Guy.[24]

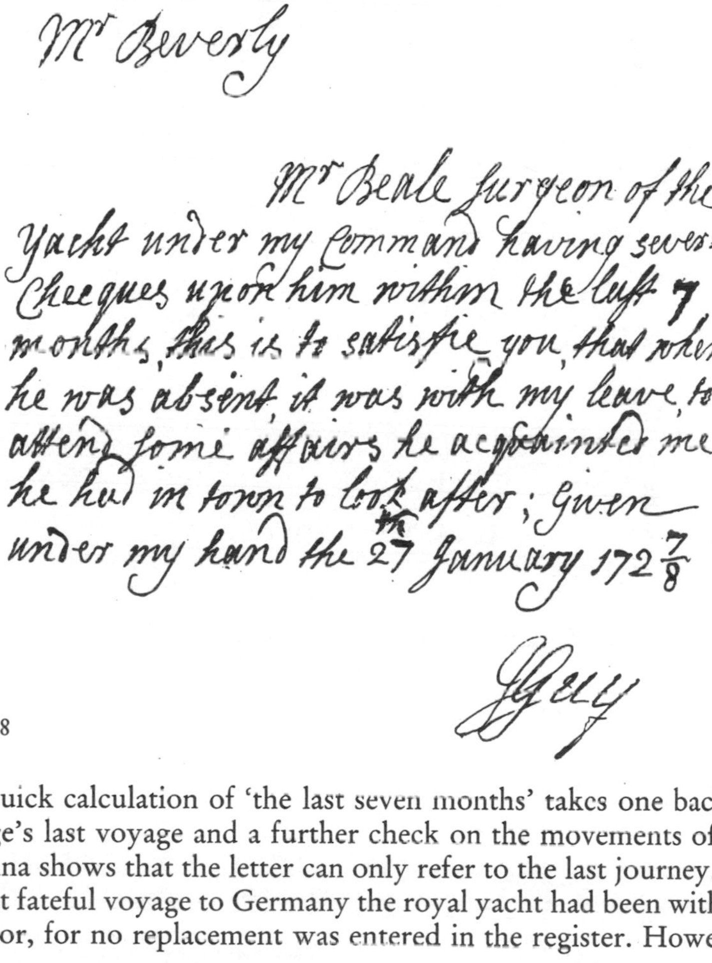

Mr Beverly

Mr Beale Surgeon of the Yacht under my Command having several Checques upon him within the last 7 months, this is to satisfie you, that when he was absent it was with my leave, to attend some affairs he acquainted me he had in town to look after; Given under my hand the 27th January 172 7/8

J Guy

Figure 8

A quick calculation of 'the last seven months' takes one back to George's last voyage and a further check on the movements of the Carolina shows that the letter can only refer to the last journey. So, on that fateful voyage to Germany the royal yacht had been without a doctor, for no replacement was entered in the register. However,

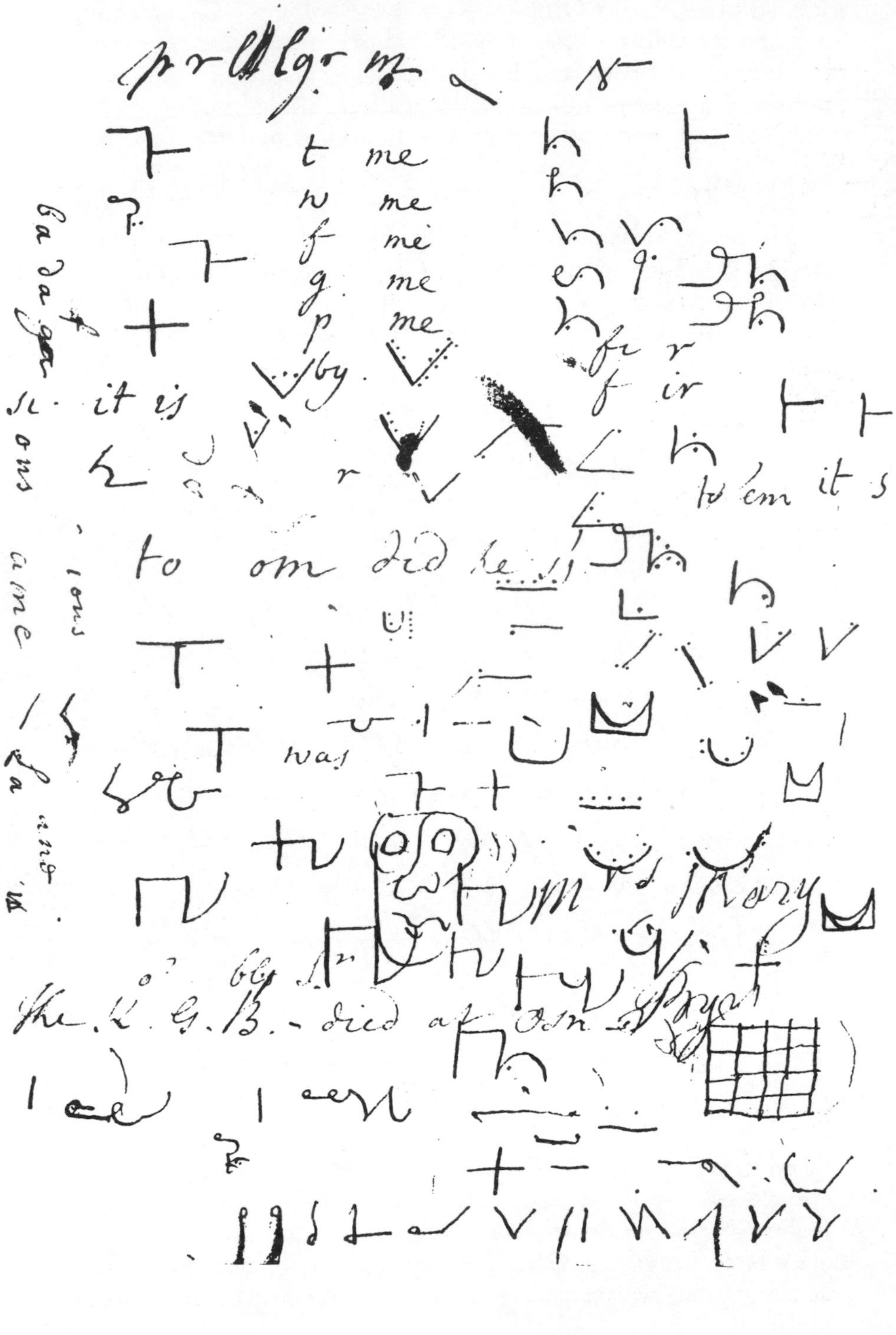

t   me

w   me

f   me

g   me

p   me

by

it is   r

to   om   did   be

was

to 'em it s

the . .G.B. – died at oon

Mary

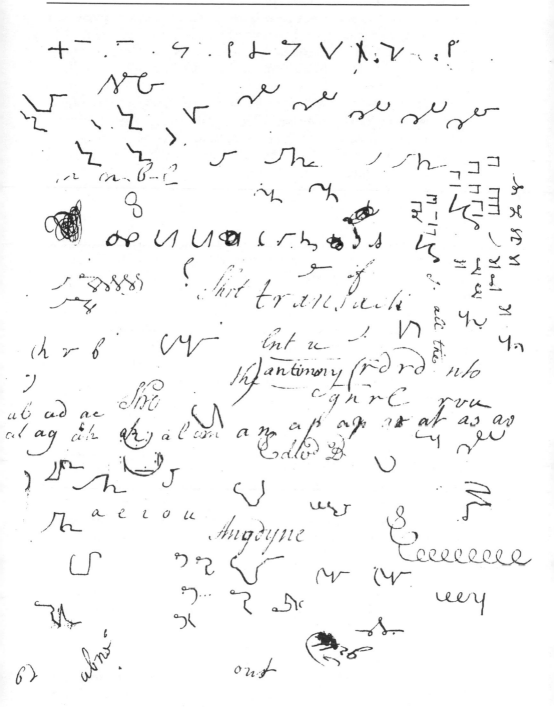

Figure 9: Byromic doodles

not only had the ship's surgeon been absent, but his absence had evidently been the cause of persistent investigation over a period of seven months. Someone, somewhere – in the Naval Office perhaps, or even higher – had insisted on checking why Beale had not been present on the King's last voyage.

The absence was caused either by inefficiency or irresponsibility, or it was deliberately contrived. The royal retinue was accommodated on several yachts for the crossing and took coach on landing as and when it could. Some preceded George while others followed him on the Carolina. This made Beale's absence even more crucial.

Several pieces of information about Beale emerge from the annals of the barber-surgeons, the lists of commissioned sea-officers in the Royal Navy and the lists of certificates granted to Navy surgeons. Richard Beale had been a regular medical officer attached to the Carolina from 1718 to 1730. Another member of the Beale family, John, had links with Byrom. (Dr Stukeley, the celebrated antiquarian and one of the early Freemasons in England, was a friend of Byrom's and visited him in Manchester. In his diary Stukeley mentioned Dr Beale, who was a fellow mason, and constituted a lodge where Stukeley claims he was chosen as Master. This lodge met at one of Byrom's old haunts, the Fountain Tavern in the Strand. He talks of it often: 'Thence to the Fountain where I had half a pint of wine and bread and cheese.')

The captain's name was Guy, and there are a number of references to Guy in the Journal. The Guys were on visiting terms with Byrom in Manchester between 1724 and 1725. Just as a succession of Beales became doctors, so several Guys took to the sea for a career. One of the Quaker Guys from Stepney is listed in the Quaker registers as a 'mariner'. Quaker Guys were friends of Byrom's in-laws. John Guy became captain of the Carolina; George Guy served as a gunner on the same boat. Thus both Guy and Beale had links with Byrom and could be the intermediaries he needed.

The general drift of Captain Guy's letter is immediately obvious, but it takes on a new significance when one knows that the name Guy is included in Byrom's list of names together with Jackson, Deacon, Falconer and Salkeld.

It suggests that the captain may have deliberately connived at Beale's absence from the royal yacht and took no steps to replace him. Since the King's own surgeon was not on board, George was conveniently and dangerously vulnerable. In such circumstances nothing would be easier than for Guy to introduce poison into the

King's food. There would have been time for it to begin to take effect while the yacht was still at sea and before any medical assistance was available. The King's gluttony helped. By devouring too much fruit, George unwittingly provided an unexpected but very convincing, explanation for his indisposition as the poison began to work. Was Guy, then, associated with the King's death, and was the box which Dr Deacon left with Byrom (so much to his alarm) for him to deliver to Salkeld in some way involved? Salkeld, too, at one time practised as a doctor. All three were Jacobites with medical knowledge.

Before news of the King's death reached England, Byrom took care to position himself in Cambridge in the surroundings he liked best. He took rooms in Trinity and busied himself playing the part of a college fellow. 'I am in commons, gown and band as orderly as if I had never stirred from hence.'[25] He was teaching fresh pupils and visiting the local gentry, but the peace of this academic interlude came to an end on Thursday 15 June. He had started a letter home to Elizabeth when, at three o'clock in the afternoon, he added: 'Just now news is come hither that expresses are going up and down with notification of King George's death; he died in Holland.'[26] It is characteristic of Byrom's deviousness that the news he had long been waiting for appears as a postscript – just that moment heard and immediately passed on.

Byrom had looked forward to a time when 'princes would expire and monarchs die'. According to Horace Walpole, on the death of George I 'Queen Caroline is said to have discovered in his Cabinet a proposal, written by the Earl of Berkeley, then First Lord of the Admiralty, to seize the Prince of Wales and convey him to America, where he should never be heard of more.'[27] It is said that George I rejected this scheme, but the very idea is an example of the intrigue which surrounded the succession of George II. It is interesting that Caroline is the person alleged to have found the document and at a time when Byrom claimed to be involved with her. Was she telling the truth? She once confessed that her character 'would never be known until after her death'.[28] In addition to the jottings in Byrom's notebook there is a reference in another poem to a 'ship doctor' visiting Cambridge to make enquiries about matters which have 'happened of late'. In the poem Byrom makes it clear that in this initiative he is acting on his own and not on behalf of any group, Jacobite, Templar or otherwise.

Whatever political objectives Byrom hoped to achieve after the

death of George I, he must have realised that the accession of the
Prince of Wales would have a dramatic impact on Caroline now that
she was Queen. He may well have felt still confident of her affections, but he could not have foreseen the extent of the change once
she had real power in her grasp. Unfortunately, the public demands
on her would now be greater, and the relationship, if it were to
continue, would do so under even more testing circumstances.

Before he had time to adjust fully to this new situation Byrom received a letter from Thomas Deacon, dated 24 June, which alerted
him to Deacon's intended departure for London. He was to take
over the practice of a Dr Cole who had recently died. The practice
was in Stepney, the home of Captain Guy, and Deacon talks of the
'very advantageous prospect' ahead. Deacon is signalling to Byrom
to read between the lines, for Guy would now be on shore-leave.
That the move to London was not dictated by any wish to further
his medical career is evident from Deacon's swift return to Manchester after six months. In fact, Deacon was at Stepney during
much of the time Mr Beverly was conducting enquiries into the
absence of Beale from the Carolina.

Unfortunately for Byrom, when Elizabeth got wind of Dr
Deacon's imminent departure, she took it as an opportunity to urge
him to take over Deacon's Manchester practice and settle down at
home. This was the last thing Byrom wanted at this point, and he
wrote at great length to refute the suggestion.

In 1718 Byrom had had the opportunity of returning to Manchester to become the librarian at Chetham's, but deliberately let it
slip. Years later, he still had no intention of relinquishing his secret
life in London. In the letter he pretends that his health is not good
enough, a ploy he often used to get himself out of a tight corner
without losing sympathy. He insists that only he knows what is best
for him despite 'the old difficulty of the opinion of others', no doubt
a reference to his father-in-law who was still anxious to see Byrom
pursuing a conventional career. His peripatetic tutoring did not
impress the old man.

In Byrom's opinion, being a doctor in Manchester was not of
much consequence. This is a far cry from the enthusiasm he expressed for 'Physic' when he was studying at Montpellier. He claims
proudly to be at the top of the shorthand tree.

Everybody commends it that learns, and longs for't that does not.
I am at the top of this affair at least, and should be so if there were

as many professors of it as of physic, there will always be patients that will employ me to administer this physic, and sure pay, and kind reception, and friendship, and interest; and much more I might say to desire your leave to proceed in it.[29]

However an unbiased reader must surely wonder why he could not get the same satisfaction from working in Manchester, where his family were. Quite simply he had to remain in London to serve his own political cause, and to be near the Queen.

Despite his reluctance to work in Manchester, Byrom returned home in the summer to be with his family. On the 11 October George II was crowned in Westminster Abbey. Byrom was quick to return to London the following month after receiving a letter on 14 November from Richard Hassell who wanted him to take part in the voting on important business at the Royal Society. This was the final outcome of Byrom's quarrel with Sloane. A ballot was to be taken on whether foreign members should be allowed to vote at meetings. Byrom opposed the motion, as did Jurin, who, as Secretary, asked for directions, citing the existing statutes. By now Jurin, too, had aroused the bitter enmity of Sloane and Sir Richard Manningham. Not surprisingly they lost and, according to the Journal, 'Byrom, Jurin and Folkes were thrown out of the Council'.[30] However, the papers of the Royal Society do not contain any record of Byrom ever being a member of the Council.

Having been out of London for the Coronation proper, Byrom lost no time in going to the playhouse to see a farcical representation of the ceremony the day he arrived in town. All he chose to record was that 'Harlequin dressed as a queen.' He made no comment on how George was treated. His obsession with Caroline led him to see the performance in terms of her rather than the King. Most people would have remembered the way the sovereign was portrayed rather than his consort, but Caroline was always uppermost in Byrom's mind.

Caroline herself was caught up in a round of new duties. Since George I's death she had been working successfully to ensure that Walpole's power was maintained. Years later, Lord Hervey recalled in his *Memoirs* Caroline's influence at this critical point. Some courtiers had tended to underestimate her when she was simply Princess of Wales:

But as soon as ever the Prince became King the whole world began to find out that her will was the sole spring on which every movement in the Court turned and though His Majesty lost no opportunity to declare that the Queen never meddled in his business; yet nobody was simple enough to believe it.[31]

It is not surprising that Caroline had little time to see Byrom.

By Christmas, Byrom had been in London for a month. He had returned to his routine of teaching, and caught up with his old circle of friends, dining with Salkeld and Deacon and spending time with the Bentleys. Martin Folkes had proposed Byrom as a shorthand teacher to Prince Frederick and Bentley saw no reason why his Jacobite sympathies should stand in his way.[32] He rallied Byrom on this, for their friendship was as warm as ever. Even so that Christmas was not a happy one. On Christmas Eve Byrom returned nostalgically to one of his regular haunts, The King's Head, not far from New Round Court. His host on this occasion was a shorthand pupil celebrating his twentieth birthday. To lighten the occasion the young man read 'a comical country love-letter that was stopped in the posthouse in the year upon suspicion of treason'. Christmas Day was solitary. He spent the greater part of it going through his papers and writing letters, confiding in his Journal: 'The worst time for me to be in London is this Christmas time.' His loneliness was a sign of what was to come. By the evening of 26 December he was sinking into a depression. He had spent the day helping to catalogue the Earl of Sunderland's library and that night wrote to Elizabeth, who was expecting their fourth child. He was tired and 'not in humour to write to anybody but thyself'. Guilt and isolation combined to make him tender for his family's welfare. 'Good night to ye all; Good night, mamma; be careful of yourselves for papa's sake.' His depression lasted for some time.

CHAPTER FIVE

Blue Nuns and Jacobites

1728–9

IN JANUARY 1728 a dispute arose between the Fellows of the Collegiate Church (now Manchester Cathedral) and the Warden, the Bishop of Chester, about the election of new Fellows. It was referred to Lord Trevor, Keeper of the Privy Seal, and Byrom attended the meetings to take down in shorthand the arguments of both sides to report back to Manchester. He concluded wryly that both parties had right on their side, but that 'might and right together may well overcome bare right'.[1] The Warden was a staunch Hannoverian appointed by George I in 1718, while many local churchmen were Tory, like Byrom. Unfortunately, at the time Byrom suffered an attack of 'what folks call rheumatism', and the pain forced him to give up transcribing the deliberations and to keep to his bed. However, two days later he 'crept out to the Royal Society', to see how matters stood for his friend Jurin, who was still under a cloud.

Since 1728 was a leap year, this February brought round an actual birthday. It is the one for which a page of the original Journal has been recently discovered. Among the passages not transcribed for the published edition was a mention of a meeting between Byrom and a relative of Bishop Peploe, whom he described as 'too zealous and obstinate', and also a reference to a bribe offered to the Fellows in return for not opposing the Warden. However, the editor did include Byrom's resolution at the end of the entry to adopt a more positive frame of mind to overcome his moods of depression 'and not suffer any sullenness to usurp upon our minds; in order to which it seems to be necessary to live so as to preserve our innocence and our health, which would naturally make us cheerful, which we perhaps could not be otherwise, by all our reasoning and thinking'.[2] It is revealing that Byrom equates health with innocence and depression with wrong-doing. His guilt and fear were now responsible for recurring bouts of moroseness.

By this time Byrom's eldest daughter, Beppy, was six years old, Edward was four and Anne two. A new infant was expected in April, but despite his wife's condition Byrom did not return home – childbirth and child mortality were, after all, everyday occurrences best left to women. He took care to end his letters with fulsome endearments, but relieved himself of any responsibility with the thought 'I suppose you are all well at your father's house and your own'. This was more wish-fulfilment than indifference. His own depression and commitments left him not wanting to think of others' woes. He was just about able to cope, when he heard that his sisters Dorothy and Betty were unwell. He wrote to his wife: 'It is a sickly time here, the weekly bills higher, they say, than has been known since the Plague.'[3] The prospect of winter and his own low state made him more sympathetic to Elizabeth: 'I am almost weary of such long absence from thee, especially when I am not satisfied of thy health, or not quite right in my own.'[4]

He did not return to Manchester until May, when he took part in the discussions between the Fellows and the Bishop, who was still trying to assert his authority by refusing to call a Chapter of the College in case the Fellows demonstrated their independence and voted against him. Byrom's intervention made him the hero of the hour. 'I was told that at all the public houses in the town they were drinking my health.'[5] This moment of local triumph encouraged him in the conviction he had a role to play in public affairs. In supporting the Tory element in Manchester he was already helping those most sympathetic to the Jacobite cause. He stayed at home for the rest of the year, and as a bonus was able to enjoy the new infant Nelly (Ellen).

He was also able to regale his family and friends with the story of his encounter with a highwayman earlier in the year. On his way down to Cambridge on 18 January his coach was held up. While two other men sought to placate the villain with a guinea apiece, Byrom proffered five or six shillings, much to the robber's anger: 'he cursed me and swore he would have gold from me'. Byrom refused to panic and took so long looking for more money that the highwayman turned upon a fourth traveller 'an honest bricklayer', who likewise proffered five shillings. Later Byrom confessed to Elizabeth: 'I never grudged to part with an ounce of silver so much in my life.' He tried to make light of the encounter and recalled ruefully his wish, when first married, to have a coach of his own, adding: 'But truly, since this rudeness, I do not much care whether I do keep one or not.' Rumour did her usual work and, after being in Cambridge a week, Byrom heard the news in London was that he had been 'robbed of all money, a portmantle full of clothes, linen, and things of value'. Little wonder that he later used the incident in a comic narrative poem addressed to Martin Folkes. It ends with the hapless travellers being rescued by the Goddess of Shorthand who advises her votaries to stick to travelling on horseback.[6]

When he returned to London the following February he chose to go back through Stafford, not one of his usual ports of call, where he stopped to teach shorthand to a member of a local family named Ward. He then moved on to Wolverhampton where he stayed the night before setting out for Birmingham. On his way he was approached by two men, one with deep red hair, intent on robbery. No doubt his earlier experience of the highwayman on the way to Cambridge had made him more wary, for this time he was travelling armed, and he fired at the two men, who made off. He continued his journey, finally deciding to put up at The Hen and Chickens in Birmingham. Snow had started to fall and the local church bell was tolling solemnly. The combination of the winter weather and mournful tones of the bell, together with the memory of the encounter on the road, played tricks on his imagination. When he saw that the hostler at the inn had deep red hair, he thought he was one of the robbers and that the landlord in all likelihood was his accomplice, the man he had shot, and that the bell was tolling for his death. He was much relieved to discover his suspicions were wrong and that the landlord was alive and well – but the incident shows how easily he was a prey to fears.

Although he had rejected the idea of a career as a doctor he found his services increasingly called upon. On his way through Wolverhampton the wife of a friend, Elwal, sent for him to discuss her illness and offered a fee for his advice which he declined. He arrived back in London on 8 January and a month later was discussing the idea of a medical career with Mr Bevan who tried to persuade Byrom to study pharmacy and chemistry with him. That was Ash Wednesday. In May he was present at Blossoms Inn when another friend, Dr Hall, had his tonsils removed without the aid of any anaesthetic by two surgeons. Byrom noted 'he bore the operation most heroically and was very cheerful after'. In June the landlady of Hindley's Inn consulted him about her three-month old child 'that had something like a rupture'. Byrom prescribed a diet of milk and water. With so many doctors among his friends and at the Royal

Society, he could hardly avoid keeping up to date with the latest scientific advances. In July he spent an evening in the company of Dr James Douglas, a celebrated anatomist whose work is still remembered today. The one thing he chose to record from their conversation was the doctor's opinion of the action of mercury upon the body. 'Dr Douglas said he thought that mercury did attenuate the blood, by breaking it.'[7] From now on Byrom developed an interest in medicines as opposed to medicine.

At the same time he became more and more concerned over the matter of diet. Byrom's attitude to health shows him to be in advance of many contemporaries. When young Nelly fell ill in May he advised his wife from London:

> the diet of the children is the only thing to look after; I do not admire vomits for them, or blisters, or anything else hardly; I like of your going into the country with her; I should think all sorts of herbage and greens were good for children as well as grass for young animals, whose machines are nourished in like manner as ours, the strongest of 'em with the simplest food and drink.[8]

Despite Byrom's advice, Nelly died later the same year. Elizabeth had to cope on her own as best she could. John wrote to console her, but continued about his business. Of course the rate of child mortality was much higher in those days and it was not as easy for Byrom to dash back home as it would be today. Although he had married for politic reasons, there are no grounds for believing he was not fond of her. She loved him and proved to be a dutiful wife and conscientious mother, bearing five children at intervals of two years. When she was forty-three and Byrom was fifty-two they had one last child, who died young.

Like most of the Byrom women, Elizabeth had a good head on her shoulders, although not as intelligent as John's sister Phebe, a genuine intellectual, often referred to jocularly by Byrom as his 'second wife'. Byrom's letters to Elizabeth contain frequent expressions of affection, but there is, too, an unmistakable tendency to talk down to her. For the most part they are informative of his day-to-day activities, or, rather those he chooses to write about. Constantly he writes of his shorthand. After all, that was his 'business' and Elizabeth, with the rest of the Byrom women, was expected to keep herself abreast of developments. She wrote scores of letters to him in reply, but only one was included in the Journal. Byrom must have destroyed them, but she religiously kept his.

She was fond of dancing and attended the Manchester Assemblies in fashionable King Street, helping to organise them. She did not give up her dancing simply because John was away from home. On one occasion when he was in Manchester she left him writing in his notebooks, and went off to the Assembly with their three-year-old daughter Beppy, who charmed the company by dancing a minuet. Submissive and competent, there was a least one occasion when she put her foot down and had her way – at the beginning of their marriage, when she objected to John keeping a coach. It was an extravagance she would not permit since it was her father who kept the purse-strings. Elizabeth hated travelling long distances in a coach, but that is hardly surprising considering the conditions of the day. For the most part she was happy to stay in Manchester, agonising over the children's ailments and sending daily reports during their illnesses. She could remember five of her eight brothers dying. Many of the other Byrom women visited London on a number of occasions. Elizabeth seems to have had no desire to see the place.

On 4 February 1730 Byrom started teaching shorthand to Edward Gibbon (father of the historian), who was then at Emmanuel accompanied by his private tutor, William Law. Byrom had visited Law for the first time the previous March at Gibbon's home in Putney. Law felt it his duty to attend one of the first lessons and was so impressed that he recommended it in Cambridge as 'the' shorthand. Unfortunately young Gibbon was an untidy writer and a poor pupil. Byrom commented: 'What a pity he should be so slow, for Law's sake!'[9] Nevertheless the lessons kept Byrom in Cambridge and cemented his friendship with Law. Apart from such pupils as Gibbon, Byrom continued to use his shorthand to develop a subversive political role.

The people prominent in his life in 1729 included figures who played an important part in the second major attempt to re-establish the House of Stuart on the throne in 1715 men such as Henry Salkeld and Charles Radclyffe. Radclyffe was the cousin of Prince James Stuart, son of James II. Radclyffe's brother James, the third Earl of Derwentwater, was the same age as James Stuart, and they had been educated together in France at the exiled court of Queen Mary of Modena, widow of the old king. The two Radclyffe brothers epitomised all that was best in the Stuart camp – they were brave, intelligent, courteous, generous-hearted and staunchly loyal. Both took part in the 1715 uprising and were captured, fighting valiantly at Preston. Despite the most powerful and moving pleas to

George I by his wife and friends, James was executed. Charles, who in his youth had been wilder and more impetuous, had likewise been condemned to die, but in July 1716 he organised an escape from Newgate totally in keeping with his audacious character. He gained permission to hold a party with thirteen fellow-prisoners to which their gaolers were invited. After getting them drunk, Radclyffe obtained a key which allowed him and his friends to pass through to the debtors' part of the prison. Here the turnkey mistook Radclyffe and his companions for visitors and showed them the way out. London was soon buzzing with news of the exploit and Radclyffe went into hiding for a while. After escaping to Paris he was appointed a secret agent by James Stuart and made several visits to London, some of which were known to the government. 'About 1730' he stayed for a time at a house in Pall Mall calling himself 'Mr. Johns'.[10] By 1732 he was moving from England to France and Rome, working for the restoration of his cousin. According to an old Lancashire tradition he disguised himself as a deaf mute on a farm near Ainsdale some months before the 1745 rebellion.

The Journal shows that Radclyffe was in London in June 1729, for he met Byrom several times that summer. On 3 June Radclyffe sent him a message by 'Mr Hanmer', probably Sir Thomas Hanmer, husband of the widowed Duchess of Grafton, through whom he would have known the Radclyffes and whose daughter-in-law, the second Duchess, was a great admirer of Byrom.[11] (Sir Thomas became Speaker of the House of Commons and, like Byrom, was a staunch Tory. At one time he had hoped to see the party regain power and had attempted to influence Caroline's husband in its favour, but without success. Disillusioned, Hanmer retired from the Commons in 1727, shortly after the death of George I.)

> Mr Hanmer came to my room about 11 o'clock when I was in bed, and told me that Mr Radclyffe had been at Richard's last night, that he wanted to see me about Captain Jones's two sons, that he should be at the Sword Blade at one o'clock.

Accordingly, Byrom 'went to the Sword Blade and found Mr Radclyffe there, and we went upon 'Change and he said he would be at Richard's tonight about seven.'[12]

Later that day Byrom went to Richard's but 'Mr Radclyffe did not come according to appointment'. Byrom had decided to miss a meeting of the Sun Club to see Radclyffe, for that same evening two members came up to him at Richard's and urged him to attend.

When he joined them later, Martin Folkes joked about his absences (there must have been others) and said 'he had been told that I had gone to Rome afoot to see the Pretender'. His Jacobite sympathies were no secret here. So keen was he to see Radclyffe that another meeting was set up for 8 June: 'To Richard's again. Mr Radclyffe there; he and I went to take a walk in Gray's Inn walks.'[13] It was safer to discuss their kind of business in the open air. The following day they met again.

> had a letter from Dr Deacon, franked by Mr Illingworth with Mrs Allen's letter about shorthand to Mr Cooper enclosed ... Mr Radclyffe, Hanmer, Mills and I went to the King's Arms and Mr Salkeld came to us and we were very merry. Mr Radclyffe said among other talk that if we had seen the Chevalier we should not be for him. I said I had seen him ... Hanmer had given Radclyffe a copy of 'My Time, O ye muses' etc. as far as the ninth stanza, which he would have me read but I would not. Mr Mills said that when he read it he kissed the book.[14]

Associated in this meeting with Radclyffe are the names of other Jacobite agents – Deacon, Salkeld, and Illingworth, a Yorkshireman based in Manchester who is also to be found in the list of Jacobites in Byrom's notebook. Radclyffe evidently wanted to make sure that all of them at this last meeting were of one mind, hence his leading comment on the Chevalier. Byrom's frank admission, 'I had seen him', made it clear that all of them could be trusted. A few months later Byrom was meeting 'Salkeld' and 'Jackson' again at the King's Arms, another link in the Jacobite spy network. Were plans being made already for the '45?

Charles Radclyffe, a man of firm conviction and energy, was a leading figure in founding the first native French lodge of Freemasonry in Paris in 1725 in the rue de Boucheries. French Freemasonry came to be known as the 'Scottish Rite', having been introduced originally by Jacobites who followed James II into exile after the defeat of the Glorious Revolution in 1688. It also claimed to have knowledge of profound mysteries which had been handed down for generations in Scotland, and was interested in such areas of speculation as the Cabala, Hermetic thought and that cluster of ideas known as Rosicrucianism. These were all subjects of interest to Byrom and the select few who formed the Cabala Club. Scottish Freemasonry in its early days was politically motivated to strengthen the old Franco-Scottish alliance and ensure continued support from France for any further attempt to restore the Stuarts.

Byrom's masonic association has been confirmed by material from The United Grand Lodge of England.[15] He was a member of the French Lodge which in 1730 was meeting at the Swan in Long Acre. This lodge was numbered 44 in the enumeration of 1729, and had been constituted originally in September 1725, when it used to meet at the Golden Lion in Dean Street, Soho. Byrom showed his interest a year earlier in 1724, while travelling to the Royal Society in a coach with the Duke of Richmond and Martin Folkes, talking 'about masonry and shorthand'. Richmond was Radclyffe's cousin and like him a mason, belonging to the No.4 Lodge at the Rummer and Grapes, Westminster. He, too, was admitted to one of the leading Jacobite lodges in Paris – the Lodge de Bussy – in 1735. Folkes became Deputy Grand Master in England as well as President of the Royal Society. A third friend, Desaguliers, was likewise both a member of the Royal Society and a Freemason, here and in France, belonging to the same lodges as Richmond. Membership of the Royal Society and Freemasonry was common to many public figures at the time and simply a sign of an innocuous interest in recondite subjects, but Byrom's masonic membership is associated with a nucleus of Jacobite sympathisers with definite political ambitions.

Byrom's connections with the Radclyffes are rich and complex. Charles had a strong link with Manchester in the person of Lady Barbara Fitzroy. Born in 1672, she was educated in Paris at an exclusive school run by the English Community of the Immaculate Conception of Our Lady, an order popularly known as the Blue Nuns because of the colour of their mantles. The convent became the most 'fashionable as well as the best organised place of education for girls' of English Catholic families in France. Years later, Charles Radclyffe sent his own children to the school.

After angering Queen Mary II, Lady Barbara spent much of her life abroad. However, it is known that she spent her last years in Manchester, with the family of William Dawson, an apothecary and first cousin to John Byrom. Dawson and his family were staunch Stuart supporters. Later, William's own son, Captain James Dawson, served with gallantry in the '45 uprising and was executed in London with the other 'Manchester Martyrs'.

Lady Barbara was eventually buried in 1734/5 in what the *Palatine Note-book* describes as the 'Radclyffe Chancel' at the Collegiate

Church, which was the 'exclusive burial place of the Radclyffes of Ordsall'.[16] On 19 January Byrom received a letter from his wife announcing 'Mrs Barbara Fitzroy dead and left Mr Dawson her effects etc.'[17] Dawson died in 1763 – the same year as Byrom – and was buried with Lady Barbara. The *Palatine Note-book* points out that these are the only two exceptions to be buried with the Radclyffes.

These links with Byrom were all strands that bound him closer to the Jacobite cause by ties of blood, personal friendship and ancient loyalties, and his connection with Charles Radclyffe shows how the Jacobite and masonic elements in his life overlap. Their meetings at this time would not have been purely social. On 17 June 1729 Byrom called on the Jacobite Salkeld, who at the time had rooms in Basinghall Street in the City. They talked about 'the absurdity of persecuting one another for our differences in opinion'. Later that month on the 28th, he dined with Salkeld 'at the tavern over against St Lawrence's church, and he said Dr Desaguliers was to be with them on Tuesday night; and he desired my company, said that the Doctor said I was a very clever fellow, that all the world said so'.[18] This was high praise indeed, for Desaguliers was a leading scientist, a disciple of Newton, who became Professor of Experimental Philosophy at Oxford and foresaw the birth of atomic theory. Desaguliers is recognised as having played a prominent part in the early history of organised Freemasonry – and his comment on Byrom is an indication of the position of influence Byrom held in Jacobite/Masonic circles. The following Tuesday Byrom called on Salkeld as arranged only to find him not at home; 'but coming back I met him and Dr Desaguliers arm in arm, and so we all went upstairs' – the comradeship between the two men is evident from this cameo. Desaguliers's high opinion of Byrom is not to be taken lightly, formed as it was from seeing him with mutual friends in the Royal Society and masonic circles. Given the known political sympathies of each of these three, it would appear that the meeting at Salkeld's house was on Jacobite business, which Byrom, despite writing in shorthand, does not commit to paper. He and Salkeld may well have thought it absurd for people to persecute each other because of different beliefs, but that did not dampen their ardour for the Jacobite cause.

Byrom continued to attend the meetings of the Sun Club, which had moved from underneath the freemasons' Lodge of Antiquity at the Goose and Gridiron in St Paul's Churchyard to the King's

Head, Holborn. This was in part due to Byrom's interventions at the Royal Society. His attitude over the form of the address to George I had marked him as politically suspect. The Premier Grand Lodge had promised allegiance to the new House of Hannover. His loyal support of Dr Jurin when his competence was questioned caused further annoyance, and the general irritation of the President, Sir Hans Sloane, and his party led to Byrom, Jurin and Martin Folkes being 'thrown out of the Council' on 30 November. Sir Hans Sloane's nephew refused to have Byrom in his house. The Sun Club's move on 5 December meant that its members did not have to come face to face with the lodge, many of whom were Royal Society men. The Sun Club settled in its new premises and stayed there until 1736.

Byrom's political activities were a continuation of the work he had been engaged in for years. The triumvirate of Deacon, Salkeld and Byrom held fast. Thomas Deacon had been a staunch Jacobite since 1716, writing the speeches of two of the rebels condemned to death for their part in the uprising. As a non-juror he refused all moves to unite his church with the established Church of England. Eventually, in 1733, he was consecrated non-juring Bishop of his small flock, which in effect constituted a Jacobite cell. James Ray, a volunteer with Cumberland's army in the '45, described it as such:

> I don't know of what body the congregation consists, they not allowing any to come amongst them but such as are of their own sort, who (like the more worshipful society of Freemasons) are under an oath not to divulge what is transacted there except it be to a just and lawful Jacobite as he or they shall appear upon examination.[19]

As for Salkeld, his Jacobite credentials have already been established, from his recusant forebear, Thomas, to his uncle Roger, 'out in the '15', and a network of spies in Cumberland. Henry and his brother, another Thomas, shared the same servant, Peter Pattinson, a resourceful and cool-headed man arrested for carrying a letter from the Young Pretender to the Earl of Barrymore, the acknowledged leader of the English Jacobites, urging the English to join with him. The Salkeld family was reared on intrigue. Byrom knew full well how reliable Henry would be. Deacon he had known from his youth. These were the two passing the mysterious box between each other, with Byrom's help, in May 1727.

CHAPTER SIX

Critical Times

1730–3

THE DISTANCE between Byrom and Caroline grew with the demands of her role as queen. Gradually he must have realised the vulnerability of his own position: strip him of his role as shorthand tutor to the great men of London and there was nothing left to protect him, a man of no substance or political office. His brilliance alone was not enough to surmount the wall of the Establishment. Nor could Caroline, now that she was queen, afford to mark him out publicly by any special favours. Besides there were other men about to enter the queen's favoured inner circle.

On 20 February 1730 Byrom's old friend Dr Francis Hooper returned to Cambridge from London to tell him that his long absence from the city had been the cause of speculation: 'I was reported to be dead of an apoplexy, that I was much enquired after.'[1] Even so, another month was to elapse before Byrom set out again for London, on 26 March. His stay was not long. He could hardly have spent a week in London. Did he in that short time see Caroline?

The final blow to the continuity of any meaningful relationship came on 7 May 1730 with the appointment of Lord Hervey as Vice-Chamberlain to the Royal Household. Hervey was one of the most colourful and witty members of the Court. As Vice-Chamberlain he held a highly important office, responsible with the Lord Chamberlain for royal receptions, birthdays, funerals, balls, anniversaries and the movement of the Court from one palace to another. He had known the King and Queen for more than ten years, and his new appointment, which gave him an apartment in St James's Palace, brought him into close contact with them during their leisure time. Gradually the Queen came to love him more than her own son, Frederick, Prince of Wales. A man of enormous charm, ambivalent sexuality and entertaining wit, he became Caroline's closest and most trusted friend. She is said to have called him 'her child, her pupil, and her charge'. His services proved invaluable. He kept her up to date with political developments the King might be planning and with all the current gossip. Their intimacy allowed Caroline to engage in such scandalous speculations as the possibility of replacing Prince Frederick in his wife's bed without her knowing it. (Caroline doubted' that the marriage had ever been consummated.) Hervey thought the proposal a possibility:

> For a month before and after I would advise the Prince to go to bed several hours after his wife, and to pretend to get up for a flux several times in the night, and to perfume himself always with some predominant smell, and by the help of these tricks it would be very easy to put the change of any man near his own size upon her that he pleased.[2]

A woman who could plot against her daughter-in-law in this way was certainly also capable of deceiving her own husband.

After Hervey was appointed, the Court moved to Windsor and he found himself comfortably installed in his own apartment at the Castle. On this occasion he was called upon to officiate in place of the Lord Chamberlain at his first important ceremony. On the Feast of St George he had to supervise the installation of the Duke of Cumberland, now nine years old, as one of the Knights of St George. Hervey had to learn all the court ceremonial for that ritual.

Byrom had recorded his eagerness to witness the preparations for the Duke's installation as a Knight of the Bath when he was still a child of four. He would have been just as keen to witness, or at least to have been told of, William's behaviour when he was made a Knight of St George. There is evidence to suggest that Byrom travelled to Windsor to learn what he could of the ceremony.

If he did not already know Hervey, Byrom would have, true to form, made every effort to become acquainted with him as another source of information about the young Duke and his mother. There is in the Journal a reference to meetings with Hervey in 1729/30. The two men apparently got on well together. Byrom recalls: 'Hervey full of compliments to me, and I submitted'.[3] These meetings took place a few days before Caroline's birthday and only a few weeks before Hervey took up his office as Vice-Chamberlain. Byrom's closeness to Caroline had led him to make reference to her birthday, but these references end in 1730. In other words, by the time the next anniversary came round, something had happened to make Byrom feel less impelled to record it. It is likely that the cause was

Hervey's growing intimacy with the Queen after his appointment. He was handsome in a pretty way and his polished manners were a perfect foil to much of the Hannoverian coarseness of the Court. His cutting wit kept Caroline amused for hours and he became practised in the art of pleasing her. At Hampton Court he rode every morning with the Queen, and on hunting days never left her side.

Hervey enjoyed one important advantage over Byrom – there was no need for secrecy in his dealings with the Queen. Apart from Byrom, no man became so close to Caroline, and, in Byrom's opinion, Hervey was the usurper of the Queen's affections. He even goes further than this. In a short poem 'Upon a Bee Stinging a Lady's Cheek by Cornet Hervey', Byrom sees himself as the Bee and Hervey as a man whose lot it was to console Caroline for the pain caused by her love affair with Byrom. In this delicate poem, Byrom seems to acknowledge that Hervey brought the Queen some peace of mind at no small cost to himself.

> To heal the Wound a Bee had made
> Upon my Kitty's face,
> His Honey in Her Cheek he laid,
> And bade me kiss the Place.
> Pleased, I obey'd and from the Wound
> Emptied both Sore and Smart.
> The Honey in my lips I found,
> The Sting within my Heart.

It is obvious that Hervey came to fill a need in Caroline's life. She was at odds with her eldest son, Frederick, whom she had grown to detest. She took advantage of her mature years to look upon Hervey as the son she wished she had in Frederick. She regarded Hervey's mother as a 'brute that deserves such a beast as my son', and complained to Hervey: 'I wish with all my soul we could change, that they who are so alike might go together, and that you and (I) might belong to one another.'[4] This is an extraordinary confession for the Queen to make, and her feelings for Hervey, whether she realised it or not, may have been more than maternal.

Byrom was powerless to hinder this deepening relationship. Hervey had so much to offer the Queen both directly in her service, and indirectly, too. She would have gained great vicarious satisfaction from observing the diverse elements in Hervey's own emotional life. There was his affair with Miss Vane, his warm friendship with Stephen Fox, and his relationship with his own wife and family (he had eight children). Hervey remained close to Caroline right up to her death and it was he who composed her epitaph, at the King's request.

The Journal reveals the names of other friends of Byrom who had access to the Queen. The frequency with which he saw these people would render Byrom's presence on the edge of the royal circle innocent of any suspicion. Some who had known Byrom from his Cambridge days must have been aware that he had refused to take the Oath of Allegiance. Among Byrom's ecclesiastical friends was Henry Wickham. Both he and Byrom had succumbed to the charms of Joanna Bentley at Cambridge. In 1724 Wickham became Chaplain to the Princess of Wales and Byrom records their encounters in the coffee houses and parks of London.

Two other clerics who visited Caroline twice a week around the period 1727-9 were Dr Samuel Clarke and Bishop Hoadley. Once again Byrom used his shorthand to gain their acquaintance. He became shorthand tutor to Hoadley's son and through him gained his father's confidence. 'This afternoon to Mr. Glover, it happened that the Bishop and Dr. Clarke were there at dinner.' Byrom was thus able to spend an 'hour or two' with them. The conversation might turn or be turned to Caroline, and no doubt it was often sufficient for Byrom to be with people simply because they had been in her presence.

There were doctors Byrom knew who were connected with the Court. Apart from Douglas, the most interesting was Dr Friend, who was once called in to treat Princess Amelia. Caroline was sufficiently pleased with his services to appoint him as her physician. Dr Friend's known Jacobite sympathies caused some unfavourable comment when he started to attend the Queen's household, but Byrom did not hesitate to associate with him. He also came to know well Dr Mead, the popular Whig doctor.

Another highly influential acquaintance whom Byrom assiduously cultivated was Philip Dormer Stanhope, fourth Earl of Chesterfield and author of the celebrated letters to his son. Stanhope became a close friend of Pope and an acquaintance of Swift.

> I showed him my alphabet and a sketch of my method, which he seemed to like very well, and said I went the right way to work, told me I had better teach it first and then print it, said he would be my scholar, and desired me to come on Tuesday morning again at ten o'clock.[5]

Stanhope was a Gentleman of the Bedchamber and, therefore, as close to the Prince of Wales as Mrs Clayton was to the Princess Caroline. During the shorthand lessons Byrom would have been able to pick up the slightest hint of any development at Court in the Prince's household, which he might not be able to learn elsewhere. When he heard that Stanhope was to receive the Order of the Bath at the same time as William in 1725, Byrom was soon knocking at his door. Again shorthand was to be his means of entry. At first the teaching went well and Stanhope was keen to learn, but before long he was having some difficulty, and postponed further lessons.

Stanhope had more pressing problems than Byrom's shorthand. He had refused Walpole's offer of the Order of the Bath and was annoyed when his brother, William, accepted it. As a result he had written some satirical verses which displeased Walpole so much that he dismissed him from office as Captain of the Gentlemen Pensioners. This would no doubt have pleased Caroline, who never appreciated Stanhope's caustic wit.

Byrom next met Stanhope five weeks later, while walking in the Mall, the day after the installation of the Knights of the Bath. It was evidently an embarrassing encounter and not simply because of the shorthand. By now Stanhope must have realised that Byrom was connected with the coterie surrounding Princess Caroline in some way, probably through the shorthand. Since the Princess and Stanhope disliked each other, the earl thought it more diplomatic to keep Byrom at a distance. Byrom felt the effect of Stanhope's behaviour but was unaware of the cause. Stanhope's advancement at Court had been through the favour of Prince George; the diplomat in Stanhope therefore made him feel it wiser not to be seen encouraging a man like Byrom whose political loyalties were uncertain.

The relationship between Stanhope and Byrom was brief. Its starting point had been, like many others, centred on Byrom's need to be near those connected with Prince William or his mother. However tenuous that link, Byrom could not let a chance slip by. The revival of the ancient Order of the Knights of the Bath had for a moment made Stanhope a desirable acquaintance. But because of Stanhope's political ambitions the friendship brought no rewards for Byrom. Stanhope's discretion paid handsome dividends. On the accession of George II he became Lord of the Bedchamber and, despite Walpole's opposition, was appointed Ambassador at the Hague in 1728.

During the early months of 1731 Byrom was in London, very much engaged in fighting the Bill proposing to set up a public workhouse in Manchester. The main architect of the plan was Sir Oswald Mosley, a Whig, though not as extreme as Peploe. As a Tory, Byrom opposed the Bill (which would have benefited the poor of the town) simply because he was afraid the workhouse would be run by the local Whigs and so further Whig supremacy in Manchester. In this instance Byrom's charitable instincts took second place to politics. He preferred there to be no workhouse than one run by the opposite faction. His vigorous opposition is clear from a letter to Elizabeth in which he claimed that 'even shorthand itself is forc'd to adjourn its concern for the present'. Nevertheless he did not neglect his own interests, for in March 1731 he was busy acquiring more aristocratic pupils with close connections at Court.

The first of these was Lord De La Warr. He had been Lord of the Bedchamber to George I and in 1731 was appointed Treasurer of the Household of George II, which meant he was automatically a member of the Privy Council. He was thus a very influential addition to Byrom's circle of aristocratic acquaintances. Byrom was with him two days before the birthday of Duke William in April: 'Lord De La Warr took me in his coach to Westminster, where I bought a box of plants 10s 6d. of Pape of Scarborough.'[6] It was an expensive purchase and no doubt a present. The Journal does not say for whom, but it looks like a gift to Caroline commemorating William's birthday. An echo, perhaps, of the present of Paradise stocks to Caroline herself.

Another new pupil was William Cavendish, third Duke of Devonshire. The Journal shows Byrom's relationship with Devonshire develop from that of tutor to friend. In March 1731 he was kept waiting the Duke's pleasure, but by 1737 he was dining with him and his family and recounts their meetings with evident pride. It was a relationship which Byrom took care to cultivate. When he first started to learn shorthand Devonshire was Lord Privy Seal, a post of some importance. The Lord Privy Seal had to approve letters patent which conferred any dignity, office, monopoly or other privilege. From 1733 until 1737 he was Lord Steward of the Household. As such he was a Cabinet Minister and presided over the examination and passing of Household accounts. This brought him into close contact with both the King and Queen. These facts are helpful in assessing Byrom's tactics. He was always conscious of his absence from home and ready to excuse it by the need to promote his shorthand. The Duke of Devonshire was a big catch, and his patronage would undoubtedly prove useful in drawing other fish into Byrom's shorthand net. Tutoring the Duke gave a perfectly respectable reason for Byrom to remain in London in April 1731 and provided another entrée into Caroline's court.

So, on 15 April, the Duke of Cumberland's birthday, Byrom writes to his wife apologising half in jest for his continued absence: 'I think I'll go live with Duke D. at Chatsworth, and then I shall be between both.'[7] He leaves her in no doubt about the value to him of such a pupil. But Devonshire's true worth was more than Elizabeth realised. All the references to the Duke learning shorthand in 1731 indicate what an apt pupil his Grace was, and one might have expected, in the normal course of events, his relationship with Byrom would cease once he had mastered the system. But this was not so; it continued for many years.

Byrom's third aristocratic pupil was Lord Paulet. He was appointed a Lord of the Bedchamber to George II in July this same year. Thus all three had close connections with the Royal Family both by birth and court appointments. No matter how much time had to be spent on the Manchester Bill, Byrom made sure he was available to teach them. As Caroline became increasingly circumscribed by protocol Byrom turned to them to try to preserve some means of access to her – but without success.

If the appointment of Lord Hervey was one blow to Byrom's already tenuous position, then the Queen's patronage of Stephen Duck was another. Duck was a farm labourer from Wiltshire whose only formal education was the village school. He was endowed with more than usual ambition for a man of his class, and educated himself in the English poets. This was no mean achievement and led him to write verses of his own, some of which fell into the hands of the neighbouring gentry and soon became talked about in London. It was not long before Stephen Duck was regarded as something of a literary wonder, gaining a reputation far beyond his worth. After hearing his verses Caroline became his patron, granting him an annuity and also a small house. In 1730 her interest in him grew as her links with Byrom slackened. That Caroline should make such a blunder in overestimating Duck's worth may not have been due entirely to her German upbringing, for she was certainly acute in her assessment of philosophers. It seems to argue some need for a protégé to fill the gap left by Byrom.

Certainly Duck's rapid advancement and social success, combined with the undeniable mediocrity of his verse, earned him the jealousy and ridicule of other writers. It was ironical that Byrom was one of the few who saw some genuine worth in the homely verses of the Wiltshire labourer. Without realising that Duck was to hasten his own eclipse, Byrom was ready to praise the new man's rise to fame.

> Dear Duck
> This comes to wish thee joy of thy good luck,
> Thy yearly pension and country seat,
> So well bestowed upon thee by the great.
> Thy verses, which have come to Lancashire,
> We read, and we commend, and we admire
> In heart a thousand and a thousand times.
> We thank thee, Stephen, for thy honest rhymes,
> Wherein thou shew'st a native genius bright,
> And poetry upon its legs set right ... [8]

Eventually Duck took Holy Orders. Caroline made him Chaplain at Kew and Rector of Byfleet. Success, however, brought no lasting good for he committed suicide in 1756. Unwittingly, Byrom foretells Duck's fate in the last lines of the poem:

> Preposterous Wits! that labour to set forth
> A vain ambitious rebel Tyrant's worth,
> Or canonise a sour self-murd'rer's pride,
> And make a hero of a suicide!
> Stephen, I vow it were a better thing
> For such as them to thresh, and such as thee to sing!

On Byrom's side, too, a number of events took place which affected his relationship with Caroline. He may have been able to accept the death of his infant daughter Nelly in 1728 with an easy, albeit sincere, resignation. The loss of his mother in 1729 was far more serious. She had always meant much to him. He had lost his father when he was an undergraduate. His mother had survived another eighteen years. He can hardly have got over her death when Elizabeth's mother died in 1730. The Journal shows 'Mother Byrom' as the centre of many activities when John was at home in Manchester. Always a man of philosophical cast of mind and once intended for the Church, he was sobered by these two deaths: his interest in religion gradually deepened and his preoccupation with mysticism grew. It is not possible to pinpoint exactly when the alteration in the relationship with Caroline occurred, but the nature of its change is known. Hervey had supplanted him. The frequency of their meetings was also affected by pressure from another quarter, one which could not be ignored.

Caroline had long made a practice of paying visits to the houses of those members of society whom she specially favoured, and, as was the custom, rewarded the servants of her host with large tips. The King, never generous with money, objected. He considered the Queen's behaviour extravagant and told her to curtail it. Lord Hervey, in his memoirs, recalls a conversation between the royal couple in 1731 which shows how offensive George could be to Caroline when he chose: 'My father,' said the King, 'when he went to people's houses in town never was fool enough to be giving away his money.'[9] The Queen's excuse was that she was simply acting on the advice of Lord Grantham. George II rounded on her: 'She was always asking some fool or other what she was to do, and that none but a fool would ask another fool's advice.' It was Lord Grantham who had provided shelter for George and Caroline when they were expelled from Court in 1717, and it was more than a little ungrateful of George to dismiss him as a fool. Hervey, who was present during the argument, intervened on the Queen's behalf. Her Majesty was simply following custom. The King retorted: 'Then she may stay at home as I do. You do not see me running into every puppy's house to see his new chairs and stools. Nor is it for you', he said to the Queen, 'to be running your nose everywhere, and trotting about the town to every fellow who will give you some bread and butter, like an old girl that loves to go abroad, no matter where, or whether it be proper or no.'[10]

The King was obviously becoming suspicious of the sums of money Caroline was spending and the amount of time she was away from the palace. George's niggardliness is well known, but the spitefulness of his remarks on this occasion shows that he felt there was something amiss. He scathingly refers to her as an 'old girl', and casts doubt on the propriety of her conduct. The metaphor behind the insult is that of a bitch ready to accept scraps from any man's table.

Hervey came to her defence. This was the rapport Byrom refers to in his poem 'Upon a Bee Stinging a Lady's Cheek'. The dispute over expenditure expressed with such venom, combined with gnawing concern over her health, pressure of state business and constant fear of discovery ultimately convinced Caroline that the time had come for the affair to end. Byrom was becoming something of a nuisance. He had no alternative but to agree.

The separation, when it came, left a void. For a while Byrom was able to lose himself in the flurry of activity surrounding the Workhouse Bill, but the blankness of the future stared him in the face. At the beginning of June he left London for a visit to Windsor with his future brother-in-law John Houghton. Ceremonies concerning Duke William drew him there. But then they moved on to Oxford and from there to Worcester and, by an unusual and lengthy route, travelled back to Manchester. Byrom finally entered Manchester on 10 June, the Old Pretender's birthday: 'The bells rang upon our coming and folks said I had done it on purpose, but I knew not what day it was ... '[11] The Jacobite anniversary coincided neatly with Byrom's return to a town where he had just defeated Whig moves to gain ascendancy. The rejoicing of his supporters over the defeat of the Bill was unmistakable. Byrom had made himself, in the words of Dr Deacon, 'the Darling of Manchester'. Let him take what comfort he could from that. He was certainly no longer the darling of the Queen. All the evidence seems to indicate that Byrom did not return to London again until December 1734. What happened during this gap of three years?

Only one brief entry from the Journal survives for 1732. It is contained in the Chetham manuscripts[12] and is dated 26 June. It shows that Byrom was with his family in Manchester and that day visited Chester. There follows a gap until 28 August 1733, when, in Parkinson's edition, he is writing from Scarborough to a young man, Thomas Houghton, who wanted to learn shorthand. In reply Byrom made a revealing admission about the state of his health:

> Sir;
> I have received from Manchester the letter you were pleased to send concerning shorthand. I esteem myself obliged to you for your good opinion of mine in particular. If my health will permit, I hope to have the pleasure of seeing at London this next winter the gentlemen who are desirous of learning it; but I am very uncertain at present whether I dare venture from home to enjoy the satisfaction of communicating it to those to whom I imagine it may be acceptable, as I have designed to do these two years past, but have been prevented; if I could have been more positive I would have acquainted you sooner ...
> > Your humble servant J.B.[13]

Evidently Byrom was still recovering from an illness which had lasted for at least two years. He was not prepared to guarantee his return to London that year, and his uncertainty proved justifiable. More than twelve months were to elapse before he could face his former routine of shorthand instruction in London. Instead he sought refuge once again in Cambridge. His many friends, the college ritual with dinner in Hall, and the comforts of college life provided him with welcome support in the next stage of his convalescence. Long illness had unnerved him, as he confessed in a letter to his wife from Trinity in October.

I am very well and hope that I shall keep so; if not I will come down again, for I do not like to be ill abroad, nor at home neither, but I can be better nursed there according to my liking.[14]

Remembering Byrom's earlier predisposition to fits of depression, it is clear that he had undergone some great crisis which affected him physically and mentally. The confident arrogance of the young man who wrote so contemptuously of Manchester in 1727 has gone. Instead he is uncertain, tentative and fearful. Years of duplicity and the weight of his secrets had taken their toll. By a cruel twist of fate it was left to Elizabeth, the wife he had neglected and betrayed, to nurse him back to health. Now, her unostentatious virtues came into their own. Capable, efficient, and with sound sense, she provided the security he badly needed during these lost years.

Christmas 1733 was a bleak one for Elizabeth, for her father died on Chrismas Eve and was buried on 27 December. In many ways he and John were diametrically opposed. The industry which John displayed in promoting his shorthand, Joseph showed in developing his business. However, John's claim to be able to make a living from shorthand did not impress his father-in-law. John was too far away from home to justify the financial returns, such as they were, and even wrote from London to his wife for money. The one thing they saw eye to eye on was their Tory principles, but that was hardly enough to excuse John to his father-in-law. Little wonder that John made no effort to hurry home when Elizabeth wrote to say her father was very ill. He did not reach Manchester until Joseph was dead and buried. In that way he was spared some pointed last-minute injunctions. As in the past, Elizabeth was compelled to cope as best she could.

For another year there is no record of Byrom's activities. On 26 December 1734 he arrives back in London, still accompanied by

John Houghton. Elizabeth must have still felt some unease about her husband's health. She had seen to it that Houghton was a frequent companion on John's travels since his visit to Windsor in 1731. Houghton was not only a good friend to John, he was to marry Elizabeth's sister, Mary. He could evidently be relied on. It was as if Elizabeth had felt for some time John could not be left to his own devices. In November 1733 she had written to him at Cambridge to suggest he should have Houghton with him and he agreed: 'To be sure I should be glad of Mr. Houghton's company; I do not find any satisfaction in prolonging my absence from my family . . .'[15] So John moved into lodgings at Mrs Abingdon's with Houghton, on 27 December 1734, the anniversary of Joseph Byrom's funeral. John had written home the day before to let Elizabeth know he had arrived safely and to wish her a Merry Christmas! Elizabeth had to find what consolation she could in her children. Byrom had other matters to attend to.

As soon as he had moved into Mrs Abingdon's, he set out to pick up the threads of his London life. Three years had elapsed since he was last in the city. He might tell Elizabeth he was glad to have Houghton with him, but after breakfast he saw to it that he and Houghton parted. Houghton visited relatives, while Byrom delivered a letter in Piccadilly. However, having delivered the letter, and free at last from all constraints, he set off to visit some of his old haunts.

The illness had had a devastating effect on his character. It was Caroline who had betrayed him, not vice versa. He needed time to rationalise the shock of that betrayal. There was no going back on the past, but how could it be assimilated into himself? There seemed only one way left, and that was through the innocence of the child born of their relationship. If his scholarship could establish a link with William, he might still be fulfilled. Even so, deviousness would still be necessary to achieve his goal. This aim gave him the inspiration to return to London, and he spent three years working to forge a link which would allow him to offer his services as shorthand tutor to William.

In 1731 a separate household had been set up for the young Duke. The full complement of tutors considered appropriate was a Governor, a Sub-Governor, a Tutor and several Assistant Tutors for specific purposes. George II chose a member of the diplomatic service as Governor, Stephen Poyntz.[16] He was also Steward of the Household and responsible for the administration of the six thousand pounds allowance which William now received each year.

Poyntz was a brilliant man who had already had a remarkable career. The son of an upholsterer, he was educated at Eton and Cambridge. Shortly after leaving college he became tutor to the Duke of Devonshire and travelled with him on the Grand Tour. He was also tutor to the sons of Lord Townsend, and later became Lord Townsend's confidential secretary. Through him he was introduced to the diplomatic service, holding a number of diplomatic appointments until he became Governor to Duke William. He remained throughout his life a trusted adviser to the Prince, and many people attributed to him the development of the Duke's character.

The Duke's Sub-Governor was Mr Wyndham, a man of whom little is known except that his wife was for some time involved in a relationship with the King himself. The principal Tutor was a Welshman, Jenkin Thomas Philips. Highly regarded for his personal qualities and a conscientious teacher, he was responsible for the Prince's instruction in Latin and saw to it that William became an excellent Latin scholar at an early age.

Another tutor was Dr Robert Smith. He was a distinguished mathematician and an astronomer, a Fellow of Trinity College, and, like Byrom, a stout defender of Richard Bentley. On Bentley's death, he succeeded him as Master. In 1749 Smith published a work on Harmonics or 'The Philosophy of Musical Sounds' which he dedicated to William. No doubt Caroline's own intellectual training saw to it that the young Prince was introduced to scientific thought. Even as a small child he attended his mother's salons and there met the greatest English scientist of all, the elderly Sir Isaac Newton. Later William studied astronomy with the Astronomer Royal, Sir Edmund Halley.

These were the chief men selected to fashion the mind and character of the boy acclaimed as the 'darling of the nation'. Byrom had to set about gaining their confidence, respect and admiration. Only then did he stand a chance of being considered as a tutor for the Prince. He had learned from Caroline how to manipulate other people and now used the same skills to persuade the royal tutors of his value to William.

Being well acquainted with the leading coffee houses, the day after his arrival, he visited a coffee house where he met Jenkin Thomas Philips. The arrangement seems to have been very carefully stage-managed. The fragment of conversation he chose to record is important:

Went to Giles's coffeehouse, there I met with Mr Philips who

taught the Duke Latin; he said the end of all learning was to be a
good man, that it was better to instruct and catechise than to
preach; we talked about Ward's drop.[17]

Nothing could show more clearly the direction of Byrom's
thoughts than this visit. The first entry in his Journal on his return is
concerned with William. If proof were needed of Byrom's personal
involvement in the fortunes of the young prince here it is. Of all the
friends and relatives Byrom could have called upon none mattered
so much at this moment as Philips. Byrom's closeness to him can be
judged from the poem he wrote entitled 'An Epistle to a Friend –
On the Art of Poetry'. The two men evidently spent much time discussing the subject.

> The Art of English Poetry, I find,
> At present, Jenkins, occupies your mind,
> You have a vast Desire to it, you say,
> And want my Help to put you in the Way.

Philips was Byrom's 'Salopian friend'; he taught him shorthand,
and their friendship was on a sound basis.

For Byrom to have recorded so simply and with such brevity the
two topics of the Prince's education and 'Ward's drop' so soon after
his arrival needs further explanation. Earlier in the Journal he gives a
reason for the kind of entries he makes and the style in which he
writes:

> I find that though what I set down in this kind of journal is non-
> sense for the most part, yet that these nonsenses help to recollect
> times and persons and things upon occasion, and serve at least to
> some purpose as to writing shorthand; therefore I must not, I
> think, discontinue it any longer, but only, if I have a mind, omit
> some trifling articles; though when I consider it is the most tri-
> fling things sometimes that help us to recover more material
> things, I do not know that I should omit trifles; they may be of
> use to me, though to others they would appear ridiculous; but as
> nobody is to see them but myself, I will let myself take any notes,
> never so trifling, for my own use.[18]

Byrom admits to writing just sufficient for him to be able to 'recollect times and persons and things'. In this instance the subjects of
the entry act as pointers to the direction in which his mind and
energy were moving. Prince William's education was to dominate

Byrom's activities for some time to come. As a youth of thirteen William was beginning to make a mark for himself. The young duke was a personable boy and both a good scholar and horseman. Like Byrom he was a very good linguist and, by the time he was twelve, completely fluent in French, German and Italian. His command of Latin, thanks to Philips, was remarkable. Philips described an occasion when two hussars, who had escaped from captivity in France, presented a petition to the Duke who was then fourteen. William was perfectly able to address them in fluent Latin, combining 'the scholar's learning with the courtier's ease'.

A little more than two weeks after talking with Philips, Byrom was in the company of another tutor, Dr Robert Smith. On 15 January he called on his old friend Dr Vernon, where he found Smith at breakfast. Byrom and Smith were already good friends and shared many interests in common – music, science and philosophy. The Journal records the development of their friendship over the years. On this occasion Smith was due to visit the young prince and Byrom took the opportunity to press his services. 'Dr. Smith went to Prince William, I told him to mention shorthand, but he was over-forward to do it, and I thought afterwards it was not for me to desire it.'[19] Byrom had evidently had second thoughts later, and his recoil after making the suggestion indicates a degree of emotional involvement. If his move had been simply that of an ambitious man in pursuit of his career, there would have been no need to be so self-deprecating. Some time elapsed before the topic was raised with Smith again.

CHAPTER SEVEN

Ward's Drop and Pill
1734–5

EQUALLY SIGNIFICANT and revealing a darker layer of his mind was Byrom's new interest in 'Ward's Drops', a medicine which took its name from Joshua Ward, a quack doctor, who brought back from France a drop and pill which he claimed could cure every known ailment. Ward had been exiled to France because he was said to have been involved in the 1715 uprising. Eventually pardoned by George II, he returned to England and gained the support of the King by the simple expedient of setting George's dislocated thumb! With Lieutenant-General Churchill as his patron, Ward was taken up by the aristocracy and made an enormous fortune from the sale of his medicines. However, they did far more harm than good and he was under constant attack for the danger of his remedies.

In November 1734 Ward was attacked simultaneously by the *Daily Courant* and the *Grub Street Journal*. The controversy grew and the *Grub Street Journal* for 9 January 1735 denounced him in the following terms:

The learned Mr. Ward, whose abilities and great success are too well known amongst the undertakers, coffin-makers, and sextons to be blasted by your slanderous pen! If he can kill by *one Drop* only, whilst others must fill phials and quart bottles to do it, it shews him the greater artist! I say a Quack is a very useful person in a commonwealth, especially if it is too populous, as ours is; and to excourage adepts, I think ought to be encouraged by a charter, and Mr. Ward to be the first master of the company. I shall only add that although I think you have done well in exposing Mr. Ward's malpractices, yet take care he don't sue you for *Scandalum Quackatum*, and conclude with this advice to all who are inclined to take this old-new-revived remedy –

Before you take this Drop, or Pill,
Take leave of friends, and make your Will,

Of late without the least pretence to skill
Ward's grown a fam'd physician by a Pill

The *Daily Courant* recalled Ward's Catholic connections and declared 'the Pill must be beyond all doubt a deep laid Plot to introduce Popery'. Byrom read the *Grub Street Journal*, and did so in Manchester as soon as the latest copy reached town. He would have seen the attacks on Ward and his remedies before setting out for London. Indeed, his darker interests would have been served by the catalogue of fatalities laid at the quack's door. Numerous deaths were caused by the administration of 'Ward's Drops', for, as doctors and analysts were quick to show, they were in essence a poison.

Certainly Byrom was not long in discussing the pills when he arrived back in London. The day he and John Houghton arrived they sent a porter to alert Mr Lloyd, a close friend from Manchester, that they were back in town. Later, at his cousin Chaddock's door, Byrom saw Lloyd again who 'came by accident'. They all went inside 'and stayed a little talking about Ward's Drops, which they commended much'. Byrom does not say whether it was the curative qualities 'they' were commending or its ability to poison.

The publicity surrounding Ward ensured that his pill was one of the main topics of conversation in the taverns and drawing rooms of London. The leading figure to whom complaints were directed was one of Byrom's closest London friends, the former secretary to the Royal Society – Dr James Jurin. On 31 December Jurin invited Byrom to dinner with two other doctors, Plumtree and Bevan. Byrom seldom refused an invitation to a meal but on this occasion chose not to go. He gives no reason for declining but perhaps it was something to do with the entry in the Journal which followed immediately: 'Dr. Jurin said that the two persons dead in Dr. Turner's account were not the same that Ward would have the world believe.'[1] Byrom was being wary. He would know the content of 'Turner's account' and, while anxious to hear Jurin's opinion, did not want to be drawn further himself. Ward's medicine was bound to be discussed at a dinner with three doctors, so he stayed away.

As part of the public outcry against Ward, Dr Daniel Turner exposed his medicine in an open letter to Dr Jurin. In 1735 he published a pamphlet entitled *The Drop and Pill of Mr. Ward considered by Daniel Turner in an Epistle to Dr. James Jurin.*

Turner cites several of Ward's outrageous claims of success. One of these was the ability of the pill and drop to cure cancer. Turner shows how ready Ward was to offer hope of a cure to those whom qualified doctors had given up.

> The last instance I will give you upon my knowledge in respect to the pretended Cures of Cancers, shall be that of C_____n W_____s lady ... Mr. Ward was consulted and gave her (if I am rightly informed) the greatest assurance of a cure, by his Butter-milk and Curds externally and his Drop and Pill internally administered; nay, when she told him she fear'd by the great stretch of the skin, the Breast would burst, he made very light thereof, and reply'd, no matter, his medicines would make it whole again.[2]

Turner's Epistle is a damning exposure; he also listed the various categories of patients most likely to suffer harm from Ward's prep-arations. He divided these into six groups. Two are as follows.

> Thirdly, such as labour under Ruptures, whether of the Navel, Groin, or Scrotum, must shun these Medicines, as they would Ratsbane. The pressure of the parts of the lower Belly, being so great under the workings of any vomit, much more such as these, that there would be the greatest danger imaginable of rendering the Malady irretrievable. Dr. D_____d told a friend of mine very lately, he had visited a woman with a navel Rupture, brought upon by the hard straining in the working of this Pill of Mr. Ward.

> Fourthly; such as have weaken'd the Tone of their Stomachs, by dram-drinking all day, Wetting in the Morning or Bottling at Night; and have brought upon them a loathing to all food, or after taking the same, immediately throwing it up again, can be no fit subjects for these Remedies; For that, besides their feeble, if not rotten viscera, with their weak and tender vessels, rendering them liable to a Breach therein, their constant Retching, more especially in the morning, which scarce any Remedy can bridle, or put a stop to, will be encreas'd; and an over-Vomiting or Purging, has-ten their deaths; of which I have had an Account of two instances in three months past.[3]

To drive home the danger of these 'medicines', Turner listed cases of fatal treatment. Case number XII concerned a Mrs Gilbert:

Mrs. Gilbert, who kept the Horseshoe Ale-House in Essex Street, of Middle Age and robust constitution, took one of the Ward's Pills the beginning of July last; it vomited her 34 and purged her 22 times. She sent for an eminent Physician and Apothecary the next Day, who found her feverish and thirsty, having continued retchings to Vomit, violent pains in her Belly, and to be short, with all the symptoms of Bowels a mortifying; and what was almost as bad, the Operation had caused a violent Navel Rupture. The Physician used his utmost Endeavours to assist her, but on the Morrow-Night she miserably died.[4]

In March 1735 Byrom was still avidly following up intriguing aspects of the Ward controversy. On Monday 31 he intended to visit some of his cronies at one of the more notorious taverns, the Fleece. On his way he called at his cousin Chaddock's house and as a result found himself leaving in the company of young Tommy Chaddock. Anxious to get rid of the boy before he reached the Fleece, Byrom took him to a picture shop in the Exchange where he bought Tommy 'three pictures to paint on glass, 6d.' and having parted from him, he met up with his friends:

They had just done dinner, Mr. Rogers, Vigor, Penn, Lloyd, Cooper, Dr. Dover, the sea captain and two more gentlemen; I had bread and butter and toasted cheese, and drank wine with them; they talked about sea-fighting, of one Long who foretold the earthquake at Port Royal, and the fortunes of others, the return of ships, of Admiral Benbow; Dr. Dover, Mr. Penn, Vigor, and another gentleman staying a bit longer than the rest, I asked Dr. Dover about his quicksilver and about Mr. Ward, and he showed us Ward's pill and his own, which seemed to be the very same, and he said had the same effects; Ward's pill he said weighed two grains . . . [5]

The most interesting person in the group was Thomas Dover M.D., a physician of dubious ability, and, at one time, a sea captain engaged in privateering. It was Dover who found Alexander Selkirk shipwrecked on Juan Fernandez in 1709, brought him back home and thus provided Daniel Defoe with his model for Robinson Crusoe. He gained the name of the 'quicksilver doctor' because of the exaggerated emphasis he placed on the value of mercury as a remedy. One of his prescriptions, Dover's Powders, remained a popular remedy until very recent years. Although his medical knowledge was not very great, he felt he deserved more recognition. In 1733 he had denounced the College of Physicians as 'a clan of prejudiced gentlemen'. Dover had taken sailors across the world to plunder in Peru and steal a Spanish ship, but Byrom now chose to talk to him about Ward's pill. Could he really expect an honest opinion? Not surprisingly Dover did not denounce Ward but set out to show that his own tablets were just as effective! What is more, and Byrom took note of this, the two preparations looked identical. This was a valuable piece of information, particularly for anyone interested in the two tablets. For a man who had turned his back on medicine as a career, Byrom was showing an uncommon interest. His enquiries were not caused by a genuine search for treatment either for himself, his family or friends. Cures for his own children lay in a careful diet rather than medicine. A preparation such as Ward's pill he would have rejected with horror. Why was Byrom so curious? Ward kept the ingredients of his medicine a secret and bequeathed them to John Page, the man who had come to his help in France. Ward himself had made a fortune; now, because of the fierce controversy, people set out to discover what those ingredients were.

An analytical chemist, Joseph Clutton, in 1736 published his analysis in 'A True and Candid Relation of the Good and Bad Effects of Joshua Ward's Pill and Drop'. Clutton outlined the experiments he made to analyse the contents of Ward's pills. These were of three different colours: blue, red and purple. Clutton was able to show that all three contained, in different proportions, antimony and cobalt and that two, the blue and red pills, also contained arsenic. The pamphlet is a fascinating account of an eighteenth-century scientist coming to grips with the dubious remedies of a quack doctor. One of the first things he does is to make clear the dangerous nature of antimony for medicinal purposes:

> The last thing I undertook was to show, to what tribe of Poisons, this nostrum belongs, and here it seems difficult to excuse the physicians and apothecaries of this city, who tacitly suffered such havoc to be made without informing the Town of the dangerous preparations of which these Pills and Drops are so apparently made. I mean the five known preparations of Antimony, which for their violence and harsh manner of working, are but very rarely prescribed by physicians. Ignorant and bold Quacks generally make these articles the basis of their packets; as they are exceeding cheap and will be sure to let poor people feel they have

somewhat for their Money. The first is Glass of Antimony this is so churlish and harsh an emetic, and cathartic, that it is hardly ever prescribed; however I have seen one grain administered at a time, and it seems to work exactly in the same manner as these Ward's Pills. It first makes the patient grievous sick then with griping, and many times great contortions of stomach and bowels, it gives an uncertain number of strong and very sick vomits; afterwards generally goes downwards, and you need not wonder, if all this brings on a powerful sweat upon the sturdiest man alive.[6]

Clutton then turns his attentions to cobalt, the other component common to all three pills:

. . . German Cobalt of the shops, Cadmia Metallica of Agricola, is a ponderous, hard, fossil substance . . . It has so strong a corrosive quality, as sometimes to burn and ulcerate the Hands and Feet of Miners, and is a deadly Poison for all known Animals.[7]

Such conclusions based on the most methodical experiments were damning. It was almost cruelly ironical that Clutton should dedicate his treatise to Queen Caroline, who in the following year fell into a fatal illness, during which she took Ward's pill.

To Queen Caroline

As thou hast at all times shewn a tender regard for the welfare of mankind, and art a true Mother of thy people, I beg leave to offer these papers to thee containing several discoveries, where in the health of the publick is concerned. That the Giver of all good may prolong thy days, and perpetuate to us these blessings in the Royal Family, to the end of time, is the sincere prayer of thy dutiful servant, Joseph Clutton.

Despite all the controversy, or perhaps because of it, Byrom's interest in Ward's pill continued unabated. Joshua Ward was related to a branch of the Staffordshire Wards, whom Byrom had visited years before, in 1729, to teach shorthand. It was with a member of this family that Byrom had discussed Cotham's death from fish poisoning.

Later, on 29 March 1736, Byrom was once more showing an interest in a sudden death. On that afternoon he called at his cousin Chaddock's house:

They were all in a hurry about Mr. Vannam, their next door

neighbour, just dead, suddenly, very suddenly indeed for he had been at the 'Change, and complained when he came home that he was not well and his wife asking him to have some drops of something, he took it, and died immediately . . . They asked me to stay to tea, but I went on.[8]

Byrom's vagueness on the nature of the drops is deliberate. It was after all at Chaddock's house that the praises of Mr Ward's Drops had been sung in 1734. If they had persuaded Mrs Vannam of the virtues of Ward's Drops, then he had every reason not to stay long that day. Within twelve months the Chaddocks moved to a new neighbourhood. Since they were known to have lived in the same house for many years, the move may have been dictated by some embarrassment.

Over many months now Byrom had become obsessed with the possibility of death by poison. In May 1736 he had a very odd conversation with his friend Dr Hartley about six prisoners in Newgate who had been poisoned: 'Dr. Hartley mentioned the six prisoners in Newgate, who I said would have recovered had they been poisoned in a manner being to save their lives.'[9] The subjects which occupied Byrom's mind at this time were becoming more sinister. What was the reason? Was Byrom preparing himself to remove some obstacle in his own path?

Just as Byrom's early studies in medicine were to develop into an obsession with poisons, so too his original interest in religion degenerated into a preoccupation with damnation. The shock of having been abandoned by Caroline affected every aspect of his character. Nowhere is this more clearly demonstrated than in the extraordinarily morbid tone of his religious thoughts. One man in particular, William Law, played an important part in directing Byrom's mind along this dark path. As so often happens, the descent into hell was gradual.

William Law was a well-known Anglican cleric who, in 1713, when Byrom was still a student at Cambridge, forfeited his Fellowship at Emmanuel College because he, too, refused to take the Oath of Allegiance. To Byrom at that time Law's fate was just another piece of university gossip. Twenty years later, however, Law had established himself as a leading opponent of the rational school of philosophy made so fashionable by Locke. Law replaced reliance on man's reason with an appeal to the spirit through his doctrine of the 'inner light'. This put him outside the mainstream of contemporary religious thinking. In 1729 Byrom bought a copy of Law's book *A Serious Call*. Writing home to his sister Phebe about the book, Byrom said: 'Mr. Law and Christian religion, and such things, they are mightily out of fashion at present.'[10] The following month he met Law and the two men got on well together. What attracted Byrom was Law's emphasis on the more mystical aspect of religion. As his disillusionment grew, Byrom found a growing affinity with some of Law's more austere teachings and around 1735 Byrom's moods became increasingly bleak.

In January that year he quoted at length from a letter written by Law to his old friend Walker in which Law discussed the 'renunciation of the world'. This was evidently a subject which occupied Byrom's own thoughts at the time. What was meant by renunciation of the world? How far was one to go to achieve it? Two days after this letter Byrom was talking about selling his library. He had almost a mania for collecting books, as he himself admitted. Now all of a sudden he seemed ready to part with them and also the medals he had started to collect. Was this an attempt at 'renunciation'? Likewise, on Good Friday he 'wandered about', as he terms it, 'considering how little the day is regarded'. He was obviously having a severe attack of religious fervour. Later that month he told a friend that he had made 'a sort of resolution not to go to the Opera or playhouses'. The phrase 'sort of' is characteristic. Even in his mood of renunciation Byrom allowed himself an escape clause. He wrote to his wife that he was keeping his vegetable diet. 'I am obliged to do it, or I should suffer.' This was in April 1735. In his new enthusiasm he talked to friends about pleasure and virtue. On reflection he concluded: 'I talk too much.'

This, however, did not prevent him from conversing on the ethics of Christianity over his customary pint of wine, and then regretting the occasion afterwards: 'To bed, but found that the wine was too much for me, that it stupifies, and moreover I smoked two pipes with them, which made me very sleepy there.'[11]

Byrom was then taken with a most extraordinary fit of charity. He often gave money to the poor, but one day in May 1735 he met a poor woman in Chancery Lane sitting on a stone in the company of a child. He gave her 1½d, to which he then added sixpence. He asked the night-watchman to help her and gave him fourpence to see her home to Drury Lane. Byrom watched and followed and, after the night-watchman had left her, gave her another shilling and a further penny to the watchman to see her home. By this stage his concern

had become almost absurd. He wrote: 'I have had many thoughts of
this poor creature, who cried "What will my end be?" . . . I wish I
had gone with her and the watchman to the place where she lived.'
Instead he had gone home and had a glass of water and went to bed
but found that he could not sleep. The next morning he had an
attack of a most peculiar breathlessness.

> While I was saying the 145th Psalm I was taken suddenly with a
> shortness of breath or fit of asthma that frightened me very much
> and threw me into a little trembling and great concern, which
> seemed to go off; it was a great difficulty of drawing in my breath
> after expiration, which was long enough, and like as if I should be
> suffocated if it was to be worse.[12]

This attack seems to have had a psychological origin. Byrom's illness had left him in a vacillating state. He feels he ought to reform
but constantly slips back. He is a vegetarian who lapses and then
worries about those lapses, a man who would abstain from drink
but does not. He is a convivial haunter of coffee houses who would
dearly love to keep a still tongue in his head but talks the hours
away. The very next day he is at the Ship Inn.

> We talked about mathematics, poetry etc., and the reflection upon
> my own vain, idle words does not please me, for being sensible
> that tavern talk is wrong, yet I go to it; it was twelve o'clock when
> we came away, and so the evening was lost.[13]

Why did he view the evening as wasted? What was wrong with
talking about mathematics and poetry with friends? Long illness had
left him vulnerable to sickness and susceptible to excessive scruples
of conscience.

The loneliness of his London existence made things worse. He
wrote to his wife in May 1735: 'My heart is at Manchester while
thou and thine are there.' More and more he turned to Elizabeth and
his family for reassurance. In this same letter he wrote:

> I pray thee, love, sit down to one letter to put me in mind of any
> or everything thou canst think of that I have to do before I leave
> London, and what to bring the children etc, for I shall forget
> somewhat or other else.[14]

He is conscious that he has not a proper home to retire to. He longs
to be back at Manchester. This is very different from his attitude
before his illness when he rented the house in New Round Court.

The whole tenor of this letter leads one to believe Byrom's return home was imminent. But what he did was to call on a pupil, Lord De La Warr, Treasurer of the Royal Household, only to learn that he had gone to Hannover with George II. That meant that Caroline was on her own and acting as Regent, as was customary in the King's absence. Accordingly Byrom did not return to Manchester but stayed in London a little longer. How often in the past had he done the same – protested his longing to be at home and still lingered? For a moment the situation must have seemed propitious for a final meeting with the Queen. But if Byrom did attempt one, he was not successful. A month later, on the 10th of June, he was on his way to visit some friends when he met Beau Nash 'who told me that *a certain very great lady* had desired him to ask for "My Time, O ye Muses" in my own hand, which I told him that I could not comply with.'[15] Usually Byrom enjoyed the pleasure his poems gave. On this occasion, however, he must have been in an unusual frame of mind to refuse the request of a 'very great lady'. Was it through pique, disappointment or because he was asked for a copy in his 'own hand'? Whatever the reason Byrom was decidedly not in the giving vein. Finally he did leave London – not for Manchester, but Cambridge.

Before this journey he spent one day, 7 June, on a visit to William Law in Putney. Making his way on horse and by foot he arrived at three in the afternoon. The two men walked together in the garden. This was a very important meeting for Byrom, for he now placed great weight on Law's views, the pessimism of which was in tune with his own darker thoughts. Law likened the world to a prison into which we had fallen: 'That we had nothing to do but get out of it, that we had no misery but what was in it, that to be freed from it was all that we wanted.'[16]

A little later Law said that it was necessary for: 'everyone to feel the torment of sin, that it was necessary for them to die in this manner and to descend into hell with Christ and so to rise again with him; that every one must pass through this fiery trial in this world or another'.

When he heard those words, Byrom could not have failed to apply them to himself and the wretchedness he felt as a result of his affair with Caroline. Whatever agonies he had endured he could now view as his portion of allotted suffering in this world. Law urged that a man suffering 'ought to abandon himself to God ... that some justice was done to God by his suffering ... that we do not know what our Lord suffered, that the sacrifice of his human body was the least thing in it.'[17] Even so, there was little comfort in such teachings; guilt left Byrom deeply confused and uncertain.

At Cambridge he had the security of mingling once again with friends of long standing, totally unconnected with his manoeuvrings in London. One of them, Turner, reminded him of something he had said twenty-six years earlier to the effect that men were happy when they had something to do. Turner told Byrom how much the remark impressed him. In the grip of his scruples once more, Byrom felt that a man had to be good before he could do good to others. For a moment he seems to have seen the attraction of a monastic existence, cut off from the temptations of the world outside: 'Query, whether to become private and religious absolutely, casting away other cares, would not be best?'[18] Although Byrom's friends thought he was wearing well, inside he was in turmoil – rising late and missing chapel. Despite his love of Cambridge he was indifferent to the fine June weather and forced to admit: 'I am uneasy to be here.'[19] For years Cambridge had provided Byrom with fresh pupils. Despite the fact that Horace Walpole started to learn during this latest visit, and others were waiting to begin, Byrom had little interest in teaching: 'I have but seen 'em little, and must leave 'em, to get away.' He did not seem able to find peace anywhere. His thoughts turned hopefully to home, and he wrote to Elizabeth: 'The College is all in the Hall at a grand feast, But I choose not to be at it. I want to feast with thee upon some of thy provision, which I like best.'[20] He stayed in Cambridge two more days and by 25 June he was back in Manchester visiting friends. Not many entries survive for those summer months. They stop on the 11 August and their content is minimal. Byrom did not think it worth the bother to carry on his Journal until the following year. It was in this dark mood of guilt, disenchantment and unease that Byrom sat down to pen his version of the poem 'Artemissia'.

CHAPTER EIGHT

Shorthand and Prince William
1736–7

IN HIS FIRST letter home after returning to London in March 1736, Byrom wrote, with more than a touch of professional pride: 'I hear that much enquiry has been made about me.' His shorthand was very much in demand, despite competition from rival systems. He nevertheless hoped to finish business speedily so that he could return to Elizabeth and his family. The following day he passed the evening 'as usual in taverns all wrong for me and my heart non in centro'.[1] His sense of isolation continued underneath all his activities. Three days later, on Ash Wednesday, the beginning of Lent, he decided to postpone teaching to go to Church. In conversation with friends the same day he shows that he has now joined the anti-theatre faction and their discussion about plays made him grieve 'in spirit for myself and them'.

Byrom's aversion to theatre-going on religious grounds had become so great that he refused the offer of a ticket for a play to be performed by the pupils of Charterhouse. This was a far cry from the days when he frequented the Opera during the early years of his relationship with Caroline. The poem 'The Session of the Beauties' includes women who were obviously actresses. His conviviality became more erratic; at times he sought out friends, at others he avoided them, recognising a friend in the street but deliberately not speaking to him.

A little over a week later Byrom noted a conversation which he had with another friend – that many died of grief – and commented, 'This but too true,' showing the topic touched him personally. The discovery of the unpublished poems reveals why.

In 1736 Byrom had been promoting his shorthand for fourteen years. In doing so he had built up a sound reputation and was readily accepted in drawing rooms, studies and private chambers throughout the city. Lawyers, doctors, scientists, members of par-

liament, courtiers, diplomats all opened their doors. He was quickly
in and out, staying long enough to give his lesson, take a glass of
wine or dish of tea, pick up the latest gossip or news, and then he
would be off again on a rapid round of further calls. Although his
moods were becoming darker, the brevity of these visits allowed
him to hide them from his pupils. Only the self-analysis committed
to his Journal over a long period reveals the true state of his mind.
His days were now gathering in momentum. The pace he set himself
on his daily round was so extreme that he appeared at times to be
like a man on a merry-go-round. The entry for 9 April 1736, is
typical of this frenzied period.

> Rose at five, very wakeful and light . . . went out about six, met
> Mrs. Whitehead in Lincoln's Inn Square, who spoke to me and
> said the pretender to Strangeways was certainly Richard Hartley's
> son, who had married a chimney sweeper's daughter at Bungy,
> that two farmers would supply this heir with money, that a man
> had died and declared upon his deathbed that he had had fifteen
> guineas and charges for his evidence for Mr. Reynolds . . . I called
> at Mr. Stansfield's and thence to Mr. Harding's, seven o'clock
> past, not up; thence to Mr. Lloyd's, he and Mr. Bateson in bed, I
> stayed there and wrote to Teddy, Beppy, Nanny, Dolly, and en-
> closed to Mrs. Byrom, and Weston two advertisements against
> Gibbs, ate a French roll there that lay upon the table, and thence
> to Mr. Harding's where I drank chocolate, and Mr. Grover, wrote
> a line or two and Mr. Harding paid ten guineas; thence to Mr.
> Lloyd's, and Mr. John Lloyd had been with them last night till
> one o'clock, Mr. Worsley called there to go with Mr. Lloyd to
> Lord Willoughby's, came away about nine, taking leave with Mr.
> Bateson and Greaves, who were to go to Oxford and Manchester
> in the afternoon . . . [2]

Was it really necessary for Byrom to rise at five o'clock? One can
hardly think so when he was knocking on the doors of people not
yet out of bed. Little wonder that he was ready to take scraps of
food from other men's tables, when he had left his own so early.
Even by his own energetic standards this itinerary was abnormal.
Through all this phase he was sustained by the aim to become shorthand tutor to William. The thought of the influence he might then
be able to exert on the young boy held him together.

However, fresh problems beset him. Byrom was now beginning
to find the behaviour of his relative Beau Byrom an increasing

source of embarrassment. He was a penniless drifter, frequently drunk and constantly turning to Byrom, among others, to relieve his distress. On the 4 April Byrom met him and, to his horror, discovered his ne'er-do-well kinsman had had the impudence to approach one of the Princes in public. On this occasion Byrom fobbed him off with half a crown. A month later Beau came knocking at his door before he had hardly finished breakfast, complaining of being 'ill and in want'. Byrom gave him a shilling. A few days later a little girl was knocking at the door just after seven in the morning with a note from Beau who had 'rheumatic pains in his lungs'. His pleas for money were usually accompanied by complaints about his health. Even so, his poverty had its comic side. Later the same day a porter came to Byrom bringing with him what purported to be Beau's final plea for help. Byrom responded by sending a pair of breeches. This was not the last he was to hear either of Beau or the breeches. A few days later still, Beau played out a scene of comic melodrama, again at Byrom's breakfast table. Taking a crust of bread he ostentatiously ate it, saying that he wondered 'how dry bread would do'. He was referring to the death of the dramatist Thomas Otway, who had died in the depths of poverty choking on a piece of bread. Later that afternoon Byrom had to go to the Anchor Inn with Beau to redeem his breeches, which he had sold for three shillings! These constant demands on his charity were almost too much and his fund of good will was rapidly becoming exhausted. One day, when talking to a friend, the name of Beau Byrom cropped up and Byrom spoke at some length about charity. But his thoughts, whatever he might say, ran along different lines: 'I talk much about charity but I wish I had it in me.' Beau's poverty was an embarrassment to all his London acquaintances and a source of scandal to his relatives in Manchester. In August 1736 Byrom felt sufficiently concerned to write to Beau's sister in Chester in an attempt to gain her assistance and financial help to persuade Beau to settle down quietly in the country away from the temptations of London. This he eventually did and Byrom, with other members of the family, provided him with a small pension.

Byrom's reputation was such that people now sought him out to learn shorthand. One was Dr David Hartley, physician and philosopher, who first approached Byrom in Richard's coffee house in March 1736. This relationship had immeasurable consequences. Hartley was some thirteen years younger than Byrom and, after studying at Jesus College, Cambridge, turned his back on a career in

the church for philosophical rather than political reasons and became a physician, although he never took a medical degree. After the
death of his first wife, Hartley settled in London in Princes Street,
Leicester Fields. He married a second time about six months before
meeting Byrom. Hartley was a man of amiable character, simple and
unaffected, very different from Byrom who was by now in the grip
of guilt and self-doubt. Hartley solved his scruples over religious
dogmas by a decidedly rationalistic approach. Byrom turned to
mysticism. Philosophically they were poles apart and, even before
giving Hartley his first lesson, Byrom was quick to argue against his
views with a mutual acquaintance. Today Hartley is chiefly remembered for the doctrine of the association of ideas which he developed
into a system of philosophy, and which had its greatest influence
towards the end of the eighteenth century, especially on Words-
worth and Coleridge. He argued that our minds are built up entirely
by the association of impressions made through the senses. It was
important, therefore, to make the right impressions and associations
in early life. This was essentially an optimistic philosophy, for
Hartley maintained that the world reflected the benevolence of
its Creator, a welcome contrast to William Law's view of the world
as a prison.

Elizabeth, Hartley's second wife, was a woman of great intelligence and something of a blue-stocking. In addition to an attractive
and lively personality, she had a fortune of some six-and-a-half
thousand pounds. On the day when Byrom arrived to give Dr Hartley his first lesson he found the doctor had gone out 'and so stayed
for him in his study according to his orders . . .' Their first meeting
took much of the day but was interrupted by Hartley's visits to and
from patients. The encounter was a distinct success and brought
with it an unexpected bonus for Byrom when Mrs Hartley also
undertook to learn shorthand. Her decision to become a pupil was a
bonus in more ways than one. A pleasant easy-going friendship developed between all three. The Hartleys were a hospitable couple
and Mrs Hartley shared many of her husband's interests. Byrom
dined with them with amazing frequency and even when Dr Hartley
was away from home he was welcome as Mrs Hartley's tutor. These
lessons gave Byrom the opportunity to observe her personal qualities, both social and intellectual. More than once he comments on
her skill in shorthand: 'after tea we had a good shorthand lecture
Mrs. Hartley having writ a good deal and prettily enough like to be
a good writer, and seemed to be pleased with it'. She evidently en-

joyed her studies: 'I stayed with Mrs. Hartley above stairs, and had long lectures about things, prpp., action, manner, about thought, word, deed, explaining the grammatical terms; she said it was very agreeable, that she had learned more in our lectures than all she had from French.'[3] Her enthusiasm was genuine and shared by her husband.

David Hartley was completely won over by the beauty, efficiency and usefulness of Byrom's shorthand. He felt it would be of enormous value for everyone and became almost compulsive in organising a campaign to publish the system. The energy Hartley displayed for this project became something of an embarrassment to Byrom, for this had not been part of his plan. He still preferred to use his shorthand more selectively so that, when he chose, it could gain him the attention of particular individuals. Thus, while Hartley busied himself with drawing up lists of subscribers and preparing advertisements for the press, Byrom tried to delay matters by quibbling over words and matters of detail. Hartley could count some very influential people among his patients, including the Duchess of Newcastle. He also attended Court. Within three weeks of meeting Byrom he was all for recommending the system to George II. In the Journal for 20 May Byrom wrote:

> I came here with Dr. Hartley from home, had a lecture with his lady, and he was about recommending the King. (At Dr. Hartley's Thursday afternoon) Here I am come from Westminster where I went with the Doctor, but was tired of staying there, the King not coming to the parliament till very late, because of some debates about the s-m-k-ling Bill they say.[4]

One would have thought that this possible opening would be regarded by Byrom as his crowning achievement, and that any reference in the Journal would show his pride and excitement at such a prospect. The truth is very different and Byrom's comment is extraordinarily casual. How was it that he could afford to grow 'tired' of waiting for the King? A royal appointment to His Majesty ought surely to have been the final accolade. Byrom's inability to be patient must be seen as either an expensive weakness or a calculated ploy to get him out of an awkward situation. While he would have to appear to Hartley to be delighted at his suggestion, Byrom's nerve failed him when it came to the point of facing up to the possibility of having to teach the husband of the woman he loved. Furthermore, he would not have relished the company of a man who had supplanted him as father to William. Byrom's Jacobite sympathies, too, would have rebelled against the idea, but he could not openly show these feelings. They had to be masked by a seeming impatience. Nevertheless, in the event he never taught the King.

This was not the first instance of Byrom's reluctance to take advantage of an entrée to the Royal Household. As early as 1731 influential courtiers were recommending Byrom to Frederick, Prince of Wales, William's elder brother. In May 1735 Byrom wrote home to his wife that Lord Baltimore, Gentleman of the Bedchamber to Prince Frederick, had been enquiring whether Byrom was in town and 'that he wanted shorthand and he believed the Prince too'.[5] Again, one would expect Byrom to be pleased, but he treated the matter almost flippantly. He goes on to describe it as a fine 'quality story' and to say that he could 'take no pleasure in Princes while absent from thee', a flattering way to end his letter to Elizabeth, but hardly true when one considers how often he postponed his return to Manchester for the sake of pupils – and pupils of absolutely no consequence compared with the Prince of Wales. It is a puzzling picture. Here is a man dedicated to promoting his shorthand to make his fortune, behaving with indifference to the Prince of Wales and the King of England. They were obviously not part of his plan.

Lessons with the Hartleys continued until the summer of 1736. Byrom left London in July, though still not at peace with himself. He was considering whether to abandon his Journal altogether; his spirits were so low. Then, while he attempted to comfort a friend in need, he was rebuffed with the charge that he did not know 'the condition of a guilty conscience'.[6] His reply showed how keenly he felt the rebuke: 'I told him I did and would gladly comfort him.' In this frame of mind he made his way to Manchester. One night, as he rode homeward, the following words came into his mind:

> My Spirit longeth for thee
> Within my troubled Breast,
> Altho' I be unworthy
> Of so divine a Guest;
>
> Of so divine a Guest
> Unworthy tho' I be,
> Yet has my Soul no rest
> But what I find in Thee.[7]

Once back in Manchester, however, Byrom was able to hide his feelings sufficiently to cope with the round of visits to family and friends. Edward was now twelve and some attention had to be given to his education. For a while Byrom entertained the idea that Edward might follow in his footsteps to Cambridge. On one of his many visits to the university he had written to Elizabeth suggesting this: 'I don't know but your son might have a scholarship for asking – send him up and try.' However, Edward had not inherited his father's exceptional intellect and the idea came to nothing. By the summer of 1736 he was learning accounting in preparation for the family businesses run by his uncles.

Byrom was lucky in that he was absolved from certain paternal duties. His late father-in-law had helped with Edward's career. It would be unfair to imply that Byrom ignored his son completely. When Edward was old enough, Byrom encouraged the boy to write to him in London. In Manchester he took him riding and on his round of visits. The Byroms were always a very close family. It must be admitted, however, that there is in Byrom's attitude towards Edward a coolness markedly different from his feelings for his daughters Beppy and Dolly, and even his own sister Phebe.

Dolly was a particular favourite. When he went to church Byrom took Dolly with him and he noted fondly that he went with '*my* Dolly to Mr. Stephen Clowes to look for Teddy'. The rest of his stay at home during that summer was not very remarkable except that he found time to take up the cause of a young girl, Fanny Henshaw, who had decided to become a Quaker, much to the disappointment of her guardians. They turned against her, and Byrom tried to offer her spiritual support during a painful and trying time. Unable to find his own peace of mind, he could still feel compassion for others.

On 3 January 1737 (N.S.) Byrom wrote a letter to his old friend Darcy Lever about rumours of Darcy's impending knighthood. In their eagerness to see him knighted, Darcy's friends had awarded him the honour before the King had bestowed it, and Byrom makes great play about this in the first part of his letter. But however jocular he pretends to be, it is not long before he is mentioning Queen Caroline and suggesting to Darcy that he should mention Byrom to her:

> Dear Darcy,
> flee from these vain honours that pursue thee, and come untainted home again; or, if you must keep Queen Caroline company this

Christmas till her rebelling spouse comes back, ask her who is to
be the High Sheriff, and send us word. Ask whether Mr. Gibb's
shorthand be come forth yet. Tell her how long it is since we first
went upon our expedition tachygraphical. Tell her the necessity
there is for reducing the law of England to some compendium of
this nature, or that we shall not be able to see the law for acts
of parliaments.[8]

While the tone of the letter is generally playful, there is tartness
and sarcasm in some of the turns of phrase. The King's return home
had been delayed by bad weather; Byrom chose to see George in the
role of a husband refusing to return home to his wife, and his later
remarks about shorthand are equally satirical. Byrom had seen
Caroline take up the poet Stephen Duck instead of him. This
memory leads him to suggest Mr Gibbs, of whom he already had
a poor opinion. It may be merely fantasy but Byrom was keen to
remind Caroline how long he himself had been a practitioner of
shorthand and how useful his services had been in the days when she
knew him as Mr Freeman and he reported the business of the House
of Commons. His brooding resentment is like a poison in the blood
ready to break out in a rash of sarcasm whenever the opportunity
occurs. This letter is an indication of the distance now between
Caroline and her erstwhile lover.

In April 1737 Prince William reached the age of sixteen. This was
to be a crucial year for him. The King and Queen had always preferred William to their eldest son, Frederick. When George and
Caroline first came to England as Prince and Princess of Wales they
left Frederick behind in Germany. He did not join them until his
father became George II and he himself could be regarded as Heir
Apparent. His behaviour constantly antagonised his parents and he
managed to be so thoroughly objectionable that Caroline loathed
him until the day she died. The mutual dislike of George I and his
son was nothing compared to the mutual hatred of George II and
Frederick.

These feelings naturally had political consequences. As far back as
1725 suggestions were being made to keep Frederick off the English
throne. At that time his grandfather, George I, was still King. The
Prince of Wales, the future George II, wanted to exclude him from
the line of succession. Lord King, the Lord Chancellor at the time,
recorded in his diary for 24 June 1725 that

Another negotiation had lately been on foot in relation to the two young Princes, Frederick and William. The Prince and his wife were for excluding Prince Frederick from the throne of England, but that, after the King and the Prince, he should be Elector of Hannover, and Prince William King of Great Britain; but that the King said it would be unjust to do it without Prince Frederick's consent, who was now of age to judge for himself, and so this matter now stood.[9]

Already the separation of the Electorate of Hannover from the Crown of England was considered highly desirable, but George I would not countenance it as a means of keeping Frederick from being King. Yet it is obvious that even at this early date, when William was still only four years old, George and Caroline saw this as a way of ridding themselves of their eldest son.

Twelve years later, in 1737, Frederick was locked in a bitter dispute with his father over the size of his annuity. He asked for £100,000 but George would offer only £50,000. According to Lord Hervey, Frederick, on the advice of his friends, then made a most surprising suggestion. He considered offering to Parliament to give up his right of succession not to the English throne but to the Electorate in favour of William on condition that he had his full annuity.

When Hervey, having got wind of this idea, reported it to Caroline, she found it difficult to believe, although she described Frederick in characteristic terms as an 'avaricious and sordid monster'. But in the end she concluded:

> Well, I thought it cruel and unjust to pull out his eyes; but if he likes to pull one of them out himself and give it to my dear William, I am satisfied; I am sure I shall not hinder him, I shall jump at it; for though, between you and I, I had as like go and live upon a dunghill myself, as go to Hannover, yet for William it will be a very good morsel; and for the £50,000 a year, I daresay the King will be very glad to give it; and if the silly beast insist upon it, I will give him £25,000 more, the half of my revenue, and live as I can, upon shillings and pennies.[10]

According to Hervey, the Queen went so far as to have some form of paper drawn up in preparation for such a scheme; 'she had burned two drafts and had now another by her; but not explaining in what manner it was done'.[11]

Nothing ever came of this idea, but it is an example of the schemes to reduce or remove the powers of Prince Frederick. What Frederick did in fact was to appeal to Parliament against his father's decision to give him only £50,000. Both houses rejected the address, and the Prince was bitterly disappointed, the more so because he was deeply in debt. He never forgave the King and he showed his resentment by neglecting to tell the King and Queen that his wife was expecting a child until the last possible moment. Then, as soon as the poor Princess's labour pains started, Frederick bundled her into a coach and had her driven away in agony from Hampton Court to the seclusion of St James's Palace.

Whatever the reasons were for this extraordinary behaviour, the child was the first born of the Heir Apparent and its arrival seemed to ensure a direct line of Hannoverian succession and thus strengthen the position of the much-hated Frederick. The King and Queen were roused in the middle of the night and at first thought that Hampton Court was on fire. When they discovered that the Princess was in labour and at St James's, the King exploded with anger and tried to blame Caroline for the flight. His words, as reported to Lord Hervey by the Queen, reveal yet again how much the minds of George and Caroline were still preoccupied with advancing the position of Duke William.

> The King flew into a violent passion, and, in German, (as the Queen told me afterward) began to scold her; saying, 'You see, now, with all your wisdom, how they have outwitted you. This is all your fault. There is a false child will be put upon you, and how will you answer it to all your children? This has been a fine care and fine management for your son William; he is mightily obliged to you. And for Ann, I am sure you deserve anything she can say to you.'[12]

George's first thought had been for the hopes he nursed of William's succession. Caroline travelled through the night and arrived at St James's at four in the morning. She had been determined all along to prevent any trickery. She was so suspicious she even refused to drink a cup of chocolate, saying to Lord Hervey who accompanied her, 'You need not fear my tasting anything in this side of the house.' However, when Caroline finally saw the infant, who was two months premature, she said she no longer doubted its parentage: 'If, instead of this poor, little, ugly she-mouse, there had been a brave, large, fat, jolly boy, I should not have been cured of my suspicions.'[13]

The she-mouse was christened Augusta on 29 August 1737. The

King and Queen were god-parents, although not present at the ceremony. Their anger with Frederick intensified when in an exchange of letters with them he pointedly refused to address the Queen as Your Majesty. This slight is an example of the perversity of Frederick's behaviour. Several times in the past he had told the Queen that he considered he took precedence over her. Once Caroline blandly assured him 'my dear Fritz, let your quality be ever so great, the King, if I was to die, would never marry you'.

The upshot of the Prince's arrogance was that on 10 September the King sent him a message ordering him to leave St James's Palace with all his family as soon as the Princess was well enough to travel. The Prince and Princess left at once, first for Kew and then to Norfolk House, St James's Square. Foreign ambassadors were advised that if they visited the Prince it would be 'a thing disagreeable to His Majesty', and a message was sent to all Peers, Peeresses and Privy Councillors that whoever went to the Prince's court should not be admitted to the King's presence.

The Lord Chancellor, Lord Hardwicke, was one of the King's chief intermediaries with Frederick during the dispute and used all his powers of persuasion to moderate the harshness of the letters sent by the King. In his own diary Hardwick added a most extraordinary note to his record of these events:

> Sir Robert Walpole informed me of certain passages between the King and himself and between the Queen and the Prince, of too high and secret a nature ever to be trusted to this narrative; but from thence I found great reason to think that this unhappy difference between the King and Queen and His Royal Highness turned on some points of a more interesting and important nature than have hitherto appeared.

This conversation took place on 5 September, five days before the Prince was banished from the Court. Years later Philip Yorke, the Lord Chancellor's son, was preparing a life of his father for publication: 'I asked my Father the meaning of the dark insinuations in this paragraph, but he protested he did not then recollect the particulars.' Whether Hardwicke's forgetfulness was real or feigned will never be known. Yorke then added a further note which shows the deep layers of mistrust in the Royal Family.

'They' (the dark insinuations) probably refer to the suspicions of the King and Queen that the Prince intended to foist a suppos-

ititious child upon them, to which the Prince's inexcusable
conduct in hurrying away the Princess from Hampton Court gave
some colour (Hervey, III, p165). The King affected to believe the
Prince himself to be a *changeling* (Ibid. p276) and in 1725 had supported a plan of excluding the Prince from the Throne, of making
him King of Hannover and of choosing Prince William to be King
of Great Britain . . . [14]

In such a fog of suspicion, innuendo and mistrust it is easy to lose
the way, but one fact stands out clearly: everything associated with
the Prince of Wales alienated the King and Queen, and the more this
was so, the more did expectations for the House of Hannover rest
with William. Now, in this same year, 1737, with Frederick more at
loggerheads with the King and Queen than ever, William's future
was of the utmost importance. Once again George II turned to his
Lord Chancellor for advice. He consulted him about the constitu-
tional problems involved in disinheriting Frederick in favour of
William. Alarmed by the proposal, the Lord Chancellor took
soundings, and one of the first people he approached was young
Duke William himself. Discreet enquiries were made as to what the
young Prince thought of the idea. To his credit William rejected the
proposal out of hand. Several people supported the idea but the
Duke would have none of it.

Byrom meanwhile, was still making a concerted effort to gain
access to William in order that he might have some means of in-
fluencing his son, however slightly, before it was too late. On 15
April 1737, Duke William's birthday, Byrom's Journal records his
continued preoccupation:

> Thence to Dr. Smith's who told me that he had spoke to the
> Duke, and that the Duke had asked Mr. Zolman if he would learn
> along with him; from him to Dr. Hartley's; thence to the park
> where I saw Dr. Smith who had been to compliment the Duke
> upon his birthday, and he was walking with Mr.J.T. Philips, who
> gave him his book of letters to the Duke in Latin . . . I went with
> Dr. Smith to Smyrna coffeehouse, chocolate 3d.[15]

The Dr Smith mentioned here is Byrom's friend Robert Smith,
tutor to the Duke. Only three weeks earlier the two men had discussed the possibility of the Duke learning shorthand. Byrom was
well aware that the young Prince's tutors would be expected to pay
their respects on his birthday. Long-standing friendship with Smith

provided Byrom with a perfectly acceptable reason for calling on that particular morning. It would be natural for the conversation to turn to the likelihood of the Prince becoming a pupil. Smith and Byrom parted company, apparently to go their separate ways, but whatever business Byrom may have had, it did not prevent him from meeting Smith a second time on his return from the royal household. Smith was now accompanied by Byrom's 'Salopian friend', Jenkin Thomas Philips, the Duke's Latin tutor, who had also been to express his birthday greeting. The entry in the Journal is deceptively simple. Byrom makes it appear as though this second encounter was almost an accident, but there is good reason to think it was not. It is clear Byrom deliberately cultivated the Duke's tutors and other members of the household.

On 28 March he had met Robert Smith 'with whom I walked, who said he would speak to Mr. Poyntz about Duke William learning shorthand'. On another occasion, when visiting Dr Hartley, Byrom was introduced to a caller who turned out to be Dr Butler, Queen Caroline's Chaplain:

> Dr. H[artley] told him that Dr. Smith was to speak to Mr. Poyntz about the Duke learning shorthand, which Dr. Butler said he thought would do very well (if I remember right).[16]

This was another fortunate encounter for Byrom, for, as her Chaplain, Butler was close to the Queen. In the conversation which followed Byrom had the pleasure of a glimpse of his young son at the age of fifteen and hearing him praised for his intelligence and quick wit:

> He told us of the Duke's forwardness, of his passing by when he (the Dr.) was reading Hobbes to a certain person and that certain person saying, well, and what do you think of this? And the Duke said that there must be right and wrong before human laws, which supposed right and wrong; and besides, wherever was there that state of nature that he talked of? Who ever lived in it? And that person (the Queen plainly) Well, but if it was left to yourself, what would you do? And the Duke said, I cannot tell what pleasures etc. might do to blind me, unless it did so and so etc.

The entry is unusual in its length, unlike so many which deal simply with daily trivia. It shows Byrom's pleasure in gleaning every scrap of information he can about William and his care in recording it.

A few days after William's birthday, on Thursday 21 April, Byrom went walking in St James's park, and came across Dr Smith again. After exchanging greetings, Smith talked to Byrom about a dinner held by the Prince's Governor Poyntz on the night of his birthday. He said that

> he perceived that I had a great many friends at Court, that dining at Mr. Poyntz's on the Duke's birthday, the discourse was about me, that Mr. Wyndham commended my shorthand from the report he had heard, that Mr. Poyntz said that he had been told of it by Dr. Butler, that he had heard that I had done a great deal of good in my own country.[17]

This entry confirms how well known Byrom was to those engaged in the Duke's education. He must have felt flattered that at William's birthday dinner he should be a topic of conversation. The care he had taken to cultivate the tutors seemed to be paying dividends. Yet his pleasure was short-lived. On the 26 April Byrom recorded:

> Mr Stillingfleet mentioned some of the royal family's learning and they mentioned the Duke, and Dr. Hartley said he believed he knew where it stuck, that it was the pence, but I suspected within myself something else, but said that I must tell him as I told some of my scholars, that I would stay till they were able to pay.[18]

Clearly Byrom did not believe for one moment that the Royal Household could not afford to pay. Characteristically, he does not expand further but leaves his concluding sally to make his point. In this denial Byrom saw the hand of the Queen, thwarting him lest he should become a confidant of their son.

Byrom had made sure that he was acceptable to the key figures in William's household. After hearing his praises sung at the birthday dinner, it must have seemed merely a matter of time before he was admitted to the presence of the Duke and established his own relationship with him. Yet, at the final moment, with success almost within his grasp, he was foiled. Despite an impeccable pedigree of patrons ready to support him, the proposition was vetoed. Did the mother bar the way to the son? All those directly concerned with the Prince's education were in favour of his learning shorthand. That it came to nothing shows the prohibition came from a higher authority – masked crudely by the excuse of expense. Could the young Duke's household, with an annual budget of £6,000, really not pay five guineas for the lessons? This rebuff was the origin of 'The Session of the Critics'. After this Byrom never resumed his campaign to teach William shorthand. There were other systems competing with his, but there is no evidence that any of them were proposed for the Duke's instruction.

Byrom's friendship with the Hartleys was as firm as ever and his visits to their home just as frequent. However, Dr Hartley was not in the best of health. He was suffering from gallstones and already had seen Cheselden, who by common consent was one of the finest surgeons of the day. Byrom was not slow to offer his own medical opinion: 'I advised him to be very attentive to his own case, that he might I thought eat chicken or plain meat without hurt that he — not try any tricks more than necessity obliged.'[19]

Even so the indisposition did not, at first, impede Hartley's campaign to get Byrom's shorthand system into print. The more enthusiasm the kind doctor showed, the more embarrassed Byrom grew. Hartley circulated many of Byrom's pupils to ask them to attend a meeting to discuss the possible publication and arrange for a testimonial to be published in the *Daily Advertiser*. By now Byrom had decided that publication was the last thing he wanted. However, because of pressure from Hartley and his friends, Byrom found himself being forced to act almost against his will. His health had improved since his breakdown, but he had not completely re covered, for under pressure he was still prone to attacks of breathlessness and chest pains. On 4 May, while discussing publication at Hartley's, Byrom felt his old symptoms return: 'and at the beginning of dinner eating the asparagus, I was put into a hurry, which Dr. Hartley took notice of and said that he believed I was not well, and I went with him into his study, having drank a glass of wine; I was not sick, it was only something stopping on my chest ... '[20]

The advertisement prepared by Dr Hartley, the claims it made on Byrom's behalf, the various alterations to its precise wording – all this was a drain on Byrom. Hartley with his energy, openness and desire to help was becoming more and more difficult to control. It was fortunate for Byrom that Hartley's health deteriorated at just the right time. On 9 May Hartley had to withdraw from yet another meeting with fellow-enthusiasts:

Dr. Hartley, who was under the medicine taking of Mrs.

Stephens, a Roman Catholic woman, for the stone, said that he thought he could not be with us on Tuesday at our meeting, and Mrs. Hartley said that she was against it because — so that I desired he would by all means look to his health and not come, though he was our chief man.[21]

Byrom must have sighed with relief when he knew his 'chief man' could not attend the meeting. It was now so much easier to oppose his proposals. This had become absolutely imperative since a Mr Gardiner had intervened with diplomatic but determined hints. The day before his crucial meeting at the Devil's Tavern, Byrom learned from one of his pupils that

> Mr. Gardiner, Bence and many more are against the scheme, that Mr. G said that there was more said of it than was true according to his experience, that he could not attempt to write as fast as anybody could read, and seemed, according to Mr. Balls's words, to be against the publication of it; I told Mr. Balls that I should be glad to have only such recommendation of it as Mr. Gardiner or any gentleman should think most proper and modest . . . [22]

Gardiner's name may have been mentioned with others, but it would be like a signal to Byrom to put the brake on Hartley's scheme and halt the rush into print. Mr Gardiner was a government agent, responsible for other political spies. One in particular was an Irishman called John Vere. Gardiner had sent Vere to Byrom two years earlier in January 1735 to learn shorthand:

> Tuesday 21st. rose at seven, went to Mr. Gardiner's according to his note that he wanted very much to speak to me. I breakfasted with him on tea and bread and butter; it was to tell me that Mr. Vere (John) to whom he had given some instructions, wanted to see me, and would have me come on Wednesday morning ten o'clock.[23]

Later Byrom notes: 'Wednesday January 22nd rose at eight, very snowy morning, put on my cloak and went to Mr. Vere's in King's Bench walks, upper end; Mr Vere paid, having had instructions from Mr. Gardiner.'[24]

Ironically, eight years after this Vere was to be the principal spy for the Duke of Cumberland during the '45 uprising. He was taken prisoner by Jacobites at Newcastle-under-Lyme in Staffordshire.[25]

Gardiner's intervention in 1737 to stop publication and Byrom's reaction to it are proof of Byrom's role as a double agent. His readiness to lean on Gardiner for the support he needed in opposing publication gives him away. Gardiner's remarks, reported to Byrom, were coded to tell him that Gardiner did not want the shorthand system to be published as a commercial venture. It was still valued as a means of confidential communication. Byrom's reply showed he understood the message. Watching Byrom's movements through the years, one is conscious of his continued sympathy and support for the Stuarts. His attempt to reconcile his Jacobite loyalties with his relationship with Caroline played no small part in his breakdown. Certainly his manoeuvres with Gardiner and Vere (however casually he attempts to record them) show the complexity of his mind.

The advocacy of his other friends was less than ever to Byrom's liking. In June he wrote: 'I have been often in great anxiety about the affair of shorthand; it seems to me sometimes as if I was got into a snare, and sometimes as if it was the only way to be delivered from a snare by printing it.' Since he knew this was impossible Byrom latched on to other problems to oppose publication. The preparation of a type had been causing difficulties for some time. A printer named Lightboun had spent a considerable amount of time and some money on the problem. Having received a letter from this man 'about his laying out eighteen or nineteen pounds to other workmen, and having been ten months at work at a guinea a month',[26] Byrom was alarmed and put his alarm to good use. He sent this letter to Elizabeth to show to her brother Josiah. In it Byrom makes out that he is frightened of being sued and that he wants the bill settled so that he could return to Manchester. Despite the success of his shorthand he apparently did not have enough money to settle it himself. He was hoping yet again to be subsidised by his wife's family. Yet he had not thought twice earlier in laying out twenty-eight pounds for a watch! Was he really so hard up, or did he simply wish to appear so to his wife and friends? In the end, the project to print was dropped. Almost two years later, in February 1739, when he was once more in the company of Dr Hartley and others, the topic cropped up. Byrom was anxious not to be blamed for frustrating the scheme. He protested:

> I had and would do all that I could, but that I could not solicit; Dr. Shaw seemed to think me not courageous, which indeed is very true, for I am tired of a subscription, if I knew how to act

properly in it I would escape from it; he said cowards were always shot, and such like, and I did not like his manner, believing that he had not much of that friendship and sentiment which I have occasion for.[27]

Obviously Byrom was hurt by the criticism of friends and wanted to see an end to the whole idea. The system was never published in his lifetime.

CHAPTER NINE

Caroline – the Power Game Ends
1737–8

JUNE 10, the anniversary of the Old Pretender, was to Byrom always a significant date. He liked his activities around this time to be especially purposeful. On 10 June 1737 he went to see the Duke of Devonshire, Lord Steward of the Household. The Duke had been a shorthand pupil six years earlier and a very apt one. He and Byrom got on well, well enough, certainly, for Byrom to be welcome at nine in the morning. The Duke was by now a highly important court official and a leading figure of the Establishment. He acted as one of the Regents in the absence of George II, and his responsibility for the examination and approval of the Household accounts brought him close to Caroline.

In his Journal for the next day Byrom makes an extraordinary comment. The first part of the entry is concerned with his shorthand. Then, for no clear reason, he writes: ' "The maid is dead, why trouble ye *the master*," comes into my mind, as to the disappointment that is met within life, that we should still pray and not faint, and do our best.'[1] These words of Christ, uttered before he raised Jairus's daughter from the dead, came unbidden into Byrom's mind. Was he seized by a sudden premonition about the state of Caroline's health which he hoped might mend? He knew of the Queen's rupture which was becoming steadily worse. Later that year she died. Or was this strange thought prompted by his meeting with Devonshire? Soon after it Byrom was taking farewell of his London friends, and a month later was on his way back to Manchester for the summer. The next entry in his Journal is dated 2 September and is concerned with another meeting with Devonshire, this time at Stockport.

Byrom was accompanied by an old friend, Thomas Reynolds of Strangeways Hall, and his son Edward: 'Was yesterday at Stockport to meet the Duke of Devonshire, gave him a watch-paper.' Since

Byrom considered it worth recording in his Journal, the gift will have had a special significance. (There are, for example, still in existence Jacobite watch papers bearing political motifs.) Byrom's account of the meeting further emphasises its importance to him.

> There were thirteen at dinner without the Duke, viz., he, the Duchess, their daughter, Capt. Vernon (the doctor's brother), Mr. Bonfoy, Lord James Cavendish, Captain Brereton, the Chaplain, one Mr. Chetham, one Mr. Hodgekins I think, Mr. Reynolds and I and two more. I ate two or three mouthfuls of venison, not having ate any flesh meat for years, and I drank some glasses of wine; they went away suddenly after dinner, in a manner. Mr. Reynolds handed the Duchess and I the young lady to their coaches, for the Duke and Duchess were in a chariot, and the young lady and maids in a coach. As I came back to the house a man spoke to me, whom I took for the landlord, and told me a long story of some wine that was shipwrecked in Ireland that Captain Vernon had seized, and he desired a line from Mr. Reynolds and me to the Duke's gentleman to speak to the Captain, and he kept me there till Lord James sent to desire my company in the parlour, and I went there and found none but Mr. Reynolds, Lord James, and Captain Vernon, and I did mention it to the Captain; and by and by he began 'The immortal memory' – 'a good health in some countries,' Lord James said, I think; and Captain said, 'Yes, everywhere almost, now;' and he filled a bumper and drank to the immortal memory of King William, and Lord James followed and took off his hat and performed the ceremony mighty devoutly; and I was thinking how to put by that nonsense, and it came into my head that I might as well take leave to go to Mr. Hoole's and so I did, and they seemed to part with me readily enough.[2]

Those present had travelled from different directions, Byrom and Reynolds had come ten miles from Manchester, the Duke and his party from his country seat at Chatsworth; all were bound to the Duke by blood, politics, business or friendship. With the Duke was a man by the name of Hodgekins or Hoskins. He was the Duke's father-in-law and Steward to the Duke of Bedford and as such was responsible during the minority of the previous Duke for letting Bedford properties. One of these was, of course, a certain house in New Round Court rented by Byrom in the name of Thomas Siddal. That all these people travelled so far simply for a meal shows that there was a serious agenda for the meeting, which was arranged on neutral ground – not at Chatsworth, but in a public inn. The Duke travelled with his family, and the young children were sent to dine in another room. Devonshire was host and ordered venison, which Byrom, now a vegetarian, did not enjoy. Poor Teddy, upstairs with the other youngsters, ate nothing at all.

However, something was evidently said or done during the meal to annoy the Duke sufficiently to make him leave with his immediate family. Byrom and his friend Reynolds escorted them to their coaches. The Duke's younger brother, Lord James, stayed on. Byrom does not mention what annoyed the Duke. Instead he digresses into a tale of shipwrecked wine. A hint, however, is given of the subject and the political sympathies of those present when he mentions the toast made by the Captain. This was couched in deliberately ambiguous words. 'The immortal memory of King William' could only refer back to the last William – William III. In other words it is neither a Hanoverian toast nor an overtly Jacobite one to the 'King over the water'. To those in the know, however, it could be taken as an indirect allusion to the plot being discussed that same year to make the young Duke of Cumberland the next King William. It is clear that Byrom found the ambiguities and innuendoes of these proceedings too much to take calmly, and he, too, became anxious to get away. Jesting in this way with William's name was not to his liking.

As Caroline's affections cooled, Byrom's hopes had become more and more centred on William, and the disappointment over his failed shorthand plan still rankled. But Byrom's jaundiced portrait of the boy's mother in 'Artemissia' shows only one side of his relationship with her. Byrom reminds us of the depth of his love for Caroline in another poem in the group, 'Damon to Celinda'. In this he adopts the role of Damon (a conventional name for the constant lover) and addresses Caroline as Celinda, whose name is a version of Selene or Artemis, the moon-goddess. The moon is used as a symbol of change and fickleness, for the poem was written when Caroline was evidently turning her attention from him to some other 'tasteless rival', most probably her favourite, Lord Hervey.

> SAY my Celinda if thy soul divines
> What ardent purpose breathes the following lines
> Does not the lover and his verse proclaim
> The idle message of a well-known flame?

Or has not yet the fair her power survey'd
And in my conduct read the waste she made?
(When fair discretion from the helm withdrew
And youth's unguarded follies blaz'd anew)
Mark'd the fond wish, and claimed the rising fires,
Something beyond what cool respect inspires
Beyond the even pulse that just admires?
Have I not lov'd in terms more clear and strong
Than all I ever said or ever sung?
Had the soft sigh no message to impart
And love no language nearer to the heart?
In beauty's triumphs, tho' we bend to you,
Some share of glory is our sex's due.
The nymph for whom no well-bred lover sighs,
No sword-knot quarrels, and no garter dies,
And only learns the lightnings of her face
From the spread canvas, or unconscious glass,
Just shares conditions with the cloyster'd fair,
Who wastes an angel's bloom in works and prayer;
Whose useless eyes the task of life forsake,
And only are employ'd to weep and wake.
'Tis yours in soft engagements to excell;
'Tis ours to lend them life by suffering well.
Embalm'd by vows, gay beauty never dies,
And lovers' incense wafts it to the skies.

Yet let the fairest of her sex beware,
Hear the soft whisper, yet suspect the snare;
Check the fond heart that offers but to glow
At the fool's incense, or the coxcomb vow.
Lest sorrowing loves the fatal waste lament,
And grudge the lavish beauties they had lent.
Perhaps betray'd (forgive a lover's fears)
To lace, to folly, impotence, or years,
Some tasteless rival shall those beauties bless,
That never lov'd, like Damon, to excess.
In vain for him has love those lustres shed,
Weav'd the soft tresses, o'er the forehead spread,
With gay delight enrich'd the damask cheek,
And turn'd the column of the marble neck.
He feels his bosom with no raptures swell,

Nor hears the music which thy lips distill;
To all that wit or beauty can endear
Lifts the fool's eye, and turns the adder's ear.
Or, oh! imagine that thy false-one flies
To light forbidden fires at other's eyes,
Unaw'd by beauty, unrestrain'd by shame,
With guilty damsels shares a vulgar flame;
Brings cold indifference to thy widow'd bed,
And starves, where love had all his plenty spread,
Then all too late, neglected, loath'd, betray'd,
To call the sex's softness to thy aid,
Thine nor thy sex's softness well can bear
The curse of pity from the happier fair.
Unmiss'd at balls, and at the ring forgot,
Slow wasting nights and silent fears her lot,
The scorn'd unnoted beauty blooms in vain,
And wants the last sad refuge to complain.
At such an hour – shall lost ideas join
And raise the image of a love like mine,
When cold reflection lifts to fatal view
Whose heart you weep for, and whose bled for you,
And the fair scale by pitying loves upborn
Weighs Damon's fondness with the husband's scorn.
Then for that awful fear one sigh may break,
Which check'd my passion when I died to speak.
One tear in many dropped for his neglect
Chide the cold distance of my dumb respect.
Then could thy wish, (did vows permit,) remove
The fool of nature for the fool of love.
When age her hoary livery shall have spread,
Those lilies faded, and those roses shed,
Or, oh! more fatal yet, when forward care
Lays waste the bloom that age had learnt to spare,
Then shall thy lover (whose unwearied eye
Now thinks it rapture but to gaze and sigh,)
Ask where the thousand loves and graces hung
That fired his bosom, and that smooth'd his song,
Shall wonder how his soul could e'er forget
What e'er the sober world calls grave or great,
Ambition, business, books, and friends disclaim,
And next to love, the best of passions fame.

'Damon to Celinda' is a genuine expression of Byrom's feelings. It is full of echoes of other poems in the sequence. When he claims his rival 'never lov'd like Damon to excess' it recalls the 'passion in excess' described in 'To The Fair Unknown'. This time, at first, Byrom feels equal to the task in hand – to point out how much he loves her. What worries him is whether Celinda/Caroline realises how sincere he has always been (his 'ardent purpose'). In one sense he sees this message as 'idle' or futile since she had obviously become interested in someone else. Does she realise what devastation that has caused Byrom? In lines, again reminiscent of 'To The Fair Unknown', he claims his love is stronger in deed than in words: 'Have I lov'd in terms more clear and strong/Than all I ever said or ever sung?'

While she may boast that it is her beauty which has been the cause of her triumph, that is only half the equation. 'Some share of glory is our sex's due'. This is the first, half-playful, warning. Women should not be so cavalier in their attitude to their admirers. For if they were not admired they would be no different from nuns locked up in a convent. It is the homage of a devoted man which gives life to the flirtatious nature of women. It is men's vows of love which immortalise female beauty. Even so he warns her to be wary of 'the fool's incense or the coxcomb vow' lest she is betrayed by inconstancy. Such a 'tasteless rival' cannot equal Damon's passion. He dwells on the wretchedness caused by his insincere rival. He will leave her a prey to 'slow wasting nights and silent fears'.

Then it will be too late, (gradually the tone of the poem becomes more serious as it proceeds). She will remember the lover cast aside 'Whose heart you weep for and whose bled for you' and gladly exchange the man who was born a fool for the one whom love made behave foolishly (in loving her too much). Byrom ends by imagining Caroline in old age, her beauty wasted in the passing years by her sufferings. He will then ask himself where is the beauty he adored and for which he had sacrificed everything normally considered worthwhile – ambition, business, learning, fame. Both of them have wasted their lives.

It was Byrom's misfortune to have fallen in love with the most complex of women. Caroline was a paradoxical figure, living a public life yet maintaining a private existence, a mother capable of hating one son as much as she loved the other, on the surface so accommodating but underneath a creature of will, truly a creature of 'infinite variety'. Tall, dignified and with great charm, she won the admiration and affection of many close to her. Chief among these was Mrs Clayton, lady of the Bedchamber and later Mistress of the Robes. On the accession of George I Caroline had done her best to give some dignity and sense of style to his gloomy and shabby court. However, after the famous quarrel of 1717, Caroline and her husband set up their own household, which she was determined would be very different.

She surrounded herself with a well-bred and well-informed set of ladies in waiting and a number of pretty, vivacious maids of honour, who added sparkle and colour to her court. One of them, Mary Lepell, eventually married Caroline's favourite, Lord Hervey. When, at the beginning, the Prince and Princess attended morning service on Sunday at the Chapel Royal, St James's, Caroline was attended by these beautiful, high-spirited girls who were not in the least inclined to worship. Soon the Chapel Royal became a fashionable venue with young gallants who came to flirt. In the end the Princess was compelled to board up the sides of the pew where the girls sat, so that they could not be seen by the congregation. To this irreverent comedy George I added a touch of broad farce. Since he did not understand a word of English he either slept through the sermon or talked loudly in his native tongue.

Caroline's quick wit, affability and wide interests won the admiration of the most accomplished young Whig aristocrats, like Stanhope and the two Herveys. Almost everyone of consequence attended the public rooms of St James's Palace, where there were receptions nearly every night. These became uncomfortably crowded. One night the Venetian Ambassadress, Madame Torn, panicked because of the crush and cried out, 'Do not touch my face!' The King heard her and remarked to a courtier, 'Don't you hear the Ambassadress? She offers you all the rest of her body provided you don't touch her face!'[3]

Happy in the knowledge of Caroline's devotion, Byrom must have decided to keep a low profile in her salons and play the 'tall nothing',[4] while other writers vied with each other for her approval. Not all the writers who thronged the salons were men of genius. Indeed Caroline's patronage of Stephen Duck showed how easily the German princess could mistake English doggerel for great poetry. In one unpublished poem Byrom comments on this with wry humour:

What can the poor pedantic Sovereign boast
Where Dullness writes at the Muse's cost?
Where Sots have just a Notion to blaspheme,
And vaunt their Doggerel in a Poet's name?[5]

Caroline shared the characteristic Hannoverian coarseness and could use a rough wit to good effect. There was nothing modest about her approach to sex. She and George shared an almost pathological interest in it, and he would write from Germany long detailed descriptions of his activities with his mistresses. George even went so far as to have one of them, Madame de Walmoden, painted in the nude and he brought the picture home to England to boast about his latest conquest.

Rightly convinced of her superiority over all other women in her husband's eyes, Caroline was clever enough to condone these affairs and make friends with her chief rival, Mrs Howard. Thus she remained the controlling influence over George's political actions. Yet she was not averse to exacting certain services from these women just to remind them of their proper station. Mrs Howard was compelled, against her will, to kneel and present the silver basin and ewer to the Queen for her to wash her hands. Caroline certainly knew how to use her husband's weakness for her own ends. Hervey, in his memoirs, describes Caroline's tactics: 'Whilst she was seemingly on every occasion giving up her opinion to his, she was always turning his opinion and bending his will to hers.'[6]

Caroline may well have used the language of the farmyard when she chose but her own sexual behaviour was said to be beyond reproach. Even so, there were the faintest whispers which have always been dismissed. The Duchess of Orleans, writing about the split between George I and the Prince of Wales in 1717, comments: 'They say that the King himself is in love with the Princess. I do not believe this, for I consider that the King has in no way a lover-like nature; he loves only himself.'[7] Later the same year the Duchess claimed that Lord Peterborough was in love with the Princess of Wales and kept telling her so, but also said that she did not encourage him. George I spread many unkind stories about the behaviour of 'cette diablesse Madame la Princesse' – no doubt out of sheer malice. Ironically, it is around this time the Princess first met Byrom and started the one secret affair of her life.

Many coarse verses satirising the Hannoverians circulated freely, which, when not openly offensive, employed innuendo and malicious speculation.

You may strut, dapper George, but 'twill all be in vain,
We know 'tis Queen Caroline, not you, that reign,
You govern no more than Don Philip of Spain.
Then if you would have us fall down and adore you
Lock up your fat spouse, as your Dad did, before you.[8]

Like a two-edged sword, this doggerel attacks Caroline as the power behind the throne while reminding the reader that George I locked up his wife for adultery, and suggesting George II should do the same. On the accession of her husband as George II, Caroline was instrumental in obtaining the office of prime minister for Sir Robert Walpole, and from that moment she was a major influence in English politics until the time of her death. A close friendship developed between Walpole and Caroline based on an affinity of mind and temperament which lasted all their lives. Both were earthy, worldly and cynical in outlook. Both loved the realities of power and, to secure these, were quite happy to allow the King to enjoy its appearances. George II made frequent visits to Hannover and when he did so he preferred to make Caroline the Regent instead of Frederick. Between them Caroline and Walpole made all the important decisions of government.

From the moment she married, Caroline consciously manipulated not only her husband but anyone she wished to use, turning calculation into a fine art. Byrom would have seen this in the steps she took to disguise their relationship. Small wonder that in his poem he likened Caroline to the 'Insidious, restless, watchful spider'. Byrom was as much a victim of her guile as George II, but, like so many others, did not realise the extent of her machinations until they were over.

As Byrom's hopes were destroyed, his mind soured further. The more he thought about Caroline's intervention to stop him teaching William, the more bitter he became. The gentle side of Byrom's nature had led him to hope that Caroline would have retained some pleasure in remembering their past affection, but this was not so. Her behaviour seemed to him unnecessarily cruel, and Byrom came to see Caroline's pursuit of power at all costs as brutally callous. He could only respond by becoming harder himself. Byrom's Jacobite sympathies provided a means of channelling his rancour towards Caroline and the circus of Hannoverians. The domestic wrangles of the Royal Family had been played out before him like a grotesque farce. Even during the heyday of his relationship with Caroline, he had never admired the rest of her family; he saw them as usurpers of the legitimate Stuarts. Ambivalent in his conduct, he grew steadily more resentful with each rebuff. At times he needed to give some expression to these pent-up feelings, even if they were carefully masked. One such occasion occurred in May 1736 when he called on a Scots friend and stayed for supper.

> To Mr. Blencowe's, where Mr. Tatham came after, and we supped there, we talked about killing of tyrants, and we read some of Shakespeare's speeches.[9]

Under the guise of a literary discussion Byrom was able to clarify a matter of conscience. Evidence suggests Byrom had been intimately concerned with the final illness of George I, and his conversation with Blencowe indicated a state of mind which allowed him to consider it perfectly justifiable to remove any obstacle in his path.

Byrom was aware that Caroline was a sick woman. She had suffered an umbilical rupture as the result of the birth of her last daughter, Louisa. For a long time she kept this secret. Hitherto it has been thought that only George II knew, but one of Byrom's unpublished poems contains a clear reference to it. Indeed, it would have been very odd if he had not known, for he was still close to Caroline when it happened. However, later, in one of his bitter outbursts, Byrom used this knowledge to denounce both Caroline's literary pretensions and her health.

> To that excess the charming turd is brought
> To this very common share of thought;
> Which malady of sense, which cankered womb
> Breaks out in verse and blisters in thy room.[10]

Did Byrom come to see Caroline as a tyrant, someone to be removed? If so, he needed the unwitting help of others. On 9 November 1737 Caroline was taken ill in her library. There is now evidence to show Caroline's original indisposition, whatever its nature, was seriously worsened by medicine taken at the outset while the Queen was still in the library.

The Queen's Library was a new addition to St James's Palace. Designed by William Kent, it stood on the west side of the palace overlooking the park until it was demolished in 1825. It was a single-storey building with a highly ornate interior. The books were housed in arched recesses set in the walls and between each pair of arches hung a bust of a former queen. The ceiling was decorated with rich mouldings. Begun in 1736 and completed in October 1737, the room was strikingly beautiful and could serve both as a library and orangery. Byrom paid a visit before it was completed, on 22 April 1737. He went with some friends 'to see the Queen's library, which I compared to a thick-rinded orange, *aurantia mala*'.[11] Byrom had been in a bad mood for much of that day and this may in part account for his dislike of the decoration of the new building. But it was inevitable that such a visit would revive painful memories, and it is little wonder he expressed his feelings with such ill-humour that it communicated to his friends. One of them, his kinsman George Lloyd, complained of feeling hot, faint and 'not wellish'. Byrom's scathing description of the handsome new building as a rotting orange carried hidden undertones of the Queen's own illness. By now she had had her rupture for thirteen years. In one sense, therefore, however handsome Caroline might still appear to be, inwardly she was decaying. In the poem 'Artemissia', Byrom describes Caroline as one who 'lies and stinks in state'. The outburst in the library was similarly motivated. His companions, however, would not understand, because they knew nothing of Byrom's involvement with Caroline or her ill health.

Shortly after his visit Byrom learned that an old Cambridge friend, Francis Say, had been appointed Queen's Librarian. They had been to Trinity together, and Say became Secretary to the Bishop of Ely. A rather colourless man whose main virtue was industry, described in an obituary as 'religious without show and learned without pedantry', he was certainly pliable enough to serve five successive Bishops. It was useful to Byrom to have such an unsuspecting friend in charge of the library.

Towards the end of August, after yet another exchange of recriminatory letters with Frederick, Caroline fell ill. She said it was gout and took to her bed at Hampton Court. Sick and fretful, she was anxious to alleviate the boredom of her confinement, so she ignored Court protocol and commanded Hervey to attend her daily in her bedroom alone. She soon recovered and gave further vent to her displeasure with Frederick, who in September was banished from St James's. Caroline looked forward eagerly to the completion of her new library. An announcement was made that all was ready for her books to be installed, but this proved premature and Lord Hervey rebuked his friend Henry Fox, Surveyor of the King's Works: 'Which of all the Devils in Hell prompted you to tell the Queen that everything in her library was ready for the putting up of her Books?'[12]

Eventually the work was finished in October and Caroline was able to enjoy her new library – but the pleasure was shortlived. She was about to enter the final phase of an illness which she had managed to conceal too long. Her treatment at the hands of the best physicians and surgeons of her day is a painful reminder of how primitive and agonising medical care was at the time.

On the day Caroline was taken ill she told Hervey: 'Here is this nasty colic that I had at Hampton Court come again.'[13] Whatever the cause of this latest attack, its course was fatally different. Thinking it was colic, Caroline took her first medicine. This must have been Ward's Drops. Historians have listed the preparations she took to relieve her pain and Ward's Drops was one of them. Lord Hervey, as one might expect, gives a detailed account of the progress of the illness, all the medicines she took in their sequence, and the treatments she received after he first learned of her indisposition. Hervey's reference to Ward's Drops is ambiguous but the inference is that Caroline took them at the onset of the illness, when, as Hervey relates, her stomach and bowels were giving her great pain. Princess Caroline, the Queen's daughter, had been taking Ward's Drops for rheumatism very recently, on Hervey's recommendation. It had proved remarkably effective and cured all the pain. The Princess had been taking the drops just before Caroline's illness, in Hervey's words: 'with the privity of the King and Queen and keeping it secret to everybody else', to save the embarrassment of the King's physicians, whose medicines had not worked. The Queen had thus been able to see how effective Ward's Drops could be by the great improvement of her daughter's health. This may have been a reason for her to take the medicine herself.

Caroline felt so ill that she left the library and returned to the main palace. There she took Daffy's Elixir, a prescription of Dr Tesier, the Royal Physician. By now she was in such pain and so uneasy with frequent vomiting that she went to bed. At two o'clock the King proposed that there should be no reception that day, but Caroline tried to make light of her illness and got up to attend the drawing room. It was here Hervey saw her. 'Is it not intolerable at my age to be plagued by a new distemper?' she said, looking so ill that Hervey asked her what medicines she had taken. When she told him, he was sufficiently alarmed to urge: 'For God's sake, Madam, go to your own room.'

Caroline insisted on staying until the King withdrew, then left herself and immediately went to bed. At seven o'clock that evening Hervey returned from visiting the French Ambassador and found the Queen alone with Princess Caroline. The Queen asked what he used to take for the colic. Hervey replied 'strong things'. An hour later the Queen felt so wretched that she said: 'Give me what you will, I will take it.' Hervey said he would bring the strongest thing he could get. He fetched some Snakeroot and Brandy and asked Dr Tesier if he could give it to the Queen. Tesier was too timid to make a decision on his own. 'He could not confirm that this very strong cordial would do her no harm', because the Queen's pulse was now very high and feverish. Hervey proposed consulting another physician, Dr Broxholme, First Physician to the Prince. Hervey's alarm at the medicine Caroline first took in the library for colic means that he regarded it as either dangerous, unsuitable or both. This further points to Ward's Drops and accounts for the concern her condition now caused.

Hervey consulted both Princess Caroline and the King, and Dr Broxholme was sent for immediately. He and Tesier agreed on the Snakeroot cordial but it took too long to prepare, for Dr Ranby, House Surgeon to the King, intervened. It was his opinion that 'no one cordial was better than another in these cases but in proportion to its strength'. Lord Hervey got some usquebaugh (whisky) immediately and it was given to the Queen. She kept it down for half an hour but then was sick. Concern was growing. 'All these strong things, twice Daffy's Elixir, mint water, usquebaugh, snakeroot and Sir Walter Raleigh's cordial' had, without easing the Queen's pain, so increased her fever that the doctors ordered Ranby to bleed her twelve ounces immediately. Matters did not improve and, early on the morning of Thursday the 10th, Caroline was blooded twelve ounces more. Hindsight shows that Caroline's symptoms were not those of colic but the result of the aggravation of the long-standing umbilical rupture. The same day two more doctors were called in: Sir Hans Sloane and Doctor Hulse. They ordered blisters and aperients. These came up, like everything else, soon after being taken.

At six o'clock on Friday morning the Queen was blooded again. The fever stopped almost completely but the frequent vomitings continued. Despite the Queen's protestations, the King insisted on telling the surgeon, Ranby, about the rupture. Although Caroline still tried to hide it, Ranby found it and said he must operate. The King ordered him to send for another surgeon, Busier, who could not be found, so Ranby returned with 'one Shipton, a city surgeon and one of the most eminent and able of the whole profession'. Then

Busier arrived. The three surgeons debated how best to operate. Should they cut a hole in the navel large enough to push the rupture back, or simply lance the swelling? They chose the latter course and let out a 'great deal of stinking stuff'. Throughout this ordeal Caroline displayed characteristic courage. When Ranby applied his knife, she showed her contempt of the pain by asking him what he would give to be able to do the same to his wife. Apparently Ranby and his wife had quarrelled and parted.

The operation was too late. By 15 November, seven days after the onset of the illness, the vomitings increased and the gut burst so that all the contents of the stomach soaked the bed. It was an appalling sign that the end was near, and the occasion of perhaps the cruellest lines Pope ever wrote:

> Here lies wrapt in forty thousand towels
> The only proof that Caroline had bowels.

At one point Caroline showed great concern for a watch she used to wear. Her agitation surprised onlookers sufficiently for Hervey to record the incident:

> . . . But even at this time, on asking for her watch which hung by the chimney in order to give it to him (the King) to take care of the seal, the natural brusquerie of his temper, even in those moments broke out. The King snapped 'Ah my God! let it alone; the Queen has always such strange fancies. Who should meddle with your seal, is it not safe there as in my pocket?'

George mistook Caroline's anxiety as a concern for the Royal seal, when she was really anxious about her watch. It may well have been the watch Byrom bought from the master-watchmaker, Graham. It would not be surprising if Caroline showed attachment to the gift in her dying hours.

On 29 November the Queen died. Lord Egmont in an un-published journal recorded the scene: 'It was Princess Amelia who read the last prayer kneeling by her bed. The queen had her read louder and stop when directed. In the midst of it she (said) 'I am going' and, clapping her finger to her mouth, expired. The King's hand was in hers.'[14]

Caroline died without taking the sacrament and still refusing to see Frederick.

The surgeons claimed that if they had known earlier about the rupture they would have had a greater chance of saving the Queen's life. However the use of Ward's Drops at the outset had done irretrievable damage.

Mrs Hartley was an advocate of Ward's Drops. She was also one of Byrom's warmest admirers, a woman who trusted him implicitly and who was related to Edmund Packe, a doctor and chemist in Covent Garden. In 1735 Packe published a paper in defence of Mr Ward's Drop and Pill, believing wholeheartedly in their efficiency. He claimed that he never knew Ward personally and this defence was written 'from no other motive than doing justice to an injured man'. He rejected the insinuation that the medicines were part of a 'Popish plot' and wrote as a respectable man, many of whose friends had taken the preparation without ill effect. No doubt Packe would have discussed this whole controversy with Mrs Hartley, who would have read his pamphlet. Apart from being related to Packe, the Hartleys were active in promoting other medical nostrums – this very year Dr Hartley had been taking Joanna Stephens's medicine for the stone. Through Packe, Mrs Hartley would have been able to provide the Queen with Ward's preparations, but the likeliest explanation is that, as a result of Mrs Hartley's advocacy, Caroline was supplied with some of Ward's medicines. Mrs Hartley would have done this in all good faith, particularly since her brother had stoutly defended their virtues. Both the Hartleys valued Byrom's opinion on all sorts of matters. They had consulted him on Dr Hartley's gallstones. Nothing would have been easier for Byrom than to sing the praises of Ward's Drops. He knew Mrs Hartley visited Court, and Caroline had been ill in the late summer, supposedly with gout. There would have been an easy opportunity for Byrom in conversation with Mrs Hartley to suggest Ward's Drops as a possible prophylactic for the Queen. Mrs Hartley's energy and enthusiasm matched her husband's, and she liked to share her interest with friends and acquaintances. In expressing her belief in Ward's Drops she would be acting perhaps naively but with the utmost sincerity. And, after all, Ward had much more distinguished champions than her. Like everyone else she was totally ignorant of the real cause of Caroline's illness. If she had known, she would not have suggested Ward's Drops for an umbilical rupture, for this was precisely the kind of illness for which it would prove fatal. Daniel Turner had clearly demonstrated this in his attack, and her brother, too, had warned: 'none in their senses offers any vomits to persons under ruptures of any sort or degree whatsoever'. Thus, when Caroline's illness was finally revealed the truth must have been a profound and devastating shock to Mrs Hartley, a shock which made her ill.

On the first day of Byrom's return to London in the summer of 1738 after the Queen's death, he made a special point of mentioning Mrs Hartley's health in a letter to Elizabeth. A week later in the second letter he mentioned her again: 'Mrs. Hartley's been very ill, is better, but very weakly.'[15] The Hartleys had by now moved out from Leicester Fields to Hammersmith. Bad weather prevented Byrom from calling.

On both occasions when Byrom mentions Mrs Hartley her name is followed by references to the Bishop of Ely, as if by a process of association. Since the Bishop's secretary, Francis Say, was Librarian to the Queen, this is not surprising. He would have been present in the new library when Caroline was taken ill. The Bishop himself was one of Byrom's shorthand pupils and, of all the many pupils waiting to start lessons, it was to the Bishop that Byrom went on his return. Say still lived at the Bishop's palace. It was probably as much to see Say that Byrom called, anxious to hear at first hand what had taken place that fateful morning in the library.

Perhaps the full story will never be known, but is it reasonable to conclude from Byrom's actions before the Queen's final illness, entries in his Journal and verses in his poems, that he was indirectly involved in the death of the Queen? He knew, only too well, medicines which would be fatal to that rupture. He had friends able to recommend treatment to the Queen at his suggestion without suspecting any ulterior motive. Was it his hope that at some time, when she was indisposed, Caroline would use Ward's Drops to relieve her symptoms? There was no need to induce an illness. Caroline might use the medicine for one of a number of complaints – gout, for instance. The important thing would be to see that the drops were easily to hand. In a sense, Byrom was leaving it to chance or, as he would prefer it, to Destiny, to provide the right occasion. He did not have to wait long. Stricken with colic, she took the drops.

As a young man Byrom had been prepared to sacrifice a promising career for the sake of principles. His love for Caroline made him compromise those principles for a while – until he realised she was unworthy of his love. This turned to a hatred which magnified her faults out of all proportion. As Caroline asserted her will, he saw her creating chaos all around; first and foremost in her rejection of him, second in her ambitious moves to promote William over Frederick, and finally in her endless will to power. He had suffered a breakdown in 1731/2, from which he had still not completely recovered. The shock of the rejection in 1737 could have caused Byrom to regress further into a deeply disturbed state of mind, and convince him that he would be furthering the Jacobite cause, which he had for so long neglected, if the alliance between the Queen Consort and Walpole could be ended once and for all.

CHAPTER TEN

The Stage Empties

1739–45

IN MARCH 1742 a pirated version of part of Byrom's shorthand
system was published under the name of William Ward. Byrom
found this reason enough to present a petition to Parliament to
bring in a Bill which would protect his shorthand and grant him the
sole right to teach and publish it. The petition was presented to the
House of Commons on 15 March and a committee appointed to
look into the matter. Byrom was called to speak on his own behalf
and given leave to present a Bill, which he did on 12 April. By 18
May it had passed through the Commons and went to the Lords.
Byrom wrote that night to bring his wife up to date with developments. He feared some opposition from the Patents Office, lest any
monopoly granted him should be seen as an infringement of their
prerogatives. In the event the Bill passed unopposed on 24 May, the
whole procedure having taken ten weeks. On 16 June George II
attended the House of Lords to give the Royal Assent to several
Bills, Byrom's among them. This unusual distinction made the
shorthand system and its inventor pre-eminent in the land, securing
for Byrom the sole right of publishing and teaching the shorthand
for twenty-one years.

The Act was one of the most important achievements in Byrom's
career. He had already taught some of the leading political figures –
both Hannoverian and Jacobite. In the process he had gained their
trust and confidences, and this had given him enormous power. The
Act gave him control of the means of spreading information secretly
and of interpreting it. By a nice irony, George II, in giving the Royal
Assent, had recognised Byrom publicly in a way which helped to
compensate for Caroline's rejection. Moreover, although he had
been denied the privilege of teaching shorthand to William, now he
brushed shoulders with him on account of it. The monopoly,
granted in 1742, was to last twenty-one years. This same year

Anno decimo quinto

Georgii II. Regis.

An Act for securing to *John Byrom*, Master of
Arts, the sole Right of publishing, for a cer-
tain Term of Years, the Art and Method of
Short-hand, invented by him.

 Whereas John Byrom, Master of
Arts, and Fellow of the Royal
Society, hath by long and studi-
ous Application invented, and is
willing to publish, a new Method
of Short-hand, by the uniform
Practice whereof, that useful Art,
being reduced to the most easy,
compendious, correct, and regular System, may be rendered
more extensively serviceable to
the Publick: And whereas by an Act made in the Twenty
first Year of the Reign of King James the First, intituled, An Act concerning Monopolies and Dispensations with
penal Statutes, and the Forfeitures thereof, it is provided,
That the said Act shall not extend to any Letters Patent,
or Grants of Privilege, of, for, or concerning Printing:
And whereas by an Act made in the Eighth Year of the
Reign of Queen Anne, intituled, An Act for the Encouragement of Learning, by vesting the Copies of printed Books
in the Authors or Purchasers of such Copies, during the Times
therein mentioned; it is enacted, That the Authors of Books
shall have the sole Right of printing and reprinting the
same, during the Terms by the said Act limited: And
whereas, though the Inventors of useful Arts deserve at
least equal Encouragement, yet the said John Byrom cannot, by the Authority of either of the said Acts, effectually

*Preamble,
reciting the
Acts 21 Jac. I.*

and 8 Ann.

7 3 2   secure

Figure 10: Act of Parliament for Byrom's shorthand

William was twenty-one. The Bill was even presented to the House of Lords close to when William became a member. In Byrom's eyes the timing could not be more auspicious.

However, whatever pleasure this association gave him, Byrom's memories of William were inevitably tainted with bitterness. As 'The Session of the Critics' shows, Byrom's ingenuous nature was viewed with contempt by some of his Cambridge contemporaries. Later, in one of his darker moods, Byrom drew a portrait of William in 'A Sov Delineated'. The picture is not flattering, and the first line of the poem recalls the slur against Byrom's own manhood:

> Six pounds of impotence at first began
> To form the mass and animate the man,
> Well weighed in scales of brass, for brass, you know,
> Strengthens the voice of mortal lives below.
> Impertinence by handfuls formed the paste
> To give the first dull lump a pungent taste.
> Two quarts of pride and patiently he takes,
> But first like Merlin quick the bottle shakes,
> That the dull seeds of innocence might arise
> To stamp the motley and enhance the prize.
> Three drams of wrangling for its own defence,
> Six grains of purity, scarce a grain of sense,
> In pity learning give to finish all,
> Each quantum sufficeth the doctor's call.
> Then beat together, through the medley of,
> And called the mighty composition Sov.

William Ward, who had published part of the shorthand supposedly without Byrom's permission, had in reality been instigated by Byrom himself, to strengthen the case for an act to protect his rights. The Wards were well known to Byrom; he had taught shorthand to several of them. However, the Act did not hasten publication. More pupils flocked to learn, but Byrom was in no mood to rush into print, although friends did manage to persuade him to have fifty copies privately printed in 1749. Three years later Byrom was still making excuses. Writing to John Houghton he said: 'My health and finances does [sic] not permit me to make promises that I cannot promise myself a fair certainty of fulfilling.'[1]

While the Shorthand Bill was going through Parliament, the Hartleys decided to leave London. Mrs Hartley's health had been uncertain since early in 1738 and the family decided to move to see if a change of environment would help. They chose Bath, still a fashionable resort for the sick and the centre of Dr Cheyne's practice. Hartley's decision to consult Cheyne is a clear indication of the nervous origin of his wife's illness. As was to be expected, the Hartleys and Cheyne became firm friends. Cheyne was now corresponding with Byrom, exchanging philosophical ideas and discussing in particular William Law. They had met originally in 1738 when John had taken his brother-in-law to Cheyne for a consultation. One of Cheyne's letters written in August 1742 contained a postscript written by Hartley. Already the Hartleys were missing Byrom and urging him to visit: 'What if you was to come to Bath, we should be heartily glad to see you if it suits your convenience ...'[2] By December the Hartleys had decided to settle permanently at Bath in a 'pleasant house in the New Square'.

Bath also acquired a more distinguished invalid – Lord Hervey. He had been dismissed from office in July and sought consolation and medical care from Cheyne's ministrations. Hervey claimed he lived the life of a recluse, conversing only with two people: his former schoolteacher, Dr Friend, and Dr Cheyne: 'with the first talk of books, with the last of health; and get instruction from both, at once improving my taste and constitution'.[3]

Cheyne's fashionable practice now contained two of Byrom's closest friends and the man who had replaced him in the affections of Caroline. Byrom became deeply concerned that Cheyne might have learned more from these people than was desirable. Among the unpublished poems in the manuscript book is one about Cheyne, cast in the form of an address and reply. Like many of Byrom's poems it circulated privately (the verses in italics sometimes omitted) and was attributed to a Dr Wynter. The complete version appears in the unpublished manuscript.

[From Dr B to Dr Cheney]
Tell me from whence fat-headed Scot
Thou didst thy system learn.
From Hippocrates thou had it not,
Nor Celsus, nor Pitcairn.

What? Tho' we grant that milk is good,
And say the same of grass,
The one for babes is proper food,
The other for an ass.

Doctor, one new prescription try,
(A friend's advice forgive),
Eat grass, reduce your bulk and die;
Your patients then may live.

[Dr Cheneys Reply]
My system, doctor's, all my own,
No others I pretend.
My blunders hurt myself alone,
But yours, your dearest friend. (hiccough by Dr Byrom)

Were you to milk and straw confined,
How happy might you be,
You might perhaps regain your mind,
And from your wit get free.

Your kind advice I cannot try,
But easily forgive.
It's natural you should bid me die,
That you yourself may live.

The unusual aside at the end of verse four hints at a more sinister meaning. The poem is part of the Caroline sequence and in it Byrom admits his fear that Cheyne might have discovered that Mrs Hartley's illness was caused by her well-intentioned but fatal recommendation of Ward's Drops to the Queen. It would not take him long to learn that Byrom had been behind the suggestion in the first place. The crucial lines come in Cheyne's 'reply': 'My blunders hurt myself alone,/But yours, your dearest friend.' Mrs Hartley was 'the dearest friend', suffering because of Byrom. If this fear was justified, then the genial Doctor was a danger to Byrom and would have to be silenced. That is the point of the paradox at the end: 'It's natural you should bid me die,/That you yourself may live.' Cheyne was already seventy-two and in the normal course of events would not be expected to live much longer. As it turned out he died not long afterwards on 13 April the following year.

The years 1742-3 saw the demise of a long list of people who had all, in one way or another, impinged on Byrom's life during the time he was close to Caroline. Some had been very close, others were linked more indirectly. But the cumulative effect was to create a void around past activities and ambitions. These deaths enabled Byrom to husband his remaining energies for fresh endeavours. Lord Hervey outlived Cheyne by only a few months. In addition to his influence with the Queen he had been very useful to Walpole, but he had always suffered from poor health and this had worsened since he went to Bath. By the middle of July he was dangerously ill and on 5 August 1743 he died. He was only forty-six.

In March Catherine, Duchess of Buckingham, had died. She was the ancient, illegitimate daughter of James II, and had lived in extravagant style at Buckingham House, fiercely proud of her royal origins. She had been a willing intermediary between Walpole and the Old Pretender in France, and one of the people who had helped the Hannoverian establishment keep abreast with the plottings of the exiled Stuarts. At one time she had seriously considered learning Byrom's shorthand, but, 'if she did, she wanted it kept secret'.

The old order was passing: first the Duchess of Buckingham and then, on 10 May, another ageing female, living in the shadows of seclusion, sickened and died. This was Melusina von der Schulenburg, the much-loathed mistress of George I. Popularly known as 'the Maypole', she was notorious for her greed. Walpole said that 'she would have sold the King's honour for a shilling advance to the best bidder'. While honest people had been ruined in the South Sea Bubble, she managed to make a fortune. Foreign, coarse and avaricious, Schulenburg symbolised all that was bad in the Hannoverian succession. She had managed to bring about a reconciliation between George I and his son, just at a time when the Jacobites were hoping to make capital out of that dissension. Worse still, she had survived George I's fatal journey to Hannover.

Autumn brought the end of one of the most formidable opponents of the Stuart cause – John Campbell, the second Duke of Argyll. He had served with the great Duke of Marlborough in the War of the Spanish Succession, and proved to be a very able and brave general. George I appointed him Commander in Chief of his army in Scotland to crush the Jacobite uprising in 1715. This he did with very little loss of life. Despite this success Argyll was suddenly deprived of his offices for no evident reason, and the Jacobites tried unsuccessfully to win him over to their side. He was soon restored to favour, however, and in 1718 became Steward of the Household. Unfortunately Argyll never achieved a political position worthy of his genuine abilities and by 1742 he had ceased to play an important part in politics. Incapacitated by paralysis, he died at Petersham in Surrey on 4 October 1743. Byrom would not regret Argyll's death, because of his suppression of the first Jacobite uprising; and his undoubted ability as a soldier would have made him a threat, even in an advisory capacity, to any future Jacobite venture.

Earlier, on 1 January 1742, Charlotte Clayton, Lady Sundon, died. Devoted to the Queen, she had been her closest confidante for many years, credited with bringing Alured Clarke and Stephen Duck to Caroline's attention. When Princess Amelia was ill, Caroline leaned heavily on Mrs Clayton, and it was to her that Caroline wrote of 'Mr. Freeman' when Byrom used that alias as her political reporter. It was a great pity that her own ill-health prevented her from being with Caroline when she was dying. Mrs Clayton's death was attributed to cancer of the throat. She, more than anyone, might have guessed the true nature of Byrom's relationship with the Queen.

In May 1742 Byrom's maternal uncle, William Chaddock, died. He had been a frequent and generous host to Byrom in his house in St Paul's Churchyard. The Chaddocks were friends of the de Vliegers, who, in turn, were near neighbours to Caroline when she had been living at Leicester House. They knew of Byrom's long-held interest in Ward's Drops. On 28 May Thomas Bentley died, the nephew of the great Master of Trinity and a great friend from Byrom's Cambridge days. He was very close to Byrom for a number of years and figures frequently in the Journals, being quick to notice little changes in Byrom's character: 'He said to me that I loved to ridicule more than I used to do.' Tom is mentioned in 'The Session of The Critics'.

Three days later, Dr Alured Clarke died. A prominent Whig clergyman and Chaplain to both George I and George II, he and Caroline got on well together and he visited her regularly. After her death he wrote a very fulsome elegy in which he went so far as to extol George's love for the Queen! On 14 July Richard Bentley, the Master of Trinity, died. As both his patron and friend, Bentley had at one time voiced uncomfortable suspicions of Byrom.

> When Dr. Walker went out for something, he asked me how many children I had and talked about the world; that the great men he had known had come to nothing, . . . [4]

Byrom watched Bentley become a great favourite with Caroline, and, although earlier he had been his champion, he resented this.

When the Bishop of Ely tried to remove Bentley from office, he was defended by Dr John Andrew, a cousin of Byrom's, and Anthony Sayer, the first Grand Master of the English Grand Lodge. Sayer also died in 1742.

In the middle of the summer, on 18 August, Darcy Lever of Alkrington died, a long-standing friend of Byrom who features often in the Journal from its beginning. Knighted in 1736/7 and at one time Sheriff of Lancashire, it was to him Byrom wrote suggesting he should remind Caroline how long Byrom had been working on his shorthand. That same year two of the Vernons died. Edward Vernon, the London merchant, at Aleppo, and Dr Thomas in London. Byrom knew both well. At Dr Vernon's chambers Byrom had approached Dr Smith to ask him to mention his shorthand to Prince William. Byrom also used his rooms in Cambridge the year he died. Another relative, Captain Vernon, was present at the famous meeting with the Duke of Devonshire in 1737. Finally, Dr Dover died in 1742. Privateer, physician and purveyor of Dover's Pills and Powders, he had discussed Ward's Pills with Byrom at great length.

When all these deaths in or around 1742 are listed they present a surprising pattern. Some might have been expected – the aged mistress of George I and the paralysed Duke of Argyll – but not all these men and women could be regarded as having come to the end of their expected span. Hervey was still young and so was Tom Bentley. When we consider the diverse group as a whole the unifying factor is their close connection with Byrom. Every one of them might embarrass him with knowledge of some part of his life he wished to keep hidden. Mrs Clayton was the woman closest to Caroline during her attachment to Byrom. Hervey had replaced Byrom in the Queen's affections . . . in short each knew more than was good for them.

For all these people to have died in the normal course of events in such a relatively short period of time was indeed highly convenient. There is no mention in Byrom's Journal of any epidemic sufficiently widespread in 1742 to account for the deaths. An outbreak of influenza throughout the country in March and April 1743 could have accounted for four deaths at the most – those of the Duchess of Buckingham, Dr Cheyne, Schulenburg and Hervey. All these deaths left Byrom able to breathe more freely, less constrained by fear of discovery, and better to plan his next move forward.

Since the 1720s the political scene had been largely dominated by Sir Robert Walpole. In 1741 he won another general election, but his position was seriously weakened. His strongest ally, Queen Caroline, was dead, and opposition had steadily grown. In February 1742 he was forced to resign after being beaten in the House of Commons in a vote which he chose to regard as one of confidence. Created Earl of Orford with an annual pension of £4,000, Walpole remained active in his retirement almost until his death.

In the spring of 1744 Walpole was attacked by an 'unremitting fever'.[5] On the advice of Sir Edward Hulse, First Physician to George II, he took 'bark', a medicine much favoured at the time. The treatment brought a temporary relief but further symptoms developed and the condition was diagnosed as 'nephritis'. Walpole decided to stay at home and rest in close retirement. Travelling now became extremely painful. Dr Ranby, Surgeon to George II, was convinced by his symptoms that Walpole was suffering from the stone. In July Walpole decided to move to his house at Houghton in Norfolk, where he kept himself 'as quiet as he possibly could',[6] travelling little and very carefully, to avoid further deterioration. At the beginning of November the King urged him to return to London. The journey took four days and was excruciatingly painful. Ranby was horrified by Walpole's worsening condition and Sir Edward Hulse was called in the day after Walpole returned to London. Hulse felt that the source of the disease lay in the kidneys. In this he differed from Ranby who remained convinced that 'the stone in the bladder was the sole cause of all this tragedy'. Walpole was opposed to surgery.

'A soft and diluting method was now again prescribed and pursued from 23 November to 15 December, the day Dr Jurin was first called to visit Walpole.'[7] Jurin was convinced there was a stone in the bladder, though he thought the kidneys might in some degree be affected as well. Because of Walpole's opposition to any form of surgery, more medicines were prescribed and administered under Jurin's supervision. By the beginning of February Ranby and one of Walpole's sons, Horace, had decided to keep a daily journal of treatment and response. Walpole's condition steadily declined and at one o'clock in the morning of 18 March 1745 he died. On 29 March, writing from the London home in Arlington Street, Horace Walpole told his friend Sir Horace Mann:

> . . . I begged your brother to tell you what it was impossible for me to tell you! You share nearly in our common loss. Don't expect me to enter at all upon the subject . . . A death is only to be felt never to be talked over by those it touches.[8]

It was Horace who had kept vigil in the house during Walpole's last illness and he was highly critical of the medicine administered to his father. With a layman's keen logic Horace questioned whether any medicine strong enough to dissolve the stone might not in the process do great harm to the internal organs. The consequences of the medicine had been a laceration such as Horace had feared, and Walpole's pain had been so great that for six weeks he had been drugged with opium.

After Walpole's death great controversy raged over his treatment. Dr Ranby published *A Narrative of the Last Illness of the Right Honourable Earl of Orford from May 1744 to the Day of his Death March 18th following.* This gave great offence to the physicians concerned, for in it Ranby utterly condemned the use of Lithontriptic Lixivium in treatment of the stone. An enquiry was held into the exact cause of Sir Robert's death. Suspicion fell most heavily on Jurin, for he had prescribed the powerful medicines which Ranby considered had contributed to the statesman's death. What basis was there for such a charge?

A graduate of Trinity College, and yet another of Bentley's distinguished protégés, Jurin has been described as one of the most learned men of his day. After a short period as Master of the grammar school at Newcastle-on-Tyne, he decided to take up medicine and made rapid and distinguished progress in his career. In London he soon gained a large medical practice and a considerable fortune. He was appointed Physician to Guy's Hospital when it opened in 1725 and held this office until 1732. Shortly before his death in 1750 he was elected President of the College of Physicians. He was one of Byrom's closest and most trusted friends since their days together at Cambridge.

Jurin suffered from gravel in the urine for some years. At first it was mild and he was able to clear it up easily, but in 1740 he, too, had a severe nephritic fit accompanied with frequent vomiting. This was followed by a stone passing into the bladder. Again he was able to clear up his symptoms, but they returned and he looked round for a more efficient form of treatment.

At this time a preparation by Mrs Joanna Stephens was being widely canvassed as a cure for gallstones. Hartley himself had taken it three years earlier and was so impressed by the relief he received that he was anxious to share his good fortune with others. Byrom had helped Hartley to prepare an act of Parliament to make known the medicine's content, and he attended the House of Commons on 14 June 1739 when the Bill was passed.

Mrs. Stephens's Bill being passed, there was a meeting of the trustees immediately, and she was ordered to give in the discovery of her medicines as soon as she could to the Archbishop of Canterbury, to be published in the Gazette. We have been (Mr. Hales the clergyman, and Mr. Roberts, apothecary with whom Mr. Lloyd lodged, Dr. Hartley and myself) putting her account in writing.[9]

Both Mr Hales and Dr Hartley carried out experiments to assess the relative value of each ingredient. It was natural that Jurin should also turn his attention to them. The conclusion of the public enquiry into Mrs Stephens's bizarre medicines was that they did have some merit and had a place in the treatment of stone, with certain provisos. An analysis of the medicines was presented in a paper to the Royal Society by Dr John Rutty in January 1741/2. Rutty was anxious to 'discourage a too great fondness of them, without detracting from their real merit'.[10] As a practical man of science Rutty maintained, 'It is not to be supposed that any remedy can be discovered of such universal use and efficacy in calculous cases that it ought to supersede the administration of all others.'[11] He also points out that there were several substances capable of dissolving stones. This had been demonstrated with stones outside the body. However, with shrewdness and caution, Rutty refused to commit himself in an area where there was a possibility of a serious margin of error:

> . . . since there is a great diversity in the several habits of the Body, and different Symptoms and circumstances which attend the disease passing under the same general name of the stone; it will still require the Sagacity of a Physician to determine which of these medicines is to be preferred . . . [12]

When it came to his own treatment Jurin showed a similar caution:

> Mrs. Stephens's medicines, I was sensible, had given great relief to many persons in my condition; and some numbers had to appearance been cured by them: But on the other hand, I considered, that of those who had died and been opened, after they were reported to be cured by taking her medicines, there had not been one, but what had a stone or stones found in the bladder. To this I added, that the number who had taken these medicines ineffectually, was very great . . .[13]

Rutty for his part concluded that Mrs Stephens's recipe contained several parts 'of little use and others plainly calculated to disguise the rest'.[14] Jurin had prepared his own version of Mrs Stephens's medicine, which he tried on himself for six months in 1740 with success. Yet, when he was called in five years later to treat Walpole he did not follow the same regime. The medicine Jurin administered to Walpole was a much stronger version of Mrs Stephens's and it was given in much heavier doses. Ranby pointed out in his *Narrative* that the dose of Lixivium was 'gradually increased to almost triple in quantity'. He calculated that Walpole had had at least thirty-six ounces of it.

More fuel was added to the controversy by the publication of an anonymous pamphlet which purported to list the charges against Doctors A, B, C, D, and E, F, 'for their treatment of one Robert of Orfud'. The allusion to Walpole was blatantly obvious. One of the charges made against the doctors was that 'the lick-liverium was potioned and prescribed into the deceased in very large quantities'.[15] Another stated that 'no man alive, unless one of the culprits, knows what this lick-liverium is'.[16] The final charge was 'that every man knows it did the disease no good, and therefore the long continuance of it was contrary to all good practice'.[17] It is obvious from all this that the circumstances of Walpole's death were viewed at the time with the greatest suspicion. That suspicion fell on Jurin, but he managed to avoid exposure because no-one was able to discover any motive.

An explanation for this is that no-one recognised the strength of Jurin's friendship with Byrom and the reason for it. Jurin appears in Byrom's Journal as early as 1723, when Byrom writes of going to see him at Tunbridge Wells to enlist him as a subscriber to his shorthand. Jurin was already Secretary to the Royal Society and the following year Byrom was elected. The Journal also records Jurin's attendance at the Sun Club from March 1726. The two men became such fast friends that they supported each other in their serious dispute with the Society in 1727. Jurin saw the sense of Byrom's complaints against Dr Ahlers. Similarly, when Jurin, as Secretary, asked for directions on whether foreign members were allowed to vote, Byrom supported him. Indeed, of all the members, Byrom alone came to his defence. Dr Bentley, their old Master, had been too cowardly to offer his support for fear of losing £500 a year. Jurin was deeply grateful to Byrom: 'Dr Jurin came to us, and told me that nobody had stood up for him but me.'[18] Behind the apparent disagreement over procedure lay the deeper division of politics. The

President of the Royal Society, Sir Hans Sloane, was a convinced Whig; Byrom, on the other hand, was a Tory. Both Jurin and Byrom were regarded with distrust, and when Jurin was dismissed, the President did not thank him for his services as Secretary. Their treatment by Hans Sloane remained a bond between Byrom and Jurin in the years to come.

It is well known that Walpole played a game of double bluff with the Jacobites. He would appear to encourage the hopes of the Pretender in order to pacify the Jacobite section of the Opposition. Lord Orrery, the Pretender's Secretary, is said to have received a pension of £2,000 a year from the English government. In this way Walpole obtained advance information of Jacobite plots. Horace Walpole in his *Memoirs* tells how Sir Robert was able to carry the Pretender's letters to his agents to George II. When the Jacobites in 1741 finally discovered that Walpole had been using them for his own ends, their fury led them to seek from the Pretender an order to remove him:

> Chesterfield was despatched to Avignon to solicit by the Duke of Ormonde's means an order from the Pretender to the Jacobites to concur roundly in any measures for Sir Robert's destruction.[19]

James Stuart, furious at having been cheated, issued his instructions. Coxe in his *Memoirs of Sir Robert Walpole* states: 'Letters from the Pretender were circulated among the Jacobites and High Tories, exhorting them to use all their efforts for the purpose of the disgrace of Sir Robert Walpole . . .'[20] This is confirmed in the letter of a friend to Walpole's brother:

> The Pretender, as this your great brother positively assured me, to his certain knowledge, sent at least a hundred letters, which were transmitted to his friends in November 1741. The purport of them was to engage them to use all possible endeavours in order to compass Walpole's demolition.[21]

In February 1742 Walpole resigned from office. Perhaps the Pretender's desire for the destruction of Walpole was interpreted too literally. The Opposition had alleged that Walpole had abused his power to make himself 'sole and prime minister' at the expense of his colleagues. The instruction from the Pretender, and his jealousy of Walpole's former influence with Caroline, would make Byrom welcome Walpole's death. Byrom himself had played an active but anonymous part in the promotion of Mrs Stephens's medicines, though he was careful not to put his name to the long list of sub-scribers he was supposedly helping to encourage. During the promotion of this treatment Byrom must have come to know the hazards and dangers inherent in it as well as the benefits claimed.

Dr Rutty, in his report to the Royal Society in January 1741/2, warned of the caustic quality of one of the ingredients in the medi-cine: 'If they are administered internally without the necessary precaution, they produce the most terrible effects; an instance of the truth of which was lately met with in this city; the powders ill pre-pared having been administered to a patient, threw him into strong convulsions.'[22] Furthermore he specifically warns that they were: 'inconvenient in ulcerations of the urinary passages', and served only to increase the pain. These dangers then were clearly known, well before Walpole's treatment, to the doctors and physicians of the Royal Society. In addition, some of Byrom's associates had also undergone Mrs Stephens's treatment with either unpleasant or fatal results – the Reverend Mr Lamplugh died in much the same drawn-out manner as Walpole. Blencowe also had first-hand knowledge of the pain these medicines could cause. Their cases were recorded when Dr Hartley was preparing evidence to obtain Mrs Stephens's medicines for the general public. Many others were printed where patients claimed benefit. But the hazards listed here, together with the serious dangers noted by Dr Rutty, are sufficient to show that, in sufficiently large quantities, the medicine would be fatal for someone with the physical weaknesses of Walpole. Byrom had the motive and the knowledge, and Jurin the means and the agent with which to remove Walpole. Despite Ranby's attack and the ensuing controversy, Jurin managed to escape prosecution and Byrom remained unnoticed in the background.

Mrs Stephens was only another in the long line of quacks who foisted their medicines on a credulous public, fearful and anxious for cures. Already by 1722 Parliament had decided it was time to take measures to protect the public. These had little effect, but in 1747 it was proposed to strengthen the power of the College of Physicians in their desire to prevent the sale of bogus cures. From now on the College was to elect each year 'ten sufficiently skilful persons' to be Examiners of Apothecaries. No person would be permitted to prac-tise the art of apothecary in London unless examined and approved by at least three of these examiners. Perhaps even more important, the examiners were empowered to enter any house where it was thought medicines were being made to examine any such 'compounds' and to destroy 'all such as they shall adjudge bad'. The need for such an act is a measure of the concern caused by the sufferings attributed to quack remedies.

The death of Walpole in 1745 removed Caroline's last and most powerful friend and ally. It has been said that Walpole 'knew the strength and weakness of everybody he had to deal with'. Byrom may well have felt that Walpole's departure was absolutely essential for the success of larger purposes.

CHAPTER ELEVEN

The '45

1745-9

AFTER THE RESTORATION of the Stuarts in the person of Charles II in 1660, the stability of the monarchy was bedevilled by the conflict between the Protestant settlement, so diligently worked for years earlier by Elizabeth I, and the later Stuarts' hankering for Roman Catholicism. Charles II, mindful of his eight years in exile, was prepared to work through Parliament, and concealed his Catholic sympathies until his death. James II, his brother, was, in the words of the Duke of Cumberland, 'a bigot to the Romish cause'.[1] His attempt to re-establish the Roman faith in this country led to widespread persecution and the ruthless suppression of Prot-estantism in an attempt to make himself an absolute monarch. Little wonder his reign lasted only three years. Replaced by Parliament with his son-in-law William of Orange and his eldest daughter, Mary – the child of his first wife, Anne Hyde – James was forced to flee. His defeat at the battle of the Boyne in a final attempt to regain the throne left William and Mary to become in reality the first con-stitutional monarchs, and the wasteful struggle between Crown and Parliament was finally brought to an end. Since William and Mary had no children, the throne passed to another Protestant daughter of James II, Mary's younger sister, Anne. She reigned for twelve years but none of her seventeen children survived. Therefore the Act of Succession (1701) ensured that the crown passed to the nearest Prot-estant relative from the family of the Elector of Hannover.

But Queen Anne had a half-brother, James Edward Stuart, child of James II's second marriage to Mary of Modena. As a Catholic he maintained his claim to the English throne from the safety of France, and first attempted to regain the throne from George I in 1715. This was badly bungled and a disaster for James. Nevertheless plans were repeatedly made to win back the English throne, but were thwarted by lack of money and dissension among the English

Jacobites. In the end James Edward lost interest and his supporters looked to his son, Prince Charles Edward, as their hope for the Catholic restoration. They had forgotten how inept the Stuart kings had been and still clung to the old belief in the 'divine right' of the Stuart succession.

The second attempt to regain the throne was by Prince Charles Edward in 1745, by then a young man of twenty-four. However, plans were laid before then, and there is evidence that the Young Pretender visited Manchester secretly the year before as part of his preparations.

This visit is described by Sir Oswald Mosley, in his *Family Memoirs*. Oswald was the traditional family name for the eldest son and the Sir Oswald Mosley of 1744 had 'imbibed from earliest infancy a high notion of the divine right of kings, and he was by no means favourable to the changes ... by which the House of Hannover had been placed upon the throne ...'[2] The memoir refers to the risk Sir Oswald ran by having 'the exiled claimant to the throne ... under the roof of Ancoats Hall in the summer previous to the Rebellion of 1745'. Although Sir Oswald (then about seventy-one) carefully avoided playing an open part in 1745 when the Prince arrived in Manchester, the memoir maintains:

> there is no reason to doubt that a secret correspondence had been carried out between him and some of the leaders of this rebellious attempt, in which Ancoats Hall was offered as a temporary asylum, to the grandson of James II.[3]

Because this secret visit had been unnoticed by historians, the memoir recounts the story's source in some detail.

It was told in 1815 by an elderly woman of eighty-four who still retained a vivid memory of her early years in Manchester when her father, a man called Bradbury, kept the principal inn in the town – the Bull's Head, which had long been a meeting place for Stuart sympathisers.

> In the summer of the year before the Rebellion, or as she used to say, before the Highlanders arrived from Scotland, a handsome young gentleman came every post-day for several weeks in succession from Ancoats Hall, the seat of Sir Oswald Mosley, where he was on a visit, to her father's house to read the newspapers. He appeared to hold no communication with any one else, but to take great interest in the perusal of the London news. She saw him fre-

quently, and could not help admiring his handsome countenance and genteel deportment; but she particularly recollected that on the last day that he came to her father's house, he asked for a basin of water and a towel, which she herself brought up, and that after he had washed himself he gave her half a crown. This circumstance was sure to make an impression upon the mind of a girl of her tender years [she was thirteen], and it caused her to take a still more attentive survey of his face and person.

In the following year, when the rebel army marched into the town, as she stood with her father at the inn door, the young prince passed by on foot at the head of his troops, and she immediately exclaimed, 'Father, father! that is the gentleman who gave me the half-crown!' Upon which, her father drove her back into the house, and with severe threats desired her never to mention that circumstance again, which threats he frequently repeated after the retreat of the Scotch army, if ever she divulged the secret to anyone.[4]

Years later when 'the fear of being charged with high treason' had subsided, her father, a zealous Jacobite, admitted that the young visitor from Ancoats had been the Prince.

It is evident that preparations had been going on in Manchester for some considerable time. According to the Broughton Manor Court records, John Byrom became Steward of the Manor, although the date given, 'about 1703', is far too early to be accurate. Later, Byrom's friend James Chetham succeeded his father George as Lord of the Manor in 1729, the very year Thomas Siddal took over the tenancy of one of the Manor farms. Siddal kept it until 1745, when he took on the more strategic post of 'Scavenger' or Inspector of Nuisances in the Market Place district of Manchester. There the Lord of the Manor was Sir Oswald Mosley and the activist Siddal's appointment is another sign of Mosley's involvement behind the scenes even at the advanced age of seventy-one.

For his part, Byrom in 1744 and early 1745 was visiting a number of towns in the North. Letters to his wife in January 1743/4 show he was travelling in Yorkshire to Halifax, Leeds, Beeston and York. In the autumn he was touring Derbyshire – Ashbourne, Buxton, Derby, Donington Park and Matlock. Some of the visits were ostensibly to teach his shorthand, others were social calls. His hosts were prominent figures among the local gentry or leading clergymen. But remembering Byrom's alleged role as the Master-Tool of the

Jacobite faction in Manchester, some of his time was no doubt given over to surveying the districts through which he travelled and assessing the likely support for the coming insurrection.

Prince Charles Edward landed on the island of Eriskay on 23 July 1745. On 19 August the Royal Stuart standard was raised at Glenfinnan, Loch Shiel. With nearly 2,000 Highlanders he made his way to Edinburgh through Dunkeld, Perth and Stirling. Edinburgh fell on 17 September and the same day, the Old Pretender was proclaimed James VIII of Scotland and James III of England. Four days later the Scots inflicted a humiliating defeat on the Hannoverian troops under Sir John Cope at Prestonpans, a victory immortalised in the poem 'Hey, Johnnie Cope, are ye wauking yet?' In victory Charles was magnanimous and humane to the enemy wounded, whom he regarded as his father's subjects – a trait which won him the devotion of his followers. The government in London was alarmed and placed several regiments under the command of the young Duke of Cumberland who was recalled from Holland, and ordered Marshal Wade of Newcastle to prevent the Jacobites from marching south. Charles lingered in Edinburgh for five weeks, denounced the Act of Union and promised a reign of religious tolerance. On 1 November the Prince set out for England and speedily occupied Carlisle (15 November), then Lancaster (25 November), Preston (26 November), Manchester (29 November) and Derby (4 December). His army had advanced 300 miles in thirty days' marching, a remarkable feat for the time – evidence that the Prince was right to make his way to London down the *west* coast. Proof perhaps, too, that Byrom and the Jacobite espionage network had done their work well.

It is an extraordinary reflection either on Byrom or his editors that the only entry in his Journal in which he writes of the '45 is a brief note on a Highlander who slept in an outhouse at his home, and on the billeting on him of one of the English officers, Lord Lempster. Either Byrom did not make any further entries or none was to be included in the printed Journal for these momentous weeks. Fortunately his daughter Beppy wrote her own vivid and direct impressions of what was happening in Manchester.[5] Her father was at home during those months. Beppy's diary commences on cue on 14 August with the news that the Pretender was on his way. An announcement of the government defeat at Prestonpans reached the town on 26 September. By 8 October she is writing 'everybody in hiding for fear of the rebels'. In her enthusiasm

Beppy, now aged twenty-three, bought a blue and white gown, the Jacobite colours, to celebrate. The Presbyterians, fearing the worst, started to evacuate their families and goods. Lord Derby arrived to put the town in readiness, as daily bulletins brought news of the progress south of the Scots. By 26 November, the day Prince William, the Duke of Cumberland left St James's in London, Manchester was deserted; 'there is hardly any family left but ours and our kin'. With shops shut and almost empty, the postmaster left next day to prevent his money from falling into the hands of the rebels. That night the Young Pretender slept in Preston, having marched at the head of his army all the way from Carlisle dressed in 'Scotch plaid, a blue silk waistcoat with silver lace, and a Scottish bonnet with J.R. on it'.

By Thursday 28 November Cumberland had reached Lichfield, and the Scots made their famous entry into Manchester:

> about three o'clock today came into town two men in Highland dress, and a woman behind one of them with a drum on her knee, and for all the loyal work that our Presbyterians have made, they took possession of the town as one may say, for immediately after they were 'light, they were beat up for volunteers for P.C.[6]

Among those ready to enlist were Dr Deacon's son Thomas, Thomas Siddal junior, and William Dawson's son James. Commissions in the Manchester Regiment were organised at the Dog Inn, Acres Court. James Dawson and Thomas Deacon each paid £50 to be captains and Dawson soon took his place as a recruiting officer at the Bull's Head, entering the names of volunteers, presenting them with the King's shilling and the blue and white cockade. Siddal hurried to the Dog Inn and, at the mature age of thirty-six, was appointed Ensign in the company to be commanded by Deacon.

As a young man Siddal had been barber-surgeon to the singing men at the Collegiate Church in Manchester; he was also a peruke-maker, a profession which made him relatively prosperous, for at one time he was said to be worth £2,000. In Easter 1745 he had given up the tenancy of his farm just north of the town when he was appointed Scavenger for the district around his home. It was an unpaid post which gave him the authority to ensure the locality was kept orderly and clean, with licence to wander at will and investigate what he thought fit. These duties took precedence over the farm. Siddal was required in the town to prepare for the second Jacobite uprising of 1745, and, as the zealous son of an equally zealous

Figure 11:
Bull's Head Yard

Jacobite, was undoubtedly seen as a valuable recruiting agent for
Stuart supporters in the town.

   Byrom's son Edward, although twenty-one years old, did not enlist. By eight o'clock more than eighty men had joined up. Byrom
brought news to his family that some men on horseback had arrived,
and he took Beppy up to the Market Cross to watch since it was 'a
very fine moonlight night'. These were part of Lord Pitsligo's troop
of horse. By now all the magistrates had fled and with them all the
lawyers except Byrom's cousin Jo Clowes. Byrom gathered with
other men of substance to decide how 'to keep themselves out of
any scrapes and yet behave civilly'. Recruiting continued the following morning and Beppy was out at the Cross again to see the rest of
the Highlanders arrive. At about o'clock the Prince came in with the
main body of his men, accompanied by the Dukes of Atholl and
Perth. It was not long before the volunteers were put to work. The
Prince, having no printing press with him, required handbills and
other propaganda material to be printed quickly and ordered a local
printer to do the work, which was done so slowly that Captain
Deacon and Ensign Siddal took a file of men and visited him to

issue threats of burning his place down if the order was not carried
out speedily. The Prince took up residence at the house of a Mr
Dickenson, the church bells were rung, bonfires lit, proclamations
made and all the town lit up. Beppy, along with her parents and
sister Dolly, walked up and down to see the spectacle. James Stuart
was proclaimed King and the family adjourned to the house of
Byrom's sister, Sarah Brearcliffe, where the women sat happily
making St Andrew's crosses until eleven o'clock. On her return
home Beppy continued making them until two in the morning and
again the next day. For her, the uprising was like an exciting play.
An officer called at the Brearcliffes' (where Beppy had returned
dressed in her blue and white gown) to take them to see the Prince –
the star of the play. She was breathless with adoration, seeing

> him get a-horse-back, and a noble sight it is, I would not have
> missed it for a great deal of money; his horse had stood an hour in
> the court without stirring, and as soon as he got on he began
> a-dancing and capering as if he was proud of his burden, and
> when he rid out of the court he was received with as much joy and
> shouting almost as if he had been a king without any dispute, in-
> deed I think scarce any body that saw him could dispute it.[7]

Still accompanied by the officer, aunt and niece went to a nearby
house to see if they could catch another glimpse of their hero:
'Secretary Murray came to let us know that the P was at leisure and
had done supper, so we were all introduced and had the honour to
kiss his hand.'[8] Byrom was not with them, but, when summoned,
put on a careful show of reluctance. 'My papa was fetched prisoner
to do the same, as was Dr Deacon . . .' The next day, 1 December,
the Prince set out on foot once more, watched, as one might expect,
by the devoted Beppy.

With the Scots went the newly formed Manchester Regiment,
never more than 300 strong, of whom it is said only 28 were Manchester Men, many drawn from the congregation of Dr Deacon,
who himself provided three sons, Thomas, Robert and Charles.
There were twenty officers in all, and the regiment was commanded
by Colonel Francis Towneley, a Lancashire man of good family
who had served with distinction for sixteen years in the French
army. He joined the rebels at Preston, and on arriving in Manchester
was appointed Colonel by the Young Pretender. The regiment was
drawn up for review by the Prince in the Collegiate churchyard and
Towneley led them forth to Derby, with the regimental flag bearing

the words Liberty and Property on one side and Church and Country on the other.

Meanwhile the Jacobite espionage network was still in operation in the North and Byrom maintained covert connection with it. An unpublished diary entry for 1730 records the name R. Jackson with the Jacobite Henry Salkeld having a private meeting with Byrom at the King's Arms in London. Now, in 1745, a Manchester man named Richard Jackson, who travelled to and from Scotland, supposedly on business, came under suspicion for his activities. He was known to have been in Scotland the weekend of 21 September when the government forces were defeated at Prestonpans. He was arrested in Cumberland shortly after for sending a letter to a former Jacobite, David Campbell, who had been involved in the 1715 uprising. The letter contained a brief account of the battle, referring to it as a 'victory' and to Charles Edward as the 'prince' not the 'pretender'. Jackson went on to ask Campbell to 'delay no time in goeing where you promised me and beg you'l send a special messenger to me at home . . . and I'l come to you . . . '[9]

All this looked very suspicious to the authorities who questioned both Jackson and Campbell, concluding that Jackson was probably one of the Manchester Jacobites liaising with the insurgents through Campbell. According to State Papers Domestic both men were charged upon suspicion of High Treason, and Campbell was probably tried, although records of his trial have not been found.[10] Jackson, released on bail like Campbell, forfeited his sureties by not surrendering at Cockermouth on 15 January 1746. Beppy Byrom in her diary for 11 January refers to an 'R Jackson' as one of 'our Manchester Men' and there was an 'R Jackson' in the Manchester Regiment. Beppy writes: 'Our Manchester Men who were at Carlisle (except Mr J Bradshaw and Mr R Jackson) are taken to York . . .' It seems likely that both references are to the same man. The absence from Carlisle and non-appearance at Cockermouth may be linked. Certainly what happened to Jackson in the end remains a mystery, but the authorities were right to suspect the existence of a network between the border region and Manchester.

That same November a grocer from Cockbridge near Cockermouth, Peter Pattinson, had travelled from Brampton to the Shropshire/Cheshire border with Wales and delivered a letter on 16 November to Lord Buttevant, son of the Earl of Barrymore, the acknowledged head of the English Jacobites.[11] The letter was written as though from Brampton by Prince Charles Edward and expressed the hope that 'all my friends in that county [Cheshire] will be ready to join us. For the time is now or never'. Angry and anxious not to incriminate his family, Lord Buttevant decided to report the matter to the Magistrates at Northwich, Pattinson was arrested and questioned. He claimed he had been travelling on business to Hexham to collect a debt, was intercepted by Highlanders, and taken to a house where 'the Pretender or his son was'. He was then told he would be set free if he would deliver a message on his way to London. Having agreed to do so because of his family and business, he set out with a travelling companion, Thomas Newby, a builder, to avoid suspicion of being found riding solo through the countryside at a time of unrest. Pattinson held to his story under repeated questioning, but was sent on to London for further interrogation with Newby and Lord Buttevant. There it emerged that it was not he who was the grocer but his wife. He had to explain how he had come to be at Brampton in the first place, and concocted the story that, hearing there were Highlanders in the area, he had gone to see them out of idle curiosity. Under further questioning it emerged that 'Since the age of eighteen he had been servant to Thomas Salkeld of Whitehall, near Wigton, and since his master's death, to his late master's brother, Henry Salkeld.' While unable to extract much more, the government prosecutors considered him an important catch and he was spared transportation. However, the charges against him were eventually allowed to drop for lack of sufficient evidence, according to a note in the Secretary of State's papers, and Pattinson was discharged on 12 November. By 18 November he had disappeared. Pattinson's link with the Salkeld family is very significant, for another servant of Salkeld's also fell under suspicion as a messenger of treasonable matter.

Henry Salkeld was apparently living quietly at home in Cumberland away from all involvement in the uprising. But in January 1746 an order was issued for the arrest of one of his servants, Anthony Sims, described as a 'spy of the Pretender'. According to an account left by Sir John Macdonald, a French citizen in the circle of Charles Edward:

As soon as we arrived at Brampton, a Catholic gentleman named Sawel [Salkeld] who had property in the neighbourhood, went to Strickland, who was a relative of his wife, to know whether his services would be agreeable, as in that case he would join the Prince. Strickland considered that as the gentleman was alone and infirm, he had better remain at home, especially as the weather was then very warm. The man who brought the message to Strickland at Brampton seeming to me to be zealous and intelligent, I asked him if he thought he could penetrate further into England.[12]

It would appear that Sims was in some way involved in passing the message on to Pattinson, who rode south to Cheshire while Sims was arrested and thrown into Newcastle gaol. Salkeld had tried to be circumspect throughout. Because of his estate he was obliged by law to contribute to the local militia, and he took care to nominate Sims as a 'rider', but this cover had proved insufficient and, fearing for his own safety, Salkeld went to Carlisle to clear his name. While he was there, the city fell to the Scots and, ironically, Salkeld was in danger of being imprisoned by them. Fortunately Strickland intervened on his behalf. Later Strickland fell ill, and in return for his help, Salkeld, who had formerly practised as a doctor, attended him – with the permission of the local justices. However, when Cumberland arrived in the city, Salkeld was imprisoned without being charged, and held for seven months. As late as July 1746 the government hoped to be able to make a case against him, but were forced to release him. Salkeld died in 1749. It is quite clear from his Journal that Byrom had been closely associated with members of the Salkeld family for at least eighteen years; and, as the leading underground Jacobite in Manchester, Byrom would inevitably be fully aware of Salkeld's real role.

It was not long before Manchester was rife with rumours of setbacks for the Prince and of his impending return. Stories were told of his magnanimity and compassion, his refusal to set fire to Edinburgh. A solitary Highlander left behind was taken prisoner by the 'Presbyterian' faction and, with news of the arrival of Marshal Wade at Rochdale, a mob gathered in the streets of Manchester threatening the houses of those who had joined the rebels. Byrom and several others tried to pacify them, but not before the mob had succeeded in smashing Dr Deacon's windows. Responsible citizens decided to set up a patrol 'to walk the streets to keep quiet' for the next week. On 6 December when the Scots were forced to retreat from Derby, Siddal was one of the officers sent on to Manchester to try to enlist more men to help. However, they were expected and Siddal was caught by the mob and chased down Market Street into St Ann's Square where he 'quit his mare' and gave them the slip. He found that the mob had broken the windows of his house with his wife and children indoors. By 9 December further measures were necessary to counter unrest and a proclamation was made in the name of His Royal Highness Charles Prince of Wales that: 'no two persons be seen walking together in the streets after nine o'clock tonight except they be guarded by some of H.R.H. own troops . . . '[13]

Lord Pitsligo sent for Byrom. Baron Forbes of Pitsligo was sixty-seven at the time and highly respected for his wisdom and prudence. His decision to join the Young Pretender persuaded 160 men from the countryside around to join forces with him. His meeting with Byrom at the Boroughreeve's house would have been to discuss Jacobite business for, interestingly, Byrom omits to mention it in his lengthy letter about these events to Mr Vigor.

On 10 December news reached Manchester that Cumberland would arrive next day. The following morning started with the church bells ringing – this time in expectation of the Duke, and the bellman went round town to appeal for provisions for his army. The townsfolk, however, were disappointed – or relieved – for the Duke was delayed, and the bellman went round town again telling people not to light up their houses yet. Next day, 12 December, Edward Byrom came to fetch his sister to see the Duke. They went up to

Figure 12: Dr Thomas Deacon's house

Aunt Brearcliffe's grand house in Spring Gardens and waited all day in vain. Cumberland had chosen another route north, through Warrington. Edward Byrom had been noticeably absent at the arrival of the Pretender, but, with the revival of the government's fortunes, displayed his Whig sympathies more openly. When Beppy returned home she found that Lord Lempster, the only son of the Earl of Pomfret, who had been Master of Horse to the late Queen Caroline, had been billeted on her father with another officer, Lieutenant Harris. Lempster was the same age as Cumberland and, since his father had been in Caroline's service, the two boys had grown up together as firm friends.

Both appear as young children in Hogarth's painting *The Conquest of Mexico*. The setting is the home of John Conduitt, Master of the Mint, who is giving a party in 1731 for the ten-year-old Duke and his younger sisters, the Princesses Mary and Louisa. Peter Quennell gives an illuminating description of the occasion in his life of Hogarth. The royal children 'are being entertained by a group of spirited young actors, Miss Conduitt, Lord Lempster and Lady Sophia Fermor, son and daughter of Lord Pomfret, and Lady Caroline Lennox, daughter of the Duke of Richmond; while, in Mr Conduitt's fine drawing-room (possibly the work of Kent) adorned with family-portraits of the previous age and Roubiliac's bust of Sir Isaac Newton, Mr Conduitt's uncle by marriage, upon the lofty chimney-piece, the actors' parents and the royal Governor and Governess, Mr Poyntz and Lady Deloraine, sit complacently surveying the show. The play that the children have selected, or that has been selected for them, is Dryden's recently revived tragedy, *The Indian Emperor or the Conquest of Mexico by the Spaniards*, and, as we learn from the prompt book held by Dr Desaguliers, they have already arrived at Act IV, Scene IV, where Cortez is "discovered bound" and the rival princesses, Cydaria and Almeria, engage in a lengthy debate across the captive conqueror's person.'

In the scene being enacted Cortez protests to Cydaria the sacrifices he has made on her behalf: 'Life, freedom, empire, I at once refused;/And would again ten thousand times for you' – words that, allowing for dramatic hyperbole, recall Byrom's sacrifices for Caroline in forfeiting all personal ambition in his devotion to her. Only the previous year, with his appointment as Vice-Chamberlain, Hervey had been able to assert his supremacy in Caroline's affections over any other rival, so this scene has an ironic poignancy in its

application to Byrom at this time. The relationship was truly at an
end. Yet here the offspring of that relationship is standing before the
fire-place, watching his friend Lempster declaim Cortez's lines.
Years later, Byrom had that same friend billeted on him in Manchester. The friendship of the Duke and Lempster had continued
down the years until they were comrades-in-arms. Hogarth was
born in St Bartholomew's Close, the son of a struggling school-
master, Richard. Later the family moved to Clerkenwell, where, in
addition to his school in Old Bailey, Richard ran a coffee house in
part of St John's Gate, once the main entrance to the Priory of Clerkenwell, the administrative headquarters of the Knights Hospitaller
of St John in England. (Today, after a chequered history, it is the
official HQ of the Venerable Order of St John of Jerusalem in this
country.) William Hogarth was a freemason, and *The Conquest of
Mexico* contains a number of masonic and Royal Society associations. The prompt for the young actors was Byrom's prominent
masonic friend Desaguliers who had praised him for his cleverness.
The bust above the fire-place invokes the brooding presence of
Newton, and Lady Caroline Lennox serves as a reminder of
Byrom's friendship with her father, the Duke of Richmond, another
notable freemason. The painting, one of Hogarth's great conversation pieces, is peculiarly rich in Byrom associations. Owned for
generations by the Earls of Ilchester, descendants of Stephen Fox,
the object of Hervey's devotion, it has now passed into another
private collection but the richness of its resonances has grown with
the new information that has emerged about the small, but striking,
central figure in the audience.

In her Journal of the '45, Beppy Byrom makes one comment
on the presence of Lempster and Lieutenant Harris in Byrom's
house: 'they are very civil, they have their man and two horses
here'. Byrom allowed himself to say a little more in a later letter to
Mr Vigor:

> . . . we treated them the best we could; and his lordship being a
> remarkably good classic scholar, we passed the time in very good
> humour and were pleased with our lot.[14]

Byrom's reticence is understandable but Lempster's choice of billet
was no accident. Who was responsible for this arrangement? Byrom
knew his father when he was Master of Horse and, just as he had got
to know all William's tutors, Byrom would know Pomfret's son.
Advantages came from those earlier days; no-one would doubt the

loyalty of the man whose praises had been sung at the Duke's sixteenth birthday celebrations. To Lempster, Byrom would appear to be one of the most reliable sources of intelligence in the north-west, and he sought him out as such. The '45 brings Byrom's double role as a Jacobite and government agent out of the shadows into sharp focus. He is dragged ostentatiously into the presence of the Young Pretender, while fully cognisant of the espionage network working on his behalf. He gives up his bed to a leading government officer, houses a Highlander in his stable and has private conversations with a leading Jacobite officer, Pitsligo. Almost symbolically, Byrom's double standards split in two with his offspring – Beppy makes her white cockades and Edward waits to cheer the Duke. Byrom's guests stayed two nights. Sunday the 15th was the first quiet day the Byrom household had experienced for a while.

Two days earlier, Cumberland had reached Preston a few hours after it had been left by the retreating Scots. Rumours proliferated: the Duke's army was about to return, an invasion of London was imminent. Amid all the uncertainty, Byrom's daughter Dolly continued with her acts of kindness to eighteen Highlanders imprisoned in the town, making sure they had meat every day. By the end of December Charles Edward had retreated back to Scotland, leaving the Manchester Regiment, which had been losing men through desertion for some time, to guard the city of Carlisle.

On New Year's Day fresh government troops arrived in Manchester under the command of the Marquis of Grenville. The anti-Jacobite feeling was running high and Dr Deacon fared so badly that he was forced to leave the town.

The town awoke on 2 January to the ringing of church bells to announce that Carlisle had fallen. All the townsfolk were ordered to illuminate their windows and a great bonfire was alight all day. The Manchester Regiment, now reduced to 114 men, together with some reinforcements from the Duke of Perth's Highlanders, could not withstand four hours of savage artillery, and, although Siddal and Colonel Towneley were prepared to die fighting, the garrison governor capitulated. All the rebels were imprisoned in Carlisle Cathedral. In Manchester the next day the Whig mob carried two effigies of Prince Charles Edward through the town. Beppy recounts their antics with scorn, telling how they:

> went to all the houses in town where any were gone from and broke their windows although lighted, and a great many more

besides that were not thick enough; they were very rude, and they carried their bunch of rags down to Mr Dukinfield's, and the Justice, out of his great courage, got a gun and shot at it, and then it was brought into the house and he wrung it by the nose, then his wife and daughter were introduced and had the honour to slap it in the face, and so on till they were all tired and drunk; for all the heads of the Presbyterians were at the Angel and gave the mob drink; then they hung it upon the signpost, then quartered it, then threw it into the fire; somebody threw a piece of it into the drink, which put them into a violent passion.[15]

Several people protested about such behaviour and Lady Lever complained at the damage done to Dr Deacon's house, which she owned. She got little sympathy from the local justices and was told to get rid of Deacon as he was unwelcome in the town. Not surprisingly, the Dawson's house, once the refuge of Barbara Fitzroy, was also damaged. Byrom in his letter to Vigor commented dryly 'The good folks who deserted the town upon their return home grew rather too valiant when the enemy was gone, and too angry at their neighbours who stayed.'[16]

The Highlanders in their retreat gave no cause for alarm – as Byrom noted they 'did not execute their wrath upon anything but meat and drink'. Dolly had raised four pounds to give the prisoners before they were transferred to Lancaster, and, despite all the turmoil, one Highlander managed to write to thank her for her kindness. Rumours abounded about an imminent French invasion, but at this point Beppy's account nears its end. On 21 January she is staying in the country, hunting and enjoying 'good sport', while in Manchester the Whigs were waiting the final victory.

The single entry about the '45 in Byrom's Journal concerns a Highlander who sheltered in his stable:

> Morton Hall, Nov, 4th, 1745. These do certify that the bearer, Alexander Macdonald, was a guard to my house at Morton Hall till this day, and is desirous to be directed forward to his country people wherever they are, because he cannot speak English. —— James D.

This note I copied from a paper which the little Highlander who came on Saturday morning to roast a piece of flesh by our fire had by him; he had three guineas quilted in the flap of his waistcoat, and one he showed me, asking if it was a good one as well as he could, for he had but very few English words; he lay in the stable, behaved very quietly, so we let him stay; said he would call upon us at his return from London to —— but we saw him no more when they all returned from Derby and were pursued by the Duke of Cumberland, when Lord Lempster and Mr. Harris lay at our house two nights, and were very civil, and had a very orderly servant, who lay in Ellen Bank's bed, my Lord in ours, and Mr. Harris in Beppy's; and two horses.[17]

Apart from this, Byrom wrote a letter in shorthand to his friend Vigor in which he describes some of the events in Manchester. It is dated 1 March 1746, Caroline's birthday, and was delivered by Byrom's trusted Cambridge friend Dr Taylor, the man he came to call the 'Vice-Master' of his shorthand society. Vigor was 'Warden' of the shorthand group in Bristol.

I thought that I should have seen you at London long before now, but the occurrences of life have obliged me to stay in the country, where a new scene of affairs has laid the same embargo upon me this winter; you will easily judge that I mean the progress of the Highland army through this place, with which, if London itself was alarmed, it is no wonder that we were so also. As they came forward, the apprehension of our people increased, a great many of them left the town and sent away their effects, and some their provisions, their bread and their cheese and their liquor, which exporting of what we and our expected visitors might want was put a stop to in some measure by sending the bellman to prohibit it. We were told one morning that they were gone to Liverpool, but it was false intelligence, for that day about noon there came a sergeant and a drummer in a Highland dress, with a woman on horseback carrying a drum, which they beat up, soon after their arrival, for volunteers. My curiosity led me to my sister's window at the Cross, where I beheld this extraordinary event of two men and a half taking our famous town of Manchester without any re-sistance or opposition, which I suppose the apprehension of the rest being at their heels might inspire us, however courageous, with the prudence not to make. That night there came in a party of horse, and the next day the whole army. The Prince (for so he has been called in all places when present, or near it, but, at a proper distance, Pretender) came in about noon, walking in a Highland habit, in the middle of a large party, and went to Mr. Dickenson's house, which his —— had that morning ordered for his lodging after viewing some others, which, for some reason or

other, they did not like so well. The officers and the men were
sent up and down to the several houses; they did not take their
billets from the constables, which made the distribution not so
equal, some having more than their share and others less, and
some houses both public and private through mistake, none at all;
amongst which ours had the fortune to be one, my name I suppose not being in the town books, being no proprietor, or not
coming within their information, so that we had only a single
Highlander, who came into the house of himself, and, behaving
civilly, we entertained him civilly, and he was content to lie in the
stable during their stay. The town was exceeding still and quiet.
The day that the Prince came in the proclamation of his father was
read at the Cross, and the two constables were forced to be there,
and one of them to repeat the words. I came by as they were at it,
but there was no great crowd or hurry about it nor any soldiers,
only an officer or two, who I suppose performed this ceremony
wherever they came. It was easy enough for friend or foe that was
curious enough to see the Prince, to have an opportunity; he rode
through the streets the day after his coming, and to do justice to
his person, whatever his pretensions may be, he makes a very
graceful and amiable appearance; he is fair complexioned, well
shaped, has a sensible and comely aspect. To account for the
beauty of the man beyond that of his father, his enemies said here
that he was the son of a very handsome pastry cook, some say
bread baker, at Paris; but the ladies, smitten with the charms of
the young gentleman, say that he takes after his mother.

There were about thirty of our neighbours that listed under
him, among whom three sons of poor Dr. Deacon, who engaged
without their father's consent as I am told, and two of them without his knowledge; his own opinion he never made any secret of,
but has done nothing in his own person that his enemies can lay
hold of him for, though they are much disposed to do it; he has
lost his lady, who died not long since, and his second son is just
dead, in conveying him from Carlisle, where he was taken with
his brothers, who are (in) London, so that his misfortune does not
want any aggravation.

The second night our town was ordered to be illuminated, but
there was no mobbing till the return of the Highlanders from
Derby, where to my surprise they ventured and came back again.
This first returning party was about thirty horse, which passed by
our house, coming into the town that way, and the foolish mob

clodded them with dirt or stones, and then I thought there would have been mischief done, but there was not. They all came in that night, and the next day laid a mulct of £5000 upon the town for the mobbing, which was moderated to half the sum, and raised with much ado. The Duke of Cumberland was expected here for three nights, and a vast mob from all parts to receive him, but he went another way, and the mob which rose soon after the Highlanders were gone did much less mischief than I expected; they broke Dr. Deacon's lamp and windows and some others upon an illumination night on the other side, for bells and candles were ready to ring and shine on all sides. I had Lord Lempster and an officer of his acquaintance and their servant and two horses quartered upon me for two nights, and we treated them the best we could; and his lordship being a remarkably good classic scholar, we passed the time in very good humour and were pleased with our lot. The good folks who deserted the town upon their return home grew rather too valiant when the enemy was gone, and too angry at their neighbours who stayed, and, if I may judge for myself, did what they could that they should suffer as little as possible by their business, which much exasperated the Highlanders, who threatened some of their houses, but did not execute their wrath upon anything but meat and drink, so that we had some reason upon the whole to be very thankful. Cousin D(awson) was here some days ago very well; she was ill at the last illumination, and her room not being illuminated for that reason, the windows were punished a little. A Highlander was shot upon the road by a fellow that for no reason but his being one, killed him as he was passing with some others; a butcher was killed in the same manner by a fellow that took him for a Highlander; nobody else killed about us on this occasion, which we thought would have slain half of us. But I am telling a long, idle story, and shall be late with my letter . . . [18]

Not only is the letter written in shorthand, it is carefully worded and presented as a 'long idle story'. It is significant that Byrom did not choose to tell Vigor that he had been summoned to see the Prince, nor that he had spoken with Pitsligo. His reference to the 'Prince' could have been incriminating, as we have seen from Jackson's letter, but Byrom explains his usage sardonically: that the nearer the man is the more he becomes the Prince – further away, he is the Pretender. Byrom would have Vigor believe that his descrip-

8 Portrait of John Byrom in middle life (from an etching by Dorning Rasbotham)

9 Thomas Deacon
1697–1753
(artist unknown)

10 'St Michael',
an allegorical engraving by
Michel Le Blon, 1615

11 Thomas Siddal
1708–1746
(artist unknown)

12 Satirical print of the
Duke of Cumberland
with the Savoyard
at Windsor

13 Prince Charles Edward Stuart with (left) Pitsligo,Chief of Clan Forbes, and (right) Lochiel, Chief of Clan Cameron (from a painting by Pettie)

tion of the Prince was gleaned from a glimpse as he rode by in the
street. He does not mention he had been close enough to kiss his
hands! Finally, the description of the Prince is a blend of sincere
compliment and spiteful gossip. He uses this old trick when he
describes the Proclamation of King James: 'I came by as they were
at it.' So often Byrom would have people think that certain events
and especially encounters happened quite by chance. Not being on
the list of property owners he escaped having a Jacobite officer billeted on him. For the very same reason he should have been spared a
Hannoverian, yet Lempster turned up, and stayed. But Lempster
was a link with earlier days at Court. Byrom, while giving the pretence of writing informally, has been very considered in what he
does and does not say. As proof of his duplicity, in the manuscript
book of poems there is one, 'On the Prince's Arrival', which shows
a very different reaction to the Prince's return to this country.

> What transport seizes us at the sudden sound
> That Britain's Prince was set on British ground!
> Had we expected, had the voice of fame
> Proclaimed the mighty blessing e'er it came,
> Watched every wave and shook at every blast!
> Anxious lest bleak and wint'ry storms should rise,
> To bar our hopes forever from our eyes!
> But e'er we knew he sailed, he reached our shore,
> We see no danger 'till he saw 'twas o'er.
> True the delight he gave had no alloy,
> And the first passion he inspired was joy.

After the fall of Carlisle, officers from the Manchester Regiment
were taken under strong guard to London to await trial, the
colonels, captains and lieutenants to Newgate, the ensigns, including
Siddal, to the New Prison in Clerkenwell, where they stayed until
the trials in July 1746. The phrase in the anonymous letter sent to the
Duke of Newcastle stating that Siddal knew 'enough to save twenty
such heads as his' had a poignantly apposite reference to the twenty
officers of his regiment.

In his dying speech Siddal made a direct comparison between the
Young Pretender and Cumberland. The Prince was

> too great and good to falsify or impose upon any people; a prince
> blessed with all the qualities which can adorn a throne, and who
> may challenge his keenest enemies to impute to him a vice which

can blacken his character; whom to serve is a duty and pleasure, and to die for an honour, and here I cannot but take notice of his royal highness, had he any of the cruelty of temper which hath so abundantly shown itself in his enemy, the pretended Duke of Cumberland, he would have shown it upon Mr John Vere when he had him in his power, and knew that he had been a spy upon the royal family abroad, and upon the prince at home almost from the time of his first landing; but the brave unfortunate young hero, with a noble compassion spared that life which has since been employed in our destruction.[19]

The John Vere named here was a government spy serving with the Hannoverian army. During the uprising Vere was captured by men from Lord George Murray's army near Newcastle under Lyme in Staffordshire. In his *Memoir of the Forty-Five* the Chevalier de Johnstone, aide de camp to Lord George, described Vere as 'the principal spy of the Duke of Cumberland'. And at the trial of Francis Towneley, Vere described himself as an officer 'sent by his Grace the Duke of Newcastle upon the publick service'.

Ten years earlier Byrom had been deliberately employed to teach Vere shorthand so that he could use it to communicate with other government officers 'in the publick service'. When one considers the double game Byrom was playing for so many years, one can understand much more clearly his unwillingness to see the shorthand system published. In a way they never suspected, David Hartley and his fellow enthusiasts did Byrom a great disservice by their constant advocacy.

The end of the uprising came with the defeat at Culloden on 16 April 1746. Here, under Cumberland's determined leadership, the Government troops dealt the final blow to the Jacobite cause. The fate of the Scots was decided in less than half an hour; William followed up his victory with a relentless pursuit of the survivors. The wounded and prisoners were either bayoneted or hanged. There was no mercy. He then rounded up the highland cattle to starve the rebels into submission. For months Cumberland's troops ravaged the countryside. The result was the destruction of the Scottish clan system. In celebration of Cumberland's victory, Handel composed 'Judas Maccabeus'. But after the initial rejoicing there was a reaction against the Duke, when his harsh treatment of the Scots became apparent. An alderman in London suggested that William should be made a freeman of the Butcher's Company, and ever since he has been known as 'Butcher Cumberland'. William sincerely believed, like Cromwell before him, that 'mild measures won't do'. Nevertheless George II admitted later that 'William had been rough with them'.

At their trial all twenty officers of the Manchester Regiment were found guilty of treason, but only nine were sentenced to death. On 30 July they were taken to Kennington Common in three sledges, each drawn by three horses. In the first were the executioner, Colonel Towneley and Captain Blyde; the second contained Thomas Deacon, Thomas Siddal and David Morgan; finally came George Fletcher, Thomas Chadwick and James Dawson. These are the nine martyrs whom Byrom writes of so movingly on the final page of the manuscript book of poems – ' Our townsmen now that they are dead and gone . . . Leave Heaven to pass the honouring sentence on.'

Their leader, Colonel Towneley, was cut down from the rope before he was dead, stripped and laid on the executioner's block. After severing his head with a cleaver, the hangman placed it in a coffin, took out the bowels and heart and threw them into a nearby fire. This gruesome procedure was repeated eight more times. At the end the executioner cried out, 'God save King George!' and the crowd responded with a shout. At home in Manchester, Siddal's widow lay expecting her last child. To preserve her life and that of the unborn babe, friends boarded up her bedroom window so that she could not see her husband's head decaying in the summer air. Next to it was placed the head of another rebel, Thomas Deacon.

Not surprisingly, when Mancheser officially celebrated the Jacobite defeat in October 1746, Mrs Siddal stayed away from the general rejoicing. Her absence was noticed and soldiers and towns-folk together attacked her house, breaking the windows and shutters. She was forced to take refuge with a neighbour while the sentinal on duty within six yards did nothing to stop it. Byrom denounced the attack in an anonymous letter to the *Chester Courant* which ended with the following epigram:

> By the bare title of this text, a laic
> Would think the times were very Pharisaick.
> Long Prayers to Heaven are in the morning pour'd,
> At night, behold the widow's house devour'd.

One more casualty of the '45 who had been close to Byrom was Charles Radclyffe. Once the rising was under way he was anxious to join the Prince in Scotland, and boarded one of two French ships taking soldiers to Scotland from France. However, Admiral Vernon captured the privateers off Dogger Bank and arrested Radclyffe and his eldest son, who, being deemed a foreigner, was exchanged. Radclyffe lay in the Tower for a year until he was finally brought to trial on 21 November 1746 at Westminster, and convicted on the charge of treason from thirty years earlier. Although he had been stripped of his English titles, Radclyffe was granted the privilege of his rank and sentenced to decapitation. Displaying the same courage and lightheartedness which had characterised his bravery in the 1715 rebellion, he mounted the scaffold on the morning of 8 December, assured the executioner of his forgiveness and gave him ten gold guineas to do his work with his best skill. He was buried in the Church of St Giles-in-the-Fields.

Byrom's Journal for 1746 to 1747 does not exist, but he seems to have spent most of that time in Manchester. His letter to Vigor dated 1 March 1746 was written from home and his next letter, on 26 February 1748, is addressed from Cambridge, where he had gone to teach shorthand. On 7 March he moved to London, and one of the first things he did was to inquire after Dr Deacon's youngest son Charles, who had been a mere youth of fifteen when he had followed his brothers and enlisted in the '45. A friend called Hudson told Byrom that he had been to see the Duke of Newcastle about Deacon and some of the other prisoners whose fate had yet to be decided. Newcastle was Secretary of State and First Lord of the Treasury, and Byrom hoped to use his friends to influence the Duke to show clemency.

A heavy cold kept him indoors for a week, but then he ventured out to the Royal Society where he talked with the Earl of Morton. During those early months of spring Byrom gave Lord Morton a refresher course in his shorthand and also taught his son. England was still at war with France over the Austrian Succession and Morton with his family had been imprisoned in the Bastille. The French had found ciphers and an alphabet on him and he had fallen under suspicion. He joked about this with Byrom at the Royal Society:

he was very merry about his examination abroad and a case of conscience about shorthand, which when they asked him to discover what he had written in it, I can't do that gentlemen, says he, for I was myself concerned in procuring an act of parliament, that nobody should discover it without Dr B.'s consent etc . . . [20]

Byrom appreciated Morton's quick-witted use of the Shorthand Act and his role in it to bluff his French interrogators and avoid any charge. This was still a time to go warily. Back in Manchester a Presbyterian minister from Rochdale, a vigorous Whig, Josiah Owen, published a pamphlet denouncing Byrom as the 'master tool of the faction' there, together with Dr Deacon and other Jacobite friends. No wonder that when Byrom heard an acquaintance repeat his ambiguous toast 'God Bless the King' and attribute it to someone else, he remained silent. When the news of Morton's treatment in Paris reached the London newspapers Byrom asked him about it again:

> he said it was very true, and it was the alphabet which I had written for him when he learnt shorthand, which he gave me, and some other papers which they had numbered and signed, he and the lieutenant-general de police at Paris, even some receipts for the shorthand subscription; but having all his papers, they found clearly that there was not the least reason for taking him up, and were ashamed of it when over.[21]

By this time Byrom was in far better health and enjoying his game of bluff and counter-bluff. He writes jokingly to his wife: 'here I am known to be a staunch and steady whig', and even shrugs off Owen's vicious attack: 'thank Teddy for his letter and friend O–n for his care of my fame and reputation; I am hardly at leisure to mind him, or perhaps I might thank him myself.'[22]

The Duke of Cumberland had taken command of British forces in Holland the previous year in the fight against the French. As one might expect, Byrom followed William's fortunes closely during his campaigns. In the same letter he writes

> Here is Lady Mer [Mar] tells me that the D(uke) of C(umberland) has but 7,000 men at his command, that the French have taken Maestricht which I have heard said elsewhere, but cannot see the probability of it, and have heard wagers offered and refused that it was not even invested . . .

Three weeks later he sent another bulletin home:

> All talk here is of peace, peace and stocks rising, but nothing certain about the conditions thereof, one report contradicting another, the D(uke) of C(umberland) said to be ill of a lethargy, like to lose an eye, and twenty ailings beside, which others

contradict; when there is anything positive worth notice I shall tell you . . . [23]

Byrom did not attempt to hide his concern over Cumberland's welfare from his wife, but could, of course, excuse it because there was a general interest in the fortunes of the British army and its commander. In July he reported to Elizabeth: 'Last night the mob were huzzaing a coach at Temple Bar, wherein they said there was the Duke of Cumberland . . .'[24] As it turned out the Duke was still abroad, but Byrom was alert to every rumour.

In fact Byrom gives himself away in writing home about Cumberland's amorous exploits as well as his daring in battle. In August 1749 William was having yet another affair, this time with a girl from Savoy. Already grown to a monstrous bulk, he was savagely lampooned with the girl in a series of cartoons (see plate 12), which led to the arrest of a number of engravers and print-sellers. Byrom took the trouble to tell Elizabeth that the girl was more attractive than the public had been led to believe. 'The Savoyard girl has made some noise and some pictures; she is a poor mean-dressed wench, but pretty enough if she was dressed out, not at all like the picture in the print where the Duke kneels.'[25]

Why should it matter to Byrom whether Cumberland's latest mistress was pretty or not? These remarks on William stand out, totally unrelated to anything else in the letter.

Nevertheless, while still keeping an eye on William's fortunes, Byrom did not forget the Manchester men still languishing in prison for their part in the '45, particularly Charles Deacon. One of his brothers had been executed with Siddal, another had died before he could be brought to trial, and Charles, Byrom learned, lay under threat of transportation with the rest of the Manchester prisoners. On the 10 June 1748 Byrom called at the house of Mr Charles Stanhope, one-time Secretary of the Treasury. Also present were Stanhope's brother the Earl of Harrington, Viceroy of Ireland, Lord Lonsdale, one of Byrom's first shorthand pupils, and the Duke of Montague.

> They asked me many questions about the Pretender, and circumstances when he was at Manchester, etc., and I told them what I knew and thought without any reserve, and took the opportunity of setting some matters in a truer light than I suppose they had heard them placed in and put in now and then a word in favour of the prisoners, especially Ch D(eacon) . . .[26]

A week later Byrom hoped to raise the matter again with the Duke of Richmond, who was one of the Council of Regency in the absence of the king abroad. Unfortunately Lady Townshend was present and delicacy made Byrom feel 'I could not well introduce the fate of Ch etc . . . as I wanted to'. Among the others present were Stanhope and his brother, Lord Baltimore, and Sir John Cope, the general so ignominiously defeated by the Scots at Prestonpans.

Byrom had another opportunity of approaching Richmond on the 14 July. There was an eclipse of the sun and Martin Folkes took Byrom to Richmond's house where they breakfasted by the river and 'peeped through glasses at it'. The house was full of distinguished people, the Dukes of Dorset and Montague, Dr Stukeley, and, strangely, James Radclyffe, the son of Charles who had been executed two years earlier. Byrom spoke to Richmond about Deacon but was met with the objection that neither father nor son had expressed any repentance – 'and that God himself did not pardon without repentance'. Byrom did not reply 'for fear of exasperating' the Duke but later raised the matter again with Stanhope.

By August Byrom was beginning to lose hope. He wrote to his tender-hearted Dolly:

I have not such good hopes as I had of the young boy being set at liberty . . . he has made some enemies or other that have represented him in so ill a light that I much question at present if he will meet with the favour which has been so long expected . . . But I am not sorry that I have spoken my thoughts about him as opportunity offered.[27]

Some of those thoughts were expressed in a Latin poem addressed to Lord Harrington. Having no copy by him, Byrom translated it from memory for Dolly. Part of it survives:

> Three brothers – I shall only speak the truth –
> Three brothers, hurried by mere dint of youth,
> Incautious youth, were found in arms of late,
> And rushing on to their approaching fate.
> ....
> The third was then a little boy at school,
> That played the truant from the rod and rule;
> The child, to join his brothers left his book,
> And arms, alas! instead of apples took.
> Now lies confined the poor unhappy lad –

> For death mere pity and mere shame forbad –
> Long time confined, and wasting Mercy's bail
> Two year's amidst the horrors of a jail . . . [28]

Deacon stayed in gaol in Southwark until January 1749. Byrom intended to visit him but again a heavy cold prevented him. By now Deacon had spent three of his nineteen years in prison, and the experience of being confined with the vilest criminals horrified him. He told his father that he felt 'as far remote from the least glimpse of Christianity, honesty, nay even common humanity itself, as black is from white'.[29] On 11 January he was taken to Gravesend together with another Manchester man, William Brettargh, and transported to Jamaica. Shortly after he arrived in April he died.

While trying to enlist help from the Establishment to save Deacon, Byrom was still seeing another member of the Jacobite triumvirate, Henry Salkeld, dining with him in July at Salkeld's request. In August 1749 he dined with him again to say good-bye before returning to Manchester. It is the last time Byrom mentions him, for Salkeld, too, died later that year.

Byrom's acquaintance with Charles Stanhope is a good example of his deliberate cultivation of men of influential standing. Stanhope was notorious because of his dishonest dealing in the South Sea shares scandal; he made an enormous fortune but survived prosecution through the protection of Sir Robert Walpole. In May 1748 he announced to Byrom that he 'had a fancy to learn shorthand'[30] and had lessons. However corrupt, Stanhope was potentially useful to Byrom in securing Deacon's pardon, and Byrom was useful to him as a source of valuable information. Stanhope was present at Rothmell's coffee house when Byrom read out an account of the arrest by the French of the Young Pretender in Paris, and he lost no time in asking for the details, sending a servant next day to wait while Byrom made him a copy. It is not known who sent the account, but it is clear that Byrom had an overview of the Jacobite rising right up to the Prince's final days in France.

Louis XV, in an effort to comply with the treaty of Aix-la-Chapelle, had asked the Prince to leave France quietly, offering him an annual allowance as an inducement. The Prince ignored the request and continued enjoying life in Paris, much to the French King's embarrassment. Louis was forced to sign a warrant for the arrest of Charles.

Tuesday the 10th December [N.S.] The Prince having dined at

home with about thirty at his table, mostly of his own people, was never seen more gay and easy, and proposed after dinner to walk in the Tuilleries, where several of his company followed him, particularly two of his Scots chiefs, one of which spoke to him in the morning concerning the reports that were a-going that he was certainly to be taken up one of these days, and as the report went, it was to be at his own house or in the public gardens, and begged of him to give him and the rest of his subjects orders; but he smiled and said, I have heard these reports for some time, but I believe there is nothing in them.

It coming on rain while we walked, he left the Tuilleries, and at stepping into his coach the two chiefs spoke to him again and told him if he had a mind to make a Bender of it, as the king of Sweden, he would not want assistance; at which he thanked them, but bid them not be uneasy. He returned home, where he stayed about half an hour, and then took his coach and went to the opera, attended by Sir James Harrington and Colonel Goring, Englishmen, and Mr. Sheridan, an Irish(man). When the coach came to the cul-de-sac, the Prince, alighting as usual, was seized in the moment by a number of the sergeants of the French bl. guards, who shut the opera door before him and the barrier behind him, while one of them insolently broke his sword in the scabbard, while two others took the little pistols out of his side pockets, then carrying him without his feet touching the ground to a room in the Palais Royal, where the Major of the French Guards, Marquis de Vandreuil, told him he had the King of France's orders. All who took him were disguised in whitish coloured clothes such as footmen out of livery wear. The Prince was in the Palais Royal bound with a rope like a common criminal and put into a remise coach, the Major and two Captains going with him, and French soldiers mounting behind with screwed bayonets. The Prince then said, 'Gentlemen, this is but a dirty office you are engaged in; I suppose I am straight on my way to Hannover!' They told him he was going to Vincennes Castle, where as soon as he arrived, he said to the Governor, Marquis de Chatelet, 'I used to come as your friend, Governor, but now I am your prisoner, I hope that you will salute me though I cannot come to you.' The Governor who was his very great friend, stormed like a lion, and ran and unbound him, but was obliged to obey orders and put him in that part of the Castle called the dungeon, a little dark hole in a place in the high tower, two captains guards within his room, and four sentries at his door. When he came into this miserable place he said it was not quite so good as his bothies in the Highland Hills. He threw himself upon the bed, but would not be prevailed upon to throw off his clothes nor eat or drink anything that night, and was frequently heard to say to himself, 'O my faithful mountaineers!' Next day he ate nothing but a little soup, but on Thursday he dined, and was taken ill after it with a violent vomiting, etc., but was perfectly well next day. He made the captains always eat with him, and spoke to them about the war, etc., and behaved with such a noble and manly courage that he so charmed the hearts of his guards that they were ready to cry when they spoke of him, and several swore they would give up their commissions rather than mount guard there any more.

He parted from Vincennes on Sunday morning by day break, where is not known; but it is said the musketeers had orders to guard him to Pont Beauvoisin on the frontiers, a place belonging half to Savoy and half to France, where it is said he will be left to go where he pleases.

The gentlemen who were in the coach with the Prince going to the opera, were put in separate hackney coaches and carried to the Bastille; his footmen went the same road, one of which, Angus Macdonald, the only Scotchman there, fired a pistol at one of the men who took the Prince.

Mr. Alexander Macleod and Stewart of Ardshiel were playing at backgammon in the Prince's house, Sir Davie Murray, etc., looking on, when the guards came to the house, and they were seized also and sent to the Bastille, as was the cook, washer-woman, and everybody within that door. Mr. Stafford, an Irish gentleman, who dined abroad, and knowing nothing of the matter, was by the guards let into the court and sent the same road as the rest. It would appear they had feared a mob, for there were guards all from the Prince's house to the Pont Royal, and above two thousand men in arms there and about the opera, and six regiments ready at call. A great many French gentlemen were put into the Bastille that night and next day for speaking of it; the people got all up in the opera to come out, but the doors were shut; everybody high and low were in tears, and I could not imagine the French were so fond of anything but their own king. *The Count de Biron* went from the Palais Royal to Court that night, and when the news was told, the Queen, the Dauphin, the

Dauphiness, and all the Madams, threw down their knives, and there was not one word spoke.

You may depend upon the truth of this paper, because I had it from the Governor of Vincennes and others of absolute credit, though it is treason now to say that he was tied or ill-used.[31]

Remembering Beppy's devotion to the young prince, Byrom sent her the gist of this account also, in a letter pointedly dated 'Prince Charles's Birth Day' (30 November). He wanted her to know that reports that the Young Pretender was dead were not true.

Apart from interceding on behalf of Charles Deacon, Byrom took the affairs of his home town very much to heart, especially when it suffered the anti-Jacobite abuse of Josiah Owen. He wrote several pieces of verse and prose to defend Manchester in the *Chester Courant*. In January 1749 Robert Thyer, Siddal's brother-in-law and Librarian at Chetham's wrote to tell him that the *Chester Papers* had been published together in a book, *Manchester Vindicated*. Great concern was felt by many prominent citizens about the damage to the town's reputation. Further harm was feared from exaggerated reports from a fight which broke out between two men at a hunt in Newton-le-Willows, which became distorted out of all recognition in London papers. Byrom's son Edward helped to provide the facts to put the record straight. Even a local M.P., Richard Shuttleworth, became involved in protecting 'the first trading town in the kingdom'. A mob of Whig louts from Wigan had been responsible for the disturbance in which one man died – with a stone in one hand and two in his pocket. Byrom was keen to see the truth published – when the New Year holidays were over 'for till then the newspaper would not be so much taken notice of'.

That year Byrom remembered St Valentine's Day, his wedding anniversary, with more genuine affection than he had shown for years. The nursing and care of his wife during his breakdown and her loyalty to him through the uprising had reminded him of her real worth.

It being Valentine Day I thought, before I stepped thither, I would just write a line to send my love and service to the lady who honoured me with her obedience some years ago upon this happy festival; so please to present my best respects to her, and let her know that I bear in grateful remembrance the felicity which befell me on this day, and has continued to be the greatest of my whole life ever since.[32]

Despite this new-found tenderness towards Elizabeth, Byrom's relations with Edward continued to be strained, lacking that spontaneity which marks his interest in Cumberland. Two weeks after the Valentine letter, he wrote again to his wife in reply to news that Edward, now twenty-four, wished to marry. His reaction is so measured that he might have been writing about some more distant relative. Being at home so little, he did not know the girl, and

> cannot judge how I should like her person and behaviour, but for my beloved son's sake, I should wish her possessed of every qualification that might justly be agreeable to thee, his sisters, uncle, aunts and friends, as well as to himself.[33]

As in the past with domestic matters, Byrom would rather leave it all to Elizabeth.

Byrom disguised his unwillingness to assume responsibility in unexceptionable sentiments. He claimed to have been thrown 'into a great but really loving concern'. It was a pity Edward's uncle and aunts had not been more enthusiastic. Byrom does not want to offend Teddy by objecting – he hopes he is making a proper choice, and 'one can think of nothing else at present than to refer to thy sentiments, which I wish thee to give me'.

That was in February; at the end of July his absence from home was more than usually felt, so much so that Robert Thyer took up the family's complaint:

> Pray, good sir, do you never intend to come down? The ladies, I assure you, cry out most terribly against such vagrant husbands, and would gladly have Mrs Byrom to come with all her family to fetch you. If you tarry a little longer, you will most certainly get within the vortex of another season, and then, I suppose you will think no more of Manchester.[34]

Another month passed before Byrom set out to join his wife once more.

CHAPTER TWELVE

Final Years

1750–63

AFTER THE DEFEAT of the 1745 rebellion, Cumberland's star, of course, remained in the ascendant. In June 1746 the House of Commons voted an increase of £25,000 to his annual income of £15,000, 'for the signal services done by his royal highness to his country'. On 12 July George II granted the Duke 'the office of ranger and keeper of Windsor Great Park ... for and during his own life, and the lives of their Royal Highnesses, the Princess Amelia and the Princess Caroline'. At Windsor William turned his attention to improving the Park with plantations of Scottish firs and cedars. He was very keen on horse-racing and founded Ascot Races. Cruel though he may have been to the Scots, he did not forget the soldiers who had served under him, founding a hospital for invalid soldiers in London and obtaining a Bill to protect soldier-pensioners from money-lenders.

When he was in London the Duke patronised Vauxhall and Ranelagh Gardens. He was never very interested in the theatre, unless he happened to be attracted by one of the actresses in a play. His favourite pastimes, as one would expect, were sport and social gatherings. He enjoyed playing cards – usually for large stakes. It was the great age of gambling, but William was not the most reckless gambler. As the years passed, the tall Duke became so big he was no longer capable of dancing but still had numerous love affairs. He never married and was quite content to have his household run by Amelia, his favourite sister.

Among Byrom's shorthand poems is one written especially for her. His interest in Amelia probably stemmed from her closeness to Cumberland, rather than any interest in the Princess herself.

Amelia's birthday was the same as that of the Old Pretender, 10 June. She became inseparable from William and any invitation to the Duke and his friends was expected to include Amelia and hers. This would be enough to prompt Byrom's lines and it is significant that he did not write poems about the other princesses.

His disillusion with the failure of the uprising must have been deep. The defeat of Culloden had been followed by the humiliating expulsion of Charles Edward from France – proof indeed that the possession of royal blood in itself was not enough. Unfortunately the Young Pretender would not face the reality of his situation. He continued living in style and cherishing hopes of another, successful, attempt. Reports of him in disguise came from all over Europe, and in September 1750 he visited London, staying in the house of Lady Primrose in Essex Street just off the Strand. At the Church of St Mary's le Grand, near what is now Trafalgar Square, he abjured the Roman Catholic religion and joined the Church of England in expectation of his return. He walked the streets telling people he would return to oust the Hannoverians. All these were empty gestures, for the cause was lost.

Byrom's involvement in the '45 had been followed by three arduous years during which he had witnessed the deaths of close companions and the bitter sufferings of old friends. The loyalty of Dr Deacon, of Tom Siddal and all the Manchester martyrs had, unlike his, been undivided, and their end came all too soon. He had attempted to make amends by interceding for Charles Deacon, and by writing in defence of the good name of Manchester. He had successfully covered his own tracks as a double agent. But in the end the strain began to tell and he returned home wearied by his efforts. He turned his back on London as the centre of power and, gradually, philosophy and religion became his consuming interests.

Once he was home Byrom became more and more content to remain in Manchester with his family.

Apart from his wife, Byrom had two daughters still living at home and he gained much pleasure from their company, as indeed he had always done. Beppy worked on the accounts ready for the family businesses. She shared her father's Jacobite sympathies. When the Old Pretender died in 1768, the Jacobites proclaimed his son 'Charles III'. Beppy bought a blue glazed teapot which still survives bearing the monogram 'CRIII' and the white rose of Stuart.

Her younger sister, Dorothy, was distinguished from her brothers and sisters by her marked artistic flair. She was remarkably clever at cutting out silhouettes from paper, and many of these survive today to show the delicacy of her skill, particularly in some delightful domestic scenes. She also completed at least seventy

portraits in silhouettes. Dolly, like Beppy, shared to some degree
Byrom's Jacobite sympathies and was his favourite daughter. It was
for her that he wrote his best and most famous religious poem,
'Christians Awake!' at the family home in Hanging Ditch as a

Figure 13: Hanging Ditch house

Christmas present in 1749. The following year a friend wrote a tune
to fit the words. He was John Wainwright, organist at Stockport
Parish church and deputy organist at the Collegiate Church in Manchester. The hymn tune has been known ever since as 'Stockport'.
On Christmas morning 1750 the Collegiate choir sang the hymn for
the first time outside Byrom's house. Later that day the hymn was
sung at Stockport Parish Church during morning service. After the
death of her widowed mother in 1788, Dolly moved to Kersall Cell.

In 1750 Byrom was fifty-eight. In the same year his son, Edward,
married Eleanora Halstead, the young woman on whom Byrom
hesitated to comment when asked for his opinion. Edward, ever a
cautious and sober young man, had known her for two years – yet
despite that his father had never set eyes on her until his return
home. The *Chester Courant* described her as a 'lady of great merit
and a handsome fortune', and the marriage was a happy one, but
sadly brief. After giving birth to four daughters, two of whom died
in infancy, Eleanora died at the age of thirty-one. Edward may
appear dull beside his father, but he was industrious and thoroughly
worthy. He ran the businesses well, adding to the family fortunes.
In the process he earned the respect of his fellow-townsmen, who

elected him Boroughreeve. The highlight of his civic duties was to conduct the King of Denmark on a tour of the Duke of Bridge-water's famous canal.

Edward is a key figure in a painting by Arthur Devis, *Breaking-Up Day at Dr. Clayton's School at Salford*. Devis was a Lancastrian painter of conversation pieces. His patrons were mostly merchants and country squires. Around 1738 he was commissioned to paint the end of term ceremony at Dr Clayton's school, St Cyprian's, sometimes called Salford Grammar School, which had been opened in 1735 for the sons of High Church Tories. As an acknowledged Jacobite, Dr Clayton is depicted dressed in a blue velvet gown with white silk. He is standing behind a round table on a raised platform in the schoolroom at Salford. Arranged around are a number of pupils who form the audience for a boy reading a poem – on this occasion Byrom's moral fable *Three Black Crows*. On the right, sitting on a stool, is the figure of young Edward Byrom following the reading with a book in his hand. Curiously, the composition of the painting has a number of similarities to Hogarth's *Conquest of Mexico*. Both painters portray spectators at a performance, Devis the recital of the poem, Hogarth the performance of a play. Rather like Desaguliers in Hogarth's setting, Dr Clayton stands ready to prompt the pupil reading immediately in front of him, indeed Clayton's eyes can follow the page as the boy reads; and just as the young Duke stares out towards the viewer, so young Teddy sits staring out of the canvas. Byrom's 'tale' is a London story, told when 'two honest tradesmen' meet in the Strand. In the middle of the nineteenth century Devis's painting adorned the Byrom country house, Kersall Cell. Now it is part of the British collection in the Tate Gallery.

Edward founded St John's Church, Deansgate, since demolished, but famous in the nineteenth century as the living of the Reverend John Clowes. He was the son of Joseph Clowes, Byrom's cousin. Among the books he inherited from his father's library were the manuscripts of Byrom's Journal and letters for 1730-2 which Joseph had carefully preserved and which fortunately later escaped Sarah Bolger and the destruction ordered by Eleanora Atherton.

Byrom's youngest sister Phebe was still involved in the family business, for when her elder brother, Edward, died in May 1740 she carried on running the shop in Market Place, which had been the start of the family fortune. No doubt she had inherited the Byrom business sense, but there was another reason, too. The register of

Baptisms at Manchester Cathedral contains an hitherto unnoticed entry for 18 October 1740: 'Thomas, son of Phebe Byrom and Rowland Colling'. Nothing is mentioned in any of the surviving family papers, but it would appear that, at the late age of forty-three, Phebe became a mother and lived with her son over the shop.

As for Byrom himself, there is a glimpse of him relaxing on an occasion in April 1750 when he became unwittingly embroiled in a different kind of political dispute. Elizabeth, who had retained her early love of dancing, had persuaded him to attend one of the weekly Assemblies. 'Not having danced there for many years, I was then invited . . . by a lady out of the country whom I had too much regard for to decline the favour; and asking her what she would please to have called for, she said, Sir Watkin's Jig, which accordingly I called for by that appellation and no other, not having the least design of giving offence to any body . . .'[1]

This dance derived its name from Sir Watkin Williams Wynn (1692-1749), a Tory MP for twenty-nine years and a persistent opponent of Walpole. He was known to have helped the Jacobites in 1745 but the government dared not touch him. Calling out his name at the dance appeared to army officers present to be an anti-government protest. One irascible and overzealous Major claimed he had heard the slogan 'Down with the Rump!' Later he blamed the 'damn'd racket' made by the 'damn'd fiddler' for his mistake, but, at the time, objected to such a dance being called. An argument followed; Byrom found himself being jostled during the dance, and the whole incident became the talk of the county. Byrom went so far as to write to Peter Bold, a local MP, in August, disgusted that the local military garrison should attempt to dictate the dances at the Assemblies, ' . . . for then the Manchester ladies would have nothing to do but to shut up their assemblies entirely'.[2] The episode reads like a comic scene from Fielding or Sterne, but is an indication of how sensitive the political climate remained for such an incident to be seen as subversive. Moreover, Byrom was still anxious to guard his own good name. However, he had used the name of the dance years earlier in an epigram written when he was at odds with Caroline over her political manoeuvrings with Walpole. He even used Siddal to add point to the jest.

> To her Majesty's presence a Barber advanc'd;
> Says he: 'Let the Jig of Sir Watkin be danc'd!
> But, as in our bosoms it raises a flame,

> Pray, let it be call'd for by some other name!'
> 'No by its true name we will call it,' says Dolly,
> 'You may, if you please, call it "Warriner's Folly".'[3]

The meaning of the last line is unfortunately lost, but the epigram shows that, when he called for the dance, Byrom was not as ignorant of what he was doing as he claimed.

In these last years Byrom became increasingly concerned with philosophical questions. One of the most enduring influences was William Law's. They had stayed friends since first meeting in 1729. Ten years later Byrom was the only man Law would entrust with his precious Syrian manuscripts which he thought had been found in a mountain and were original, genuine gospels, although outside the accepted canon of the New Testament. Law owned five and allowed Byrom to borrow each one in turn, insisting that he 'should not transcribe them, nor let anybody know of them, but the matter should pass between him and me only'.[4] Byrom agreed and each manuscript was read and discussed by the two men. Byrom went back to Law with the first, 'his first MS of *Athan*', on the 28 August and in the course of the discussion Law

> mentioned the philosopher's stone as what he believed to be true, and I think as if some had had it, or, had it – not to be found by philosophers; we agreed it could not possibly be forgery.[5]

This shows how close Byrom was to Law. It is proof, too, that Byrom had already begun to discuss the 'philosopher's stone' with his closest friends – an idea which is explored in geometrical form in the drawings in the Byrom Collection concerned with 'spiritual alchemy'. When Byrom borrowed Law's third manuscript, *The Apocalypse of the B.V. Mary*, he drew attention to the Virgin's prayer 'Keep me with thee' as 'a natural proof of no forgery'. However, it has been accepted since by Biblical textual scholars that the works published under the name of Dionysius Areopagita are not genuine. Byrom, to his credit, questioned the authenticity of the Greek text. Law valued his comments and, when Byrom one day said that it would be a pity if the manuscripts were lost, he replied, 'I'll leave you my executor.' At first Byrom assented, but quickly changed his mind. 'No, I do not desire to be your executor, I wish you to live.'[6]

Law never married but lived a life of uncompromising simplicity and, as far as possible, practised the principles he taught. Already he had denounced the stage without reservation. Such was his austerity that Byrom noted: 'I find the young folks of my acquaintance think Mr Law an impracticable, strange, whimsical writer, but I am not convinced by their reasons.'[7]

In 1727 Law had founded a school at King's Cliffe for fourteen girls, and later, in 1740, added eighteen boys who were to be brought up according to his devout Christian principles. He believed that all money which was not strictly necessary for one's own needs should be spent on charity, and this, naturally, drew an abundance of beggars to his house – much to the annoyance of neighbours, who presented a petition to the local magistrates. Law refused to accede to their objections. He corresponded with Byrom regularly up to the year before he died.

By 1760 both men were ailing, and Byrom wrote to Law that he was confined by his ill-health. In his reply, the last of his many letters to Byrom, Law comforted him:

> your body is the prisoner and you are its jailer. It is because your mind has all your care, and you are always travelling with it as high and as far as you please, that your body goes nowhere, and has only the liberty of travelling such journeys as your two-armed chair takes.[8]

So close had the two men become that physical infirmity and the miles separating them meant nothing.

Byrom also engaged in religious discussions with John and Charles Wesley. He records meeting Charles Wesley in 1737 after his return from his unsuccessful mission to Georgia. Both brothers were influenced strongly by Law and both learned Byrom's short-hand, writing most of their manuscripts and hymns in it. In March 1738 Byrom complimented Charles on being such an excellent pupil: 'You are so complete a master that I shame at my writing when I see the neatness of yours.'[9]

While they became friends they did not always see eye to eye, for Methodism was a cause of controversy. The Church of England was still the guide for moral behaviour in British culture. It was a natural subject of discussion in drawing rooms whenever issues of right and wrong were debated. Most people were still believers.

Byrom's attitude to faith is seen most clearly in a conversation he had in March 1737 with Dr Joseph Butler. This discussion more than any other shows how Byrom viewed life and the basis on which he made his decisions. He was visiting Dr Hartley when they were interrupted by the arrival of a friend, John Lloyd, and, later, by Dr Butler. His great work the *Analogy of Religion Natural and Revealed* had been published a few months earlier and in 1736 he had been appointed to the household of Queen Caroline as her spiritual adviser. By special command he attended the Queen every evening from seven to nine until she died in 1737. His closeness to Caroline and, through her, his access to William, now approaching sixteen, had made Butler a figure of special interest to Byrom – just at the time he was hoping to become William's shorthand tutor. When the topic was raised at the beginning of this meeting Butler supported the idea himself, although, of course, unaware of Byrom's motives. So he was doubly welcome – because of his connections at Court as well as his book, in which he attempted to apply reason to religious belief.

After discussing the ideas of Sir Isaac Newton on prophecy and the writings of Pascal, the conversation opened up into a wider discussion of reason and authority. Naturally Butler argued for reason, while Byrom championed authority based on the consent of the Christian Church. He argued that faith was 'a thing impossible to reason . . . that man had a heart capable of being faithful as well as a head capable of being rational, and that religion applied itself to the heart'.[10] Byrom became quite impassioned, faced with someone close to Caroline and, no doubt, feeling the force of his own guilt at failing to live up to the faith he proclaimed. Nevertheless he persisted that, if people believed, they did so not because of reason, but because they had been moved by reading the life of some devout Christian. Byrom's decision to become a non-juror had been based on the authority of a body of doctrines which proclaimed the divine right of kings. Reason would have dictated a sensible accommodation with the new Hannoverian establishment and brought the reward of an assured career. He said to Butler:

> I was born in the Church of England, and therefore Providence having placed me under authority; I had it not to search for, and that as reason sent me to no particular place, that did; that I considered a man how he was born under the parental authority, that if a man should invite a child to leave his father's house, . . . still that child would stick to parental authority.

The argument contains the very essence of his religious beliefs. Religion was a matter of the heart, which in his own case had directed him away from self-interest. It is perhaps the supreme irony of

Byrom's life that the dictates of that same heart led him into a temptation which brought about the betrayal of the beliefs he held so dear. If he had compromised like a rational man, he might have been truer to his faith.

Given his faith, Byrom read widely; both orthodox Christian and non-Christian writers. Apart from the early fathers of the Church, he studied the works of many Jewish writers, the Neo-Platonists of the Renaissance, exponents of the Hermetic tradition, the Rosicrucians and early alchemical writers. All this served to broaden his outlook while he remained firmly in the Church into which he was born, having, as he confessed, no taste for 'hasty turners'.

One of the most secret parts of Byrom's life concerned the activities of his Cabala Club. This was formed from a select group of friends in the Sun Club, among whom were the two Grahams, senior and junior, both key men and regular in attendance. It was the younger Graham who first drew Byrom's attention to the extraordinary device for cutting jewels and the mysterious papers owned by Falkoner in St Bartholomew's Close. Graham accompanied Byrom when he first went to see Falkoner, sensing the potential of Falkoner's tools and papers for the work of the Cabala Club. He communicated this excitement to Byrom and the Journal entries suggest that a particular kind of intimacy had grown up between Byrom and young Graham, one born of shared but exclusive interests which they wished to further.

Byrom had probably been a mason since 1725, and there is a document in the possession of the freemasons called the Graham MS which is dated 1726. Part of it consists of an examination procedure for a mason, but about half deals with a lengthy exposition of legendary material concerning Noah, Bezaleel and King Solomon, some of which is not to be found in either the Bible or Talmud. The manuscript is important to masons as part of the material possibly concerning a mythical pedigree to Biblical times. It may well be that the bond between Graham and Byrom lay in a shared knowledge about the existence of the manuscript, and that even within the Cabala Club they kept that knowledge to themselves and a small group, but were always on the alert for corroboration or other related material. One reason for thinking this is a third link Byrom had with the Graham MS – through the Robinson family in Rokeby, for the Graham MS came to light in 1936 when the owner, the Rev Hilary Robinson of Londesborough Rectory, Yorkshire, was initiated into the Masonic Brotherhood.

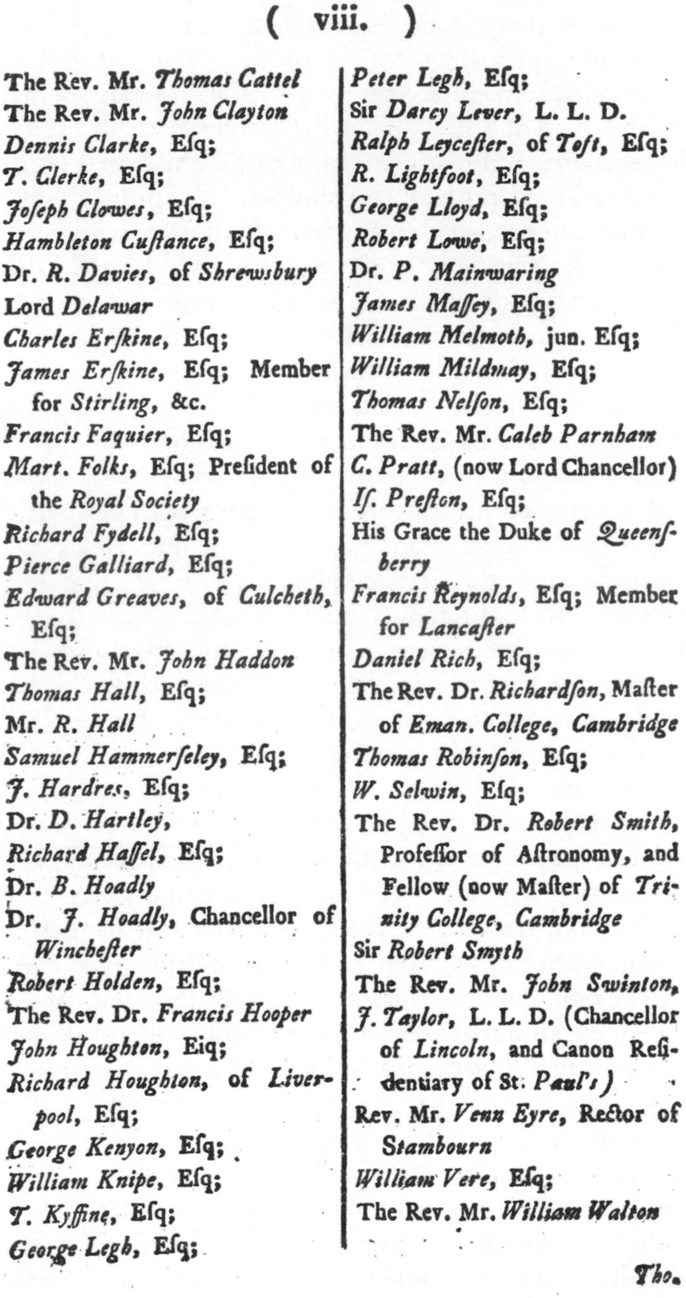

(viii.)

The Rev. Mr. *Thomas Cattel*

The Rev. Mr. *John Clayton*

Dennis Clarke, Efq;

T. Clerke, Efq;

Joseph Clowes, Efq;

Hambleton Cuftance, Efq;

Dr. *R. Davies*, of *Shrewsbury*

Lord *Delawar*

Charles Erfkine, Efq;

James Erfkine, Efq; Member for *Stirling*, &c.

Francis Faquier, Efq;

Mart. Folks, Efq; Prefident of the *Royal Society*

Richard Fydell, Efq;

Pierce Galliard, Efq;

Edward Greaves, of *Culcheth*, Efq;

The Rev. Mr. *John Haddon*

Thomas Hall, Efq;

Mr. *R. Hall*

Samuel Hammerfeley, Efq;

J. Hardres, Efq;

Dr. *D. Hartley*,

Richard Haffel, Efq;

Dr. *B. Hoadly*

Dr. *J. Hoadly*, Chancellor of *Winchefter*

Robert Holden, Efq;

The Rev. Dr. *Francis Hooper*

John Houghton, Efq;

Richard Houghton, of *Liverpool*, Efq;

George Kenyon, Efq;

William Knipe, Efq;

T. Kyffine, Efq;

George Legh, Efq;

Peter Legh, Efq;

Sir *Darcy Lever*, L. L. D.

Ralph Leycefter, of *Toft*, Efq;

R. Lightfoot, Efq;

George Lloyd, Efq;

Robert Lowe, Efq;

Dr. *P. Mainwaring*

James Maffey, Efq;

William Melmoth, jun. Efq;

William Mildmay, Efq;

Thomas Nelfon, Efq;

The Rev. Mr. *Caleb Parnham*

C. Pratt, (now Lord Chancellor)

If. Prefton, Efq;

His Grace the Duke of *Queensberry*

Francis Reynolds, Efq; Member for *Lancafter*

Daniel Rich, Efq;

The Rev. Dr. *Richardfon*, Mafter of *Eman. College*, *Cambridge*

Thomas Robinfon, Efq;

W. Selwin, Efq;

The Rev. Dr. *Robert Smith*, Profeffor of Aftronomy, and Fellow (now Mafter) of *Trinity College*, *Cambridge*

Sir *Robert Smyth*

The Rev. Mr. *John Swinton*,

J. Taylor, L. L. D. (Chancellor of *Lincoln*, and Canon Refidentiary of *St. Paul's*)

Rev. Mr. *Venn Eyre*, Rector of *Stambourn*

William Vere, Efq;

The Rev. Mr. *William Walton*

Tho.

Figure 14: List of subscribers to Byrom's shorthand manual

The list of subscribers to Byrom's shorthand manual in 1767 contains the name of Thomas Robinson. He had known Byrom for thirty years and had drawn up the form of wording for Dr Hartley's unsuccessful attempt to raise a subscription for an edition in 1737. He was also one of the people with whom Byrom liked to discuss mathematics – and the drawings in the Byrom Collection are all rooted in geometry and mathematics. Byrom makes frequent references to several Robinsons throughout his Journal. Thomas Robinson had connections with Henry Salkeld, living in rooms above him in the City. In April 1737 Byrom records calling on Salkeld, 'but he was not within . . . Mr Robinson spoke to me out of his window, and so I went up there after that Mr Salkeld was not within, and sat with him a little'.[11] The Salkeld archives in the Cumbria Record Office, Carlisle, show Mr Thomas Robinson as an agent for Mrs Margaret Salkeld, Henry's widow, advising her on her properties and mines from at least 1756 to 1766, by which time he is referred to in the documents as a 'Man of Fortune' and a Member of Parliament.

The Journal shows that the Robinson who knew Salkeld was the same man whom Byrom first met as a shorthand writer in the House of Commons, and other references indicate that he was a member of the Robinsons of Rokeby. Tall and thin, he was nicknamed 'long Sir Thomas' and Byrom on meeting him in 1725 measured himself against him to find that 'he was about two inches shorter than I'. One of his brothers was Captain Septimus Robinson, who, after a distinguished army career serving under Marshal Wade in the '45 and under Marshal Ligonier in Flanders, became tutor to the two sons of Frederick, Prince of Wales. In April 1735 Byrom records: 'thence to Westminster Hall, saw Mr Robinson there . . . went with Mr Robinson into the park, met Prince Frederick . . . walked home with Mr Robinson, very warm weather, and dined with him . . .'[12] Another brother, Richard, became Primate of All Ireland in 1760 but was appointed Prebendary at York in 1738. In 1744, when Byrom was touring Yorkshire in readiness for the '45, he visited York and twice dined with Captain Robinson. By then Byrom had got to know all the chief members of the Robinson family.

In addition to being in control of a confidential shorthand system, Byrom seemed to be carrying out a highly secret quest for knowledge of a different kind, knowledge that had come to be regarded as either unfashionable, unprofitable or even unacceptable, but which to others – many men of great intelligence and probity such as Sir

Isaac Newton and Robert Boyle – may have still contained, within
its outmoded forms, truths which were worth preserving, insights
which the more 'rational' movement of the times had failed to
appreciate. This was the reason for Byrom's interest in the extraordinary geometrical drawings which came into his possession.
Jacques Christophe Le Blon, who had been concerned with that collection, had left England, and in 1735 Byrom cuts a solitary figure in
an upstairs room at Abingdon's, 'at the old work about the proportions'. That was the 9 April; the next day he 'stayed at home
proportioning, and there is still no end of it (query, whether to
meddle with it any more while in London, but keep to the square
hypothesis).[13] But he did stick at it: on 16 April he returned to
Abingdon's, where in the peace of an upstairs room, he was 'proportioning the compendium', and at the end of another busy day he
sat 'compendiuming' from eleven o'clock 'till the watchman went
past twelve'. Byrom was totally engrossed by this activity and on
the 19 April he returns to Abingdon's, 'went up stairs, proportioning till past one o'clock'. After breaking off to visit a friend, Byrom
resumed his work until midnight. It is obvious that he was very
anxious to understand and master the skills necessary to interpret
and use the drawings he was studying, now that he could no longer
rely on Le Blon's help through the amazing intricacy of the figures.
The use of mathematics and geometry to formulate abstract philosophical thought goes back to the ancient Greeks and even to
Babylonian times. Byrom, as a mason, would be aware of the basis
of much masonic teaching in geometry and architecture and of the
importance to masons of such buildings as the Temple of Solomon.
The Byrom Collection contains within it drawings connected with
the beginnings of Freemasonry. It may well be that the Graham MS,
with its 'uncanonical' legends, was looked on as part of the same
body of teachings. Papers belonging to the Rev. Hilary Robinson
show his descent from a Thomas Robinson, and the possible links in
his genealogy help to account for Byrom's interest in the family.

Another document connected with the masons, the *Multa Paucis
for Lovers of Secrets*, is an account of the founding of The Grand
Lodge in England and was published anonymously about 1763, the
year of Byrom's death. Records show that the French Lodge to
which he had belonged was 'erased 23.3.1745' – before the beginning
of the uprising. However, Byrom, in the solitude of his study at
Hunter's Croft, could reflect on his years as 'John Shadow' and his
work behind the scenes in London. As he neared his end he would

want to leave his affairs in order. Could the publication be part of these arrangements? In June 1763 the copyright granted to his short-hand for twenty-one years by George II expired. His manual had still not been published, but the confidential matter hidden until now in the cipher could be properly revealed by anyone privy to the system. This laid Byrom himself open to exposure and he must have felt the last vestiges of his power slipping away.

Byrom had suffered from asthma for many years and in 1763 there was a sharp decline in his health and he became completely house-bound. Sarah Brearcliffe, the sister who provided the first glimpse of him as a youth on the banks of the river Irwell left a short diary for September and October of that year, and from it his last weeks can be followed.

It begins on 1 September:

My brother John Byrom called Dr Byrom was removed from his own house in Hunters Croft to his sons House in ye key Street for the sake of more or Better Air.[14]

John Houghton, his friend and literary executor, came to visit him every day for a fortnight. On Friday the 23rd, after a bad night, he made his Will. On Sunday his condition deteriorated and all his family came to see him, and at about six o'clock the following morning he died 'very resigned and easy'. The next day his Will was read. Sarah records:

27 (September) left his son ye estate that his Cozn Worthington left him   his son to pay the charge upon Kersall to his sisters and then Kersall Estate be wholly his two Daughters – he left 10 servants 40s apiece and to Ned Normand share forty shillings ye year for his life and to the infirmary one hundred pound.[15]

Byrom had never been a man of wealth but had great compassion, and always gave help to those in need. Apart from the annuity to his servant, he left a total amount of £201. Most of that went to charity, but he also remembered the family servants. The Will contains no mention of his library of books and manuscripts nor his own papers. Edward inherited one piece of property, his father's interest in the remainder ceased when he died.

He was buried on St Michael's Day, Thursday 29 September. The funeral celebrations could not have been better timed if they had been stage-managed. Indeed, perhaps, towards the end, the immi-nence of the saint's feast day seemed auspicious, for St Michael had

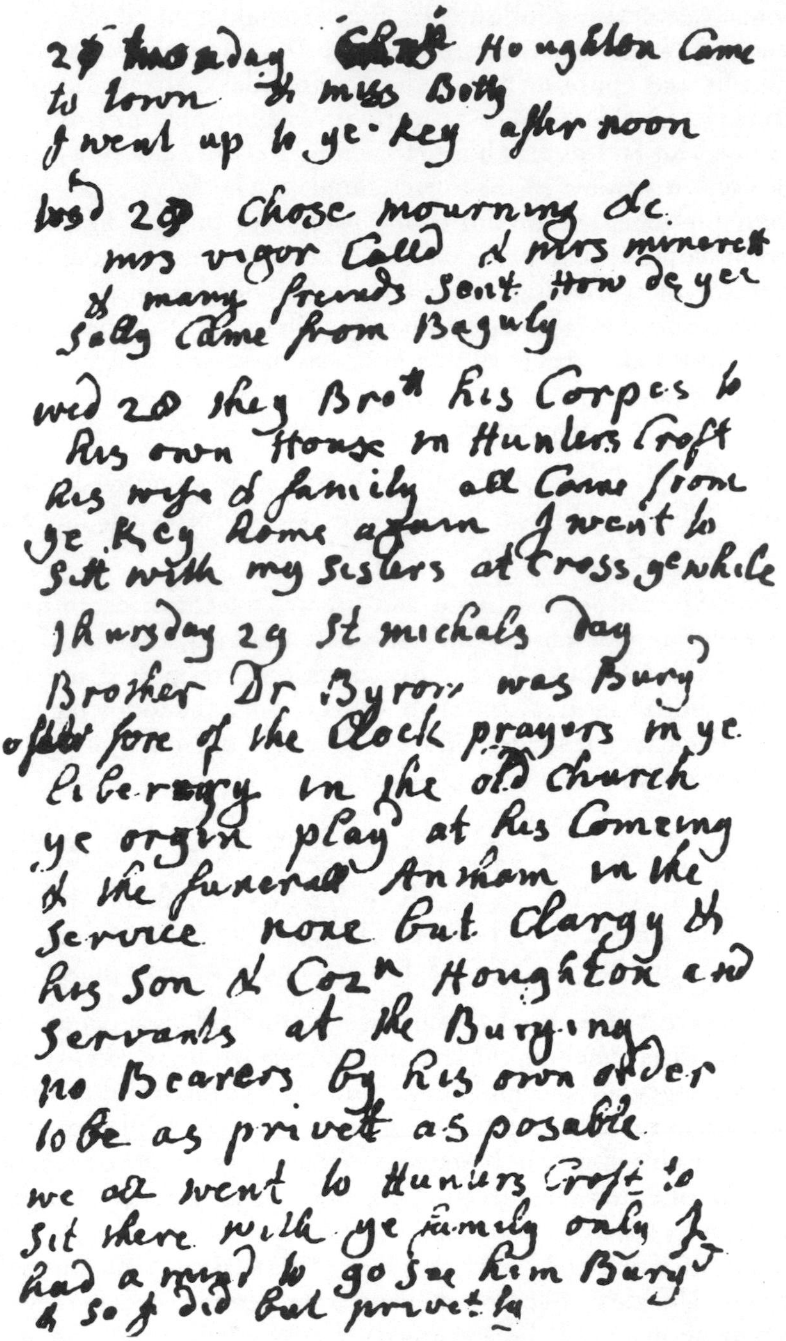

2? tuesday ~~christ~~ Houghton came
to town & miss Betty
I went up to ye key after noon

tues 2? Chose mourning &c.
mrs vigor Call'd & mrs minerett
& many freinds sent How de yee
Sally came from Beguly

wed 2? they Brot his Corpes to
his own House in Hunters Croft
his wife & family all came from
ye Key home again I went to
Sitt with my Sisters at Cross ye while

Thursday 29 St michals Day
Brother Dr Byrom was Bury'd
before fore of the Clock prayers in ye
Liberary in the old Church
ye orgin play at his Comeing
& the funeral Anthem in the
service none but Clargy &
his Son & Cozn Houghton and
servants at the Burying
no Bearers by his own order
to be as privet as posable
we all went to Hunters Croft to
Sit there with ye family only I
had a mind to go See him Bury'd
& So I did but privet ly

Figure 15: St Michael's Day

featured significantly in the course of his work with the collection of geometrical drawings in his custody. Some are directly related to an allegorical engraving filled with early masonic symbols and dominated by the figure of St Michael fighting with Lucifer – the role allotted to him in the *Book of Revelation*. A detailed analysis of the symbols can be found in *The Byrom Collection*, but the engraving has very important historical implications for Freemasonry, as it clearly pre-dates the formation of The Grand Lodge in this country. Byrom would also be aware of St Michael's role in the Church as the protector of Christians, especially at the hour of death, when he conducts the soul to God. Sir Hans Sloane is known to have owned a copy of the engraving, and Byrom possessed drawings designed to fit in geometrical patterns embedded in the picture.

The funeral took place at four o'clock in the afternoon with prayers in the library of the 'old church'. In memory of his love of music, 'the organ played at his coming' and a funeral anthem was sung. He was attended by his son Edward, John Houghton and servants; the whole ceremony was as simple and 'as private as possible'. The women were asked to stay away, but Sarah, who had carefully chosen to ignore that wish, watched the interment in the family vault, hidden by the deepening shadows of the late September afternoon. Byrom had lived the life of a solitary man and even at the end showed his independence in the manner of his burial. On the 7 October a local Justice of the Peace fined his estate five pounds, because, contrary to the law, he had insisted on being buried 'in a shirt shift sheet or shroud not made of sheep's wool'. Half the fine went to the poor of the town, the other to the informer.[16]

What did Byrom achieve? What was his legacy? Certain tangible things can be put forward, such as his shorthand and the verse. The shorthand in its elegance and simplicity was one of the most efficient to be evolved. It continued in use well into the nineteenth century and is a forerunner of the system devised by Isaac Pitman. The diaries and poems have long been valued as historical sources for the political, social and religious currents of thought of his day. They have a photographic realism which balances the more malicious *Memoirs* of Lord Hervey. But the newly discovered manuscripts shed a fresh light on his writings, and certain salient events such as the '45 rebellion need to be reappraised. Only now can his role as a grey eminence stalking the corridors of power be truly appreciated. He was never able to take centre stage himself, but operated from the wings in more than one drama. All through his life the force and charm of his personality impressed men of acuity and judgment as widely different as Hans Sloane, Charles Radclyffe and William Law, and made him welcome to great aristocrats such as the Dukes of Richmond and Devonshire. Lacking all vanity and seeking enlightenment, he valued above all else the gifts of mind and spirit. These he searched for in the Royal Society, the Sun Club, in Freemasonry and his Cabala Club. They brought riches which belied the final simplicity of his solitary funeral.

The fine exacted on his estate was a reminder that Byrom could not escape the consequences of all his actions. He knew before he died it would be incurred, just as he believed he now had to face his Maker and be judged. The final verse in the shorthand manuscript is a plea to his fellow-townsmen martyred in the '45 whose cause he had betrayed. He died awaiting their judgment too.

> Our townsmen now that they are dead and gone
> Leave Heaven to pass the honouring sentence on,
> Martyrs are not still, he who keeps the keys
> Of its blest gates may open if he please.
> Strive to get in thyself, ne'er mock I wrote
> On the wrong side, to keep thy neighbour out.

Perhaps the most enduring legacy is the lesson to be learned from his life. It is a tragic reminder of our flawed nature. Byrom began endowed with enviable gifts – a superior intelligence, admirably fine feelings, and high moral scruples, but, once he was tempted and lost direction, his career was a parable of wasted powers. Like the hero of a Greek tragedy, he reminds the spectator of the need to know one's boundaries, to understand clearly what one gives assent to. His infatuation for the 'fair unknown' was all the stronger because of his innocence and ignorance; he was the victim of his own 'cloistered virtue'. Once enthralled, he was unable to resist the force of the emotion Caroline had unleashed. Understandably, he tried to justify his actions to himself, but he was fatally compromised, and his efforts to remain loyal to his first political principles were doomed. Fate dealt him a cruel hand: the woman he loved rejected him, the cause he espoused failed, the son he had fathered was denied him. The efforts to salvage something from the wreckage of his aspirations came to naught. He knew this and withdrew to the seclusion of Manchester where he drew strength and support from his family's roots. There he spent his remaining years, coming to terms with the past. In his study of number philosophy Byrom learned that seventy-two was of paramount importance, expressing profound concepts. Perhaps his death at the significant age of seventy-two and his burial on St Michael's day should be regarded as the Grand Master's final salute to those ancient truths.

The Enigma Persists

T HIS STORY of John Byrom's life started almost incidentally, aris-
ing out of enquiries into the life of Thomas Siddal. That
particular search ended on Kennington Common with a nagging
question still unanswered – what did he know that was worth the
lives of twenty men like him? The new facts which have emerged
about Byrom suggest a number of solutions.

First and foremost, there was the house in New Round Court
rented by Byrom in Siddal's name. Was the loyal barber ever aware
of this relationship? Did he keep it secret because of his unswerving
loyalty to the Stuart cause? Perhaps he saw Byrom's relationship
with Caroline as a cynical piece of political manoeuvring, a means
whereby he could penetrate to the very heart of the Hannoverian
establishment. Or was it that, having been weaned on Jacobite principles since the death of his father in 1716, Thomas was so involved
with the preparations for the '45 that he, more than anyone, saw the
truth in the description of Byrom as 'the master-tool of the faction'?
Was he aware of Byrom's interest in the deaths of George I and
Walpole? Despite the grief he knew his death would bring his
family, Siddal would not betray Byrom. Moreover, the Young Pretender had escaped, hoping to return . . . he would need men like
Byrom still in place.

The secret may have centred on the presence in Manchester of
Lady Barbara Fitzroy, whose connections with the Radclyffes in her
formative years in Paris may have made her a stronger focus for
Stuart allegiances in the North than people have realised. She was
the illegitimate daughter of one of Charles II's mistresses, Barbara
Villiers, by John Churchill, first Duke of Marlborough, the hero of
Blenheim. Charles Radclyffe's involvement in the foundation of
French Freemasonry makes his contribution to the '45 even more
significant, adding political intrigue to his personal bravery. Cer-

tainly the Young Pretender, secretly visiting Manchester, had been led to believe the town was filled with supporters ready to rally to his flag. In truth, Byrom had a part in so many intrigues it is difficult to know which of them Siddal was party to. However, there are other areas of Byrom's life which are mystifying even today. They are connected with his Cabala Club and the knowledge he had been led to believe these studies would uncover. There is also his connection with the French Ordre du Temple.

The Science Museum in London has in its custody a manuscript notebook concerning geometric solids once owned by Robert Boyle and now part of a larger collection associated with George III.[1] The small vellum-bound book is similar to those Byrom used for his shorthand notes, but Sir Robert Boyle (1627-92) died the year Byrom was born. Even so, the similarity of the two sets of drawings is immediately obvious and is explained by the fact that these particular drawings were prints, with various modifications and additions made by hand. Their presence in Boyle's papers is explained by his interest in the Christian Cabala; one of the prints has, superimposed on the geometrical pattern, a Tree of Life bearing the figure of the crucified Christ.[2] Boyle, always a devout Christian, was therefore working on similar material thirty years before Byrom. We know, too, that Sir Hans Sloane had drawings related to Byrom's. They were source material for the Cabala Club, and Byrom obtained his supply of drawings mainly from Jacques Christophe Le Blon and others from Jonathan Falkoner. The collection is too vast and complex to do justice to it here, but part is concerned with scientific and philosophical inquiries into the nature of the universe and of matter, in attempts which still married science with religion.

In addition to the notebook, the Boyle Collection contains an extraordinary range of three-dimensional objects – brass models of the five regular solids as well as representations on brass plates of astronomical, astrological and mathematical delineations. One link between Boyle and Byrom is Stephen Demainbray (1710-82), a scientist of Huguenot extraction who wrote to Byrom in 1750. As an orphan he had lived in London with John Desaguliers, another Huguenot scientist, member of the Royal Society, freemason in England and France, and the third Grand Master of freemasonry in this country. Newton thought highly of Desaguliers and he, in turn, had the highest regard for Byrom. Some of his work foreshadowed present-day theories about the atom. Indications are that Desaguliers was aware of the nature of Boyle's work with the drawings and shared that knowledge with Byrom for the Cabala Club.

In Byrom's Collection there are copies of drawings identical with some of Boyle's. One has the same 'flaw' in it. They had evidently been printed from the same plate. Moreover, in the Boyle Collection there is a plate for this drawing which has the figure of a unicorn neatly incised in the metal by some man-made process. Close examination shows that it is not a blemish, but a deliberate motif which appears to have been added. For centuries the unicorn has been a symbol of purity and strength. It became the emblem of a group of religious heretics in twelfth-century France whom the Church felt it necessary to suppress. The geometrical drawing on the back of this plate was also printed, and Byrom's copy has written on it shorthand symbols, including the letters 's', 'p', 'r', 's' . . . 'suppress'.

Had Byrom (who began his investigations with the intention of bringing what he discovered out into the open) at some stage come across ideas so troubling that he found himself censoring them? There were other facts which Byrom might have helped to suppress.

In 1869 one James Chetham, shoemaker, of Greenheys, Manchester petitioned the Lord Chancellor in the Chancery Court for the return of all lands and properties once owned by Humphrey Chetham in 1650, and of which he believed he had been wrongfully deprived.[3]

The cause of all the trouble started not long after the '45 uprising. Two successive owners of the estate, Samuel Chetham and his brother Humphrey, died without leaving issue in 1744 and 1749 respectively. They should have been succeeded by Timothy Chetham, the son of a cousin, but he had died the year before Humphrey in 1747/48. In normal circumstances Timothy's son, William, should, therefore, have inherited. But, instead, the estates went by a collateral line to Edward Chetham of Manchester, Counsellor or Barrister at Law, and, incidentally, a friend of Byrom who often stayed in his rooms in London. The facts of the dispute reveal an extraordinary saga of alleged fraud and even murder.

Family tradition was that Timothy had been removed by poison – one year before bachelor Humphrey died. His son, William, was a soldier in the army of George II and remained in the service until 1761, helping to fight the Scottish rebels and later abroad. It was claimed that during his absence in the army Edward Chetham seized the estates immediately Humphrey died and arranged to have the marriage register at Holy Trinity Church, Salford, 'cut torn and mutilated and otherwise tampered with' to remove the evidence of Timothy Chetham's marriage to William's mother, Hannah Ashton, thus destroying the evidence of William's legitimacy and right to inherit. Edward was also accused of keeping Humphrey's Will on some legal excuse and of providing a forged 'copy' for inspection. However, not long after Edward took over, William's uncle, James Chetham, commenced a search for evidence of the marriage. To forestall exposure, Edward is alleged to have bribed James with a small pension to abandon the search.

In 1761 William returned home from the army and set about establishing his claim to the estates he should have inherited twelve years earlier. But he was unable to find proof of his parent's marriage and, as a result, lost the action he brought against the dastardly Edward at Lancaster Assizes. In 1769 Edward committed suicide and died intestate. The much-disputed lands were taken over by his two sisters, Alice Bland and Mary Clowes, wife of Samuel Clowes of Smedley. James Chetham, now without his pension, joined forces again with his nephew to help him with his claim. They had by now established William's pedigree but still lacked proof of Timothy's marriage. Both men died, and the next claimant was only thirteen years old, but, on reaching his majority he, too, tried to prove his rights to the estates. He died young, leaving a third claimant, an infant of three and a half.

The skulduggery was not yet over, for when the third claimant (another William) was old enough to serve in the Navy, he fell victim of a plot whereby he was drawn into a fight, brought before Justices of the Peace and, without being allowed to defend himself, sentenced to ten years' service abroad in a man-of-war. On his discharge he recommenced his claim on the estates, searching, like all the claimants before him, in the Diocesan Register at Chester for proof of the marriage, but to no avail. After a succession of legal moves he got his son, James, to write in 1851 to one of the heirs of Mary Clowes's portion of the lands, one William Leigh Clowes, who denied any connection with the dispute. James Chetham developed the habit of walking over Clowes's property, particularly the park, with Clowes's knowledge and, in or around 1852, Clowes partially admitted the claim on him by promising to raise James up 'as one of the family'. Later this was denied. He was also said to have given him a present of five pounds, and, on being shown the pedigree, to have said 'Prove it, prove it', meaning the marriage of

Timothy and Hannah. Later he suggested a settlement of £30,000 to £40,000, but died without doing anything about it.

In March 1868 James Chetham searched again in the Diocesan Register but without success. However, he happened to have forgotten some article, and, on returning to claim it, the clerk on duty suggested he should look in an 'ancient Index to Licensed Marriages (very little known even to antiquaries)' where he found Timothy Chetham's name and the number of the marriage return made in 1725. The register transcript was eventually found to contain a record of the marriage for 21 November 1724 at Holy Trinity Church, Salford. On further examination, the page where the marriage entry had been written was seen to have been pasted to the next page so well that they looked like one. James checked the church register and found that the whole leaf for 1724 had been carefully torn out, and that the numbers of the nearby entries had been altered. Such were the lengths Edward Chetham had been prepared to go to in order to gain possession of the Chetham estates. The Plaintiff made all these allegations in Chancery but they were not upheld, despite the evidence offered, because the claim was barred by the Statute of Limitations: too much time had elapsed in bringing the case to court. After all these efforts the penniless shoemaker never gained control of the lands and wealth he claimed.

The dispute over the Chetham estates is not a self-contained interlude in the drama of Byrom's life. It has implications which reflect on his conduct at the time. Byrom was steward of the Broughton Manor, which was part of the Clowes estate in Manchester. The farm Siddal tenanted from 1727 to 1745 was on Clowes property. Byrom was related to the Clowes family and a close friend of Joseph Clowes. He confided in Joseph and constantly used his chambers when in London. Joseph knew about the Cabala Club, including that part of Byrom's investigations which he thought better to 'suppress'. Joseph would know, or at least suspect, Edward Chetham's part in the dispute over the Chetham estates. It would be quite clear to everyone concerned at the time what would be the outcome of two brothers inheriting in succession and dying without issue. The legal heir was Timothy. However, his family had declined in status and prospects. Hence it was necessary to remove Timothy *before* the death of Humphrey, and then to destroy any chance of the poor relations inheriting. The villain of the piece, Edward, and his two sisters were contemporaries of Byrom. When Edward was driven in the end to suicide and died without issue, his sisters shared the estates – one half going to the Clowes family and enriching them considerably. Joseph could not fail to have been aware of all the accusations and justifications this newly acquired wealth brought his family. As Steward of Broughton Manor, Byrom no doubt had his suspicions. He knew Edward Chetham well. But he kept quiet. He had enough guilty secrets of his own to hide, and, by not questioning the probity of other prominent members of Lancashire society, either tacitly or explicitly was bargaining for his own security. It is an example of the truth of the old adage that people in glass houses should not throw stones. The Chetham and Clowes families could justify their conduct in the interest of preserving the status quo. Byrom, too, could find reasons to justify his behaviour. Years earlier in London he had discussed clinically the rightness of 'removing' tyrants. Already, by the time Edward Chetham seized the estates, Byrom had made so many accommodations to his conscience that one more was easy to make. Moreover, he was a lover of secrets and, in the collection of drawings, had come across some he had not expected and which were far more important to him than disputes over land.

Closely connected with the collection of drawings is an engraving by Michel Le Blon which was commissioned in 1615 for a manual on fencing by Gerard Thibault (1574-1627). A copy of it can be found with the St Michael engraving in a book owned by Sir Hans Sloane. Highly allegorical and filled with figures taken from Greek mythology, it is dominated by Zeus who is surrounded with the chief gods from Olympus, four of them representing the elements of fire, air, earth and water. The border is decorated with the signs of the zodiac. It clearly belongs to the hermetic tradition, using symbols of art, music, science and self-knowledge. It is more fully analysed in *The Byrom Collection* and is directly connected with geometrical cards among Byrom's drawings cut out to the same size and shape or drawn to reveal the underlying geometrical structure in the engraving. That structure was intended to convey information to those well-versed in the 'mysteries' of the tradition.

The basic pattern is also the same as that in the cosmati pavement in the Sanctuary at Westminster Abbey. This originally had a Latin description set in the stones, which included a list of animals and ends by declaring: 'Here is the perfectly rounded sphere which reveals the eternal pattern of the universe.'[4] The creatures listed feature in the engraving. The geometry of the pavement and

Byrom's cards evidently come from a common tradition of learning connected with the Jewish Cabala and ancient Greek and Egyptian thought. The pavement dates from 1272, the engraving from 1615, and other drawings were being created for Byrom's Cabala Club in and around 1732. Thus the tradition to which they belong extends in this country for a period of at least 460 years during which time it evolved and found expression in many different forms – architecture, philosophy, alchemy, science and even politics.

In the 1720s the dean of Westminster Abbey was Francis Atterbury, the Jacobite Bishop of Rochester. He worked on repairing the structure of the Abbey with Sir Christopher Wren (himself associated with early masonic movements in England), and he also instigated one of the Jacobite attempts to regain the throne, when Prince Charles Edward was born in 1720, thus providing an heir to the direct Stuart line of legitimate inheritance. His attitude was in keeping with High Church belief in the divine right of kings. Byrom, we know, shared that belief and was aware of Atterbury's strong convictions while still an undergraduate. Atterbury was arrested, imprisoned and exiled. He lived in Paris at the court of the Old Pretender along with other exiles like Charles Radclyffe, but, when he died in 1727, he was buried in the south aisle of Westminster Abbey, at his request 'as far away from Kings and Caesars as the space will admit of'.

In unravelling all the complexities of Byrom's story, certain names of people and places recur like themes in music, some more clearly than others. Michel Le Blon was a student of the Cabala and a disciple of the German mystic Jacob Behmen. Byrom admired Behmen's work greatly and his interest coincided with his work in the Cabala Club. Le Blon belonged to a famous firm of Huguenot publishers in Frankfurt who originally came from Liège. Liège was home for a while to Prince Charles Edward and Clementina Walkinshaw, who gave birth there to his daughter Charlotte. Later, in 1758, the Prince moved to Bouillon where he made fast friends with a M. Thibault. Some of these echoes are coincidental, others are part of a much larger pattern.

That pattern extends to events in France which began in 1891 in the tiny French village of Rennes-le-Château. The local priest, while working on the restoration of his church, discovered four parchments preserved in sealed wooden boxes inside a hollow column. Two of these parchments are said to have comprised genealogies, one dating from 1244, the other from 1644. The remaining two documents, apparently composed in the 1780s, were pious Latin texts. The priest, Berenger Saunière, reported the finds to his bishop who sent him to consult scholars in Paris. Among these was a young man, Emile Hoffet, with a high reputation as a linguist and palaeographer but also well-grounded in the esoteric tradition. What transpired in the meeting with Hoffet and his colleagues is not known, but Saunière returned to his village, where he remained until he died in 1917, leaving his possessions to his housekeeper. The full story of these documents and the extraordinary wealth which suddenly befell Saunière after their discovery is told in *The Holy Blood and the Holy Grail*. The central thesis of the book is not the concern of this epilogue, nor is its validity or otherwise an issue. The facts related so far are those which Henry Lincoln first learned in 1969 and which started him off on a detective hunt with his colleagues Michael Baigent and Richard Leigh.

Material about the Rennes-le-Château story and its implications began to appear in France in 1956, some in books, some in privately printed papers. In the Bibliothèque Nationale a series of documents has been lodged under the title of *Dossiers Secrets* which consists largely of genealogies attributed to Henri Lobineau, apparently the pseudonym of an Austrian historian and antiquarian, Leo Schidlof. What is of interest in the context of Byrom's drawings is that one of the genealogies in Lobineau's compilation is a list of 'Grand Masters' of a secret society, which originated in France in 1188 and is alleged to be still operating today, called the Prieuré de Sion. The complete list given by Baigent, Leigh and Lincoln is as follows:

Jean de Gisors	1188-1220
Marie de Saint-Clair	1220-66
Guillaume de Gisors	1266-1307
Edouard de Bar	1307-36
Jeanne de Bar	1336-51
Jean de Saint-Clair	1351-66
Blanche d'Evreux	1366-98
Nicolas Flamel	1398-1418
René d'Anjou	1418-80
Iolande de Bar	1480-83
Sandro Filipepi	1483-1510
Léonard de Vinci	1510-19
Connétable de Bourbon	1519-27
Ferdinand de Gonzague	1527-75

Louis de Nevers	1575-95
Robert Fludd	1595-1637
J. Valentin Andrea	1637-54
Robert Boyle	1654-91
Isaac Newton	1691-1727
Charles Radclyffe	1727-46
Charles de Lorraine	1746-80
Maximilian de Lorraine	1780-1801
Charles Nodier	1801-44
Victor Hugo	1844-85
Claude Debussy	1885-1918
Jean Cocteau	1918-(1963)[5]

The relevant people on the list are those whose period of office coincides with the dates of the drawings in *The Byrom Collection* or whose work is part of its provenance – Robert Fludd, J. Valentin Andrea (also known as Andreae), Robert Boyle, Isaac Newton and Charles Radclyffe. This section of the pedigree is strikingly apposite.

Fludd, a reforming physician in the reigns of James I and Charles I, was an exponent of the Hermetic tradition. His work owes much to the ideas of Christian Cabalism; Byrom's collection contains drawings directly related to his theories of the universe. One even bears the name of Fludd and his great work *The Microcosm*. Boyle had drawings that were companions to Byrom's. Newton was still President of the Royal Society when Byrom was elected, and spent a considerable amount of time testing the validity of the ideas of the alchemists. Like the Masons, he was fascinated by the dimensions of the Temple of Solomon and its symbolism; Byrom's collection contains a series of drawings which examine the proportions of the Temple. Radclyffe knew Byrom, and, as a senior freemason in France, would have been conversant with the esoteric ideas which occupied speculative masonry at the time. All four men were closely linked with a corpus of inter-related ideas which find geometrical expression in Byrom's collection.

I knew of Andreae's part in that tradition on the continent, but had not attempted to place him directly as a formative figure in the context of the drawings. However, shortly after the publication of *The Byrom Collection* I received, through the publishers, a letter from a reader who had been prompted to write because he had instantly recognised the similarity between drawings in the book and in one which he himself possessed. The book in question is one of Andreae's rarest works, *Mathematicum Memoriale* – so rare in fact that I have not been able to trace a copy in a public library anywhere in the British Isles. Published in 1614, it consists of 110 geometrical drawings divided into ten decads, each containing eleven drawings, but with no commentary. I have studied the book and copied drawings from it, and the relationship of Andreae's book to drawings in the Byrom Collection is unmistakable. Moreover, the separate decads in Andreae's book correspond very closely to divisions I had worked out in ordering the mass of material I had worked on – architecture, technology, fortification and science. A companion volume, written by Andreae, and published with a commentary in 1614, is in the Library of Tübingen University. Andreae spent some years as a Lutheran pastor in Tübingen. The discovery of *Mathematicum Memoriale* and its relationship to the collection reaffirmed that the drawings are part of a wider, European movement of ideas, and authenticates the interpretation of certain aspects of the collection.[6]

It also completed the small section of the pedigree listed in *The Holy Blood and the Holy Grail* which had attracted my attention. Perhaps it should not be surprising that people known to be members of an acknowledged esoteric tradition should be singled out as leaders of a secret society. They could be deemed to have just the right qualifications to give it credence. But the point is not that the drawings confirm the existence of M. Lobineau's secret society, but that quite independently five of his Grand Masters, one after another, occur in the pedigree of material *known to exist* in one collection and which had for the most part been kept secret to the initiates. There are perfectly sound reasons for that secrecy. Some of the material is concerned with alchemy, the precursor of chemistry. Before science emerged from the shadows, it rubbed shoulders with magic. People working in this grey area were often men of the highest integrity, while others were evidently quacks. Even Boyle experimented to find out if it was truly possible to transmute base metals, and was told by Newton, no less, to keep his findings secret.

The five names on Lobineau's list had a contemporary relevance when I discovered that, in 1955, three Englishmen applied to the French Consulate in London for an export licence to bring three of Saunière's mysterious genealogies to this country.[7] It is said they were deposited at the International League of Antiquarian Booksellers, 39 Great Russell Street, later to be placed in a strongbox at

Lloyd's Bank Europe Ltd. The men concerned were Viscount Leathers, C.H., Captain Ronald Stansmore Nutting and Hugh Murchison Clowes. It was intended that the documents remain for twenty-five years to be studied and then be returned to France. Hugh Murchison Clowes was a solicitor and, among other things, a director of his family's firm of printers in London. It specialised in printing Bibles and had been responsible for the catalogue of the British Library. To commemorate its 150th anniversary, a history of the firm, entitled *Family Business*, was published in 1953 which contained a genealogy of the founder's family. It shows that the founder's father's great-grandmother was grandmother of John Byrom as well as Joseph Clowes. I was intrigued that Hugh Murchison Clowes was interested in studying documents associated in the eighteenth century with Charles Radclyffe, especially since Radclyffe himself knew John Byrom and through him the earlier Joseph Clowes, John's cousin and constant companion. In his Journal for June 1729 Byrom records meeting Radclyffe at the Sword Blade in the City just after leaving Joseph Clowes's chambers.

Hugh Murchison Clowes was a partner in Hunter's, an old and highly respected firm in Lincoln's Inn, founded in 1715 by one Ambrose Newton. As a relative put it, Hugh was a solicitor 'only in a very grand way'. By tradition, a partner in the firm had served as Clerk to the Worshipful Company of Masons since 1741. The Masons' Company is concerned with the maintenance of cathedrals and other ancient monuments originally built by operative masons, and, in so doing, is involved in the continuity of the building traditions which created them. One of the liveried companies of the City of London, it resembles the Law Society, having been formed to regulate the work of stonemasons from the point of view of the employees. Hugh Murchison Clowes was Clerk to the company for some twenty years until 1947, and according to his successor, the late Alan Philpotts, was the chief administrator, keeping the accounts and records of company meetings. In June 1953 Hugh was sworn in as Upper Warden, and the minutes for a meeting held that month show the nature of the company's work:

> The Clerk reported that during the restoration of Canterbury and Rochester Cathedrals lectures would be given upon the construction of these buildings and it was thought that they would be of value to all stonemason apprentices. It was agreed in principle that, when details of the lectures were available, they should be

communicated to the London Association of Master Stonemasons and, if there was sufficient interest, the Company would make a contribution towards the expenses of taking the apprentices to either Canterbury or Rochester.[8]

The Masons' Company is distinct from the Freemasons now, but this was not always so. The speculative Freemasons separated in 1717 with the foundation of The Grand Lodge, but its origins lay with the masons. A Lodge of Accepted Masons known as The Acception was visited by Elias Ashmole in 1682, when other men were present who were not members of the Masons' Company, and its existence can be traced back in the Company's accounts to 1630.[9] It is obvious that the two bodies have common antecedents and some shared interests – for example in the skills of the operative masons. Byrom, of course, was a Freemason, interested in the mysteries which accrued around the Temple of Solomon and other masonic lore. Hugh Murchison Clowes, employed in part on Masons' Company business, no doubt developed interests which coincided with some of Byrom's. There is evidence that he was involved in obtaining Saunière's documents on an extended loan for study. They may have contained, in his opinion, information relevant to his position in the Masons' Company, of which he was now Upper Warden. Equally, the knowledge he gained in the Masons' Company may have been relevant to the mystery surrounding the genealogies from France.

The two men who joined Clowes in applying for the export licence for the documents were Viscount Leathers, a close friend of Winston Churchill and Minister of War Transport in World War II; and Captain Nutting, a prominent figure in the shipping and banking world, and a former member of MI5 – both distinguished men. So Hugh Murchison Clowes would not have been acting solely for himself, but on behalf of a group, even if it were a group of three.

The link involving members of the Clowes family from different generations should not be ignored either. The collection of drawings in Byrom's custody formed a nucleus of material which joins together in a meaningful way five of the men on Lobineau's list of Grand Masters. From Robert Fludd to Charles Radclyffe an intellectual pedigree can be traced. A similar link may connect lawyer Clowes, in 1730, with Hugh Murchison Clowes more than two hundred years later – not such a far-fetched idea when the tradition which links the Great Pavement in Westminster Abbey with

Byrom's drawings 460 years later is considered. Joseph Clowes had in his possession the papers, diary extracts and manuscripts of John Byrom which included his long letter on the Cabala to Ralph Leycester. They went to his son, the Reverend John Clowes, and with them may have been other material dealing with the same tradition which has not survived, or which is still waiting to be discovered. The 'banishment' from Manchester of William Clowes by his father – because of his unsuitable marriage[10] – may have been the means whereby certain knowledge was transmitted to the southern branch of the family from which Hugh Murchison Clowes sprang. That knowledge could have become family lore and surfaced again with Hugh. Family secrets certainly have the power to survive for generations and, if those secrets were concerned with issues too important to ignore, their survival is guaranteed.

Appendix I

BYROM'S POEMS

The total number of Byrom's published poems comes neatly to two hundred. Most first appeared in the 1773 edition prepared by John Houghton and printed in Manchester by J. Harrop. Byrom was born with an almost dangerous facility for verse-writing. He confessed in 'An Epistle to a Friend on the Art of English Poetry' that from his youth he was

> Smit with delight, full negligent of Prose,
> And thro' mere liking, tempted to compose.

Moreover he lived in an age when much verse and prose was published anonymously or under obvious pseudonyms. Byrom enjoyed this convention, for it suited his love of subterfuge. But it causes certain problems for a biographer, which is why in the Preface to the first edition John Houghton felt it necessary to assure the reader 'That the Poems here presented are the genuine Productions of Mr Byrom . . . carefully transcribed from his own Manuscripts!'

The two volumes comprised 152 poems. Volume I contains verse on a wide range of miscellaneous topics, serious and witty. Volume II consists entirely of devotional verse. This same broad division was repeated in the 1814 edition published in Leeds by James Nicols, and again in the 1894 edition. This was edited by Adolphus William Ward for The Chetham Society in Manchester, and ran to four volumes. A further volume was published by the Chetham Society in 1912 (also edited by Ward), containing forty-eight more poems, and miscellaneous letters to and from Byrom. Byrom's love of versifying led him to translate almost any aspect of his life into verse, from humdrum domestic nonsense to serious religious and philosophical argument.

He circulated his verses anonymously among friends, relishing the amusement they caused and the mistaken guesses over their authorship. However, sometimes this backfired on him, to his own annoyance. In 1725 Byrom wrote his famous epigram about the feud between Handel and the Italian composer Bononcini. A few years later he was having to assure friends that he was the author, and it was still being attributed to Swift and Pope as late as the 1860s. So it is not surprising that poems in the unpublished MS book have also appeared in print attributed to other men.

The first poem, 'To The Fair Unknown. After Seeing Her at the Musick Booth at Sturbridge Fair', appears on page eleven, and, at the bottom of the page, someone has added in longhand, amid other scribbling, the name Taylor. The sheet has every sign of having been cut from the notebook and stuck back in. Overleaf, down the right-hand margin, is written 'mr please to send', which is not a translation of any of the shorthand on the page, but looks more like a memorandum to send the torn sheet to someone, almost certainly John Taylor. This poem appeared in print in 1786 in *A Select Collection of Poems* by John Nichols (volume 8), where it was attributed to John Taylor, a Fellow of St John's College, Cambridge who had died twenty years earlier in 1766. He is mentioned frequently in the Journal, appearing as early as 1729, when he was twenty-six. Byrom referred to him as 'Mr Taylor, my disciple', he was a great advocate of Byrom's shorthand and in 1748 Byrom calls him 'my shorthand Vice-Master'. Not surprisingly his name appears among the subscribers to the Manual, which appeared in 1767. In Cambridge he regularly attended meetings of Byrom's shorthand circle at the Hoop tavern. Another member was John Houghton himself, who was at the time a youth of eighteen in his second year at St John's.

Taylor remained associated with Byrom until he died. Knowledgeable and trustworthy, and a good friend, active in the cause of Byrom's shorthand, he is likely to have had copies of Byrom's poems since it is known Byrom liked to circulate them privately.

Taylor has also been credited with the last poem in the first section, 'Damon to Celinda'. A version of this appeared in *The Gentleman's Magazine* for 1779, thirteen years after his death. It may be coincidence that the two poems attributed to Taylor come at the beginning and end of the section, telling of the onset and conclusion of an affair. Yet none of the other poems recounting stages in the story has been traced to him. The inference is that Taylor at some time acquired copies of these poems from the sequence but not the rest.

Two other poems in this sequence have been wrongly attributed for very much the same reasons. 'On A Spider' appeared in *The Gentleman's Magazine* in July 1737 entitled 'The Spider and Poet' and attributed to 'Mr Littleton'. 'A Letter from Cambridge to Atone' (under the title 'A Letter from Cambridge to a Young Gentleman at Eton School') appeared in later miscellanies as the work of Edward Littleton. He was a scholar of King's College, Cambridge who became Chaplain to George II in 1730. He died in 1733. Both poems were credited to him after his death but no other poems by him have been published. In 1735 his sermons appeared, dedicated to Queen Caroline, to raise money for his widow and children. Littleton's biographer, Dr Thomas Morrell said: 'Whether his academical studies checked his poetical flights, and he rejected these trifles for the more solid entertainment of philosophy I know not, but I could meet with nothing more of this kind.' It is much more likely that Littleton, like Taylor and so many others, acquired copies of Byrom's poems and kept them among his papers. The published version of the 'Cambridge' poem contains a number of important differences. In Byrom's shorthand MS book the poem is longer and much more personal to Byrom himself. It is addressed to 'Dear Hall', a Fellow of King's College and a member of the French Lodge of Freemasons to which Byrom belonged. This all points to Byrom's authorship.

English verse of the eighteenth century is filled with classical allusion and figures taken from Greek/Roman history and mythology. Byrom made good use of this convention in recounting his relationship with Caroline. The identity of Caroline can be established in part from the subtitle to 'Artemissia' where she is referred to as 'the Queen', as well as from the description given in the body of the poem. But the name Artemissia (herself a Queen) immediately calls up the goddess Artemis, and Byrom is able to ring the changes on this in other poems in the sequence by calling the loved one 'Celinda' ('Damon to Celinda') and 'Delia', when 'On a Young Lady Stung by a Bee' was published anonymously. Celinda and Delia are alternative names for Artemis, and, in an age of such thorough classicism, the allusions would be readily understood. Similarly, when Byrom refers to himself as 'Damon', the classical figure of Damon as a Pythagorean scholar and faithful friend who valued friendship more than life would come to mind. When Byrom calls on Phoebus, as in the line 'Could Phoebus like the fair unknown' ('To the Fair Unknown'), he is reminding the reader that

Phoebus is the twin-brother of Artemis and that he is the god of song and music. The purity of Byrom's love is also subtly emphasised, for the name Phoebus alludes to the bright and pure nature of Apollo.

BYROM'S PLACE IN THE HISTORY OF BRITISH SHORTHAND

Historians generally date the beginnings of shorthand with the Greek historian Xenophon, who used it in writing a memoir of Socrates. In 63BC a Roman, Marcus Tullius Tiro, devised a system in Latin which lasted a thousand years. After the end of the Roman Empire this skill gradually came to be associated with witchcraft and by the Middle Ages fell into disuse. In England Thomas à Becket (1118-80), when he was Archbishop of Canterbury, encouraged attempts to rediscover Tiro's system and interest in shorthand grew. In 1588 Thomas Bright devised an English system, which he called *Characterie*.

The seventeenth century saw the development of a number of systems, each building on what had gone before. The first steps towards a phonetic system were taken by John Willis in the *Art of Stenographie*, published in 1602. In 1633, using a system closely based on this, Henry Dix tried to improve on the representation of vowels. In 1638, Thomas Shelton published his *Tachygraphy*, a method of shorthand which was widely used. It was this system Pepys employed to write his famous *Diary*. In 1646, Jeremiah Rich published *Charactery*, which was slightly more phonetic in that it dispensed with the letter C and substituted signs for either K or S depending on whether the sound was 'hard' or 'soft'. Then in 1672, William Mason published the first of his three systems, based on Rich's work. His final method, *La Plume Volante*, was taken over by Thomas Gurney and developed into *Brachygraphy* (1750) which became the official system used at the Old Bailey. Gurney established a dynasty of shorthand writers who eventually, in 1806, were appointed shorthand reporters to both Houses of Parliament. Charles Dickens describes learning this method in *David Copperfield*. It was not easy to use, however, and required 'considerable manual dexterity . . . as well as mental energy'. Byrom's system, on the other hand, was, according to E.H. Butler, 'so superior to all others that it earned him the enmity of his fellow authors'. He was anxious to achieve a smooth-flowing script, without awkward joins between the signs, and as phonetically accurate as possible. Even the abbreviations were based on 'the properties of the language' and not on 'any arbitrary marks'.

Several more systems were developed in the eighteenth century and Byrom's biggest rival was James Weston who issued a fifty guinea challenge to him through the press to prove whose method was speedier and more legible. Byrom ignored the challenge, but in 1725 he judged a contest at the Chapter coffee house between Weston and another rival, Anthony Clayton. Byrom and his friends had great fun at the expense of both men, neither of whose method was as simple and elegant as his. Byrom's system appeared in several editions in the nineteenth century, and holds an honourable place in the evolution of British shorthand. However, in 1786 Samuel Taylor achieved great speed in writing with an alphabet of nineteen letters made almost entirely by simple strokes. Although not phonetic, its ease made it very popular. In 1837 Isaac Pitman published his *Stenographic Sound-Hand* which incorporated phonetic features into Taylor's system.

In 1852, Pitman's brother, Benn, introduced the system to America. Later, in 1888, an Irishman, John Robert Gregg, produced his *Light-Line Phonography* based on a study of Taylor's and Pitman's work. In 1893, Gregg also took his method to America, and for a long time Gregg's and Pitman's systems led the field both there and in England. In 1968, further advance was made in the search for the most efficient rapid writing with the publication of *Teeline Shorthand*. This system employs streamlined versions of the letters of the conventional alphabet (omitting vowels and 'silent' letters). Its simplicity soon won it many advocates and it is now widely in use.

BYROM'S LIBRARY

Byrom collected an impressive library of 3,327 books and 41 manuscripts which reveal in their breadth and diversity the extent of his learning. It was housed at Kersall Cell, the country home in Salford which he enjoyed in his later years, and remained there until the death of Eleanora Atherton in 1870, when she bequeathed it to Chetham's Library. It contained books and papers rare even in Byrom's day and Miss Atherton arranged for a catalogue to be privately printed in 1848 as a record of its treasures. However, during the twenty-two years between the publication of the catalogue and her death, Miss Atherton is believed to have given various books away to admirers of her famous forebear so that, unfortunately, the library never received the collection intact.

As one would expect from a man originally intended for an ecclesiastical career, there are a great many books on theology, church history and liturgy, with Bibles in Latin, Greek and Hebrew, and innumerable commentaries. He had twenty-six books written by his friend, the mystic William Law, but there are also first editions of important works from the hermetic tradition such as Henry Cornelius Agrippa's seminal text *De Occulta Philosophia* (1533) and John Baptist Porta's text on *Natural Magick* (1591). Many of Byrom's manuscripts and books on necromancy and witchcraft, together with Reuchlin's *De Arte Cabbalistica*, Hermes Trismegistus's *The Divine Pymander* and John Dee's *Monas Hieroglyphica*, are part of the background study to his work in the Cabala Club. Similarly his library contained many standard works connected with the revival of mathematics and geometry in this country – Rudd's edition of Euclid with the famous Preface by Dee (1651), later works by Descartes and texts on trigonometry. His study of science begins with medieval alchemists like Roger Bacon and continues up to the work of Robert Boyle and Isaac Newton. There are contemporary texts on electricity and magnetism. His exceptional linguistic ability is shown by the dictionaries of the seven languages he had at his command and the grammars of fourteen he studied. This area extended logically into shorthand and ciphers, and he possessed a rare copy of John Falconer's early work on codes, *Cryptomensis Patefacta* (1685). His interest in medicine can be seen in a number of books and manuscripts ranging from Galen and Paracelsus to a manuscript of Elizabethan medical recipes and contemporary work on inoculation. The Rosicrucian writers Johann Valentin Andreae, Michael Maier and Thomas Vaughan rub shoulders with orthodox Christian apologists like Aquinas and Thomas à Kempis. Pharmocopeias, histories of France and treatises on fortification all had a bearing on activities and studies which Byrom pursued either in private or public. The library was truly representative of his formidable intellect.

Appendix II

Genealogies collated from *The Private Journal and Literary Remains* of John Byrom, Volume II, Part 2; church records, and public and private family papers

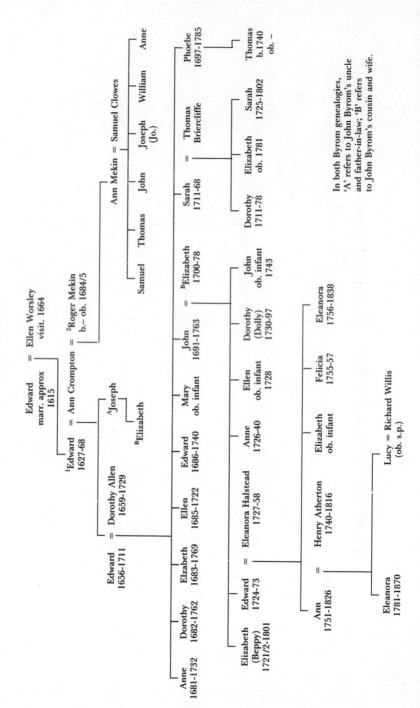

THE BYROM FAMILY
of
MANCHESTER

In both Byrom genealogies,
'A' refers to John Byrom's uncle
and father-in-law; 'B' refers
to John Byrom's cousin and wife.

BYROM OF SALFORD – Collateral Line

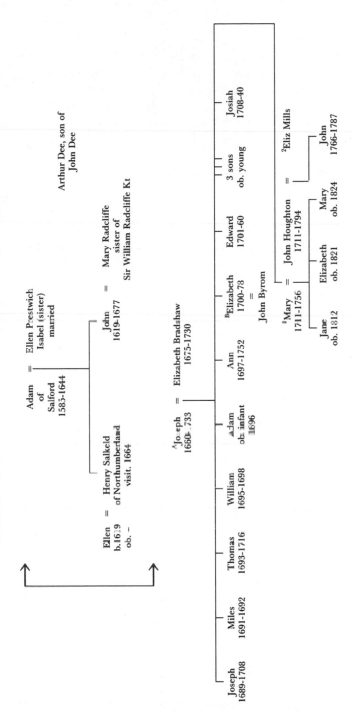

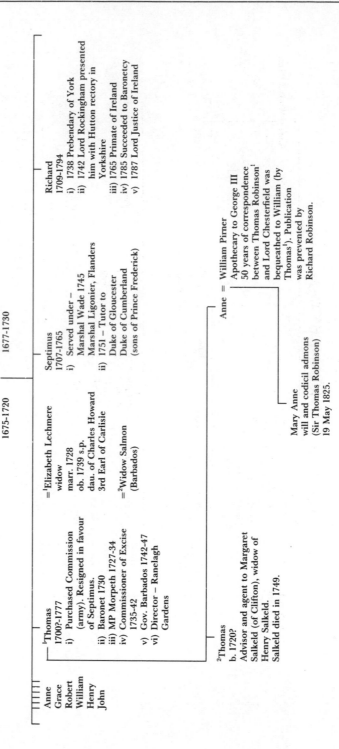

ROBINSON
of
ROKEBY

William = Anne Walters
1675-1720   1677-1730

Anne
Grace
Robert
William
Henry
John

¹Thomas
1700?-1777
i) Purchased Commission (army). Resigned in favour of Septimus.
ii) Baronet 1730
iii) MP Morpeth 1727-34
iv) Commissioner of Excise 1735-42
v) Gov. Barbados 1742-47
vi) Director – Ranelagh Gardens

=¹Elizabeth Lechmere
widow
marr. 1728
ob. 1739 s.p.
dau. of Charles Howard
3rd Earl of Carlisle

=²Widow Salmon
(Barbados)

Septimus
1707-1765
i) Served under –
Marshal Wade 1745
Marshal Ligonier, Flanders
ii) 1751 – Tutor to
Duke of Gloucester
Duke of Cumberland
(sons of Prince Frederick)

Richard
1709-1794
i) 1738 Prebendary of York
ii) 1742 Lord Rockingham presented him with Hutton rectory in Yorkshire
iii) 1765 Primate of Ireland
iv) 1785 Succeeded to Baronetcy
v) 1787 Lord Justice of Ireland

²Thomas
b. 1720?
Advisor and agent to Margaret Salkeld (of Clifton), widow of Henry Salkeld.
Salkeld died in 1749.

Anne = William Pirner
Apothecary to George III
50 years of correspondence between Thomas Robinson¹ and Lord Chesterfield was bequeathed to William (by Thomas¹). Publication was prevented by Richard Robinson.

Mary Anne
will and codicil admons
(Sir Thomas Robinson)
19 May 1825.

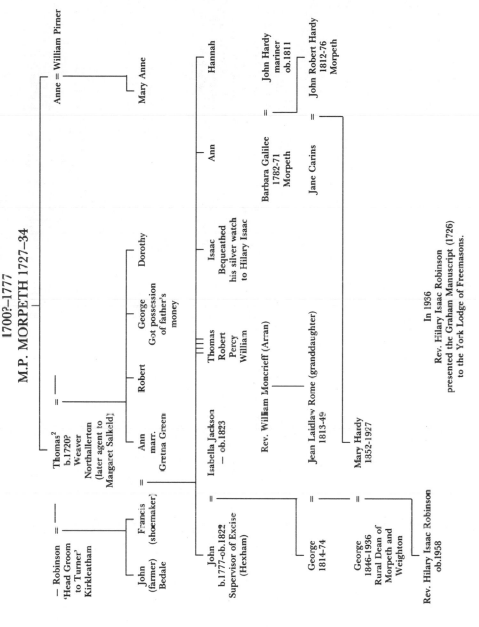

SIR THOMAS ROBINSON[1]
1700?–1777
M.P. MORPETH 1727–34

In 1936
Rev. Hilary Isaac Robinson
presented the Graham Manuscript (1726)
to the York Lodge of Freemasons.

CLOWES
with Byrom connections

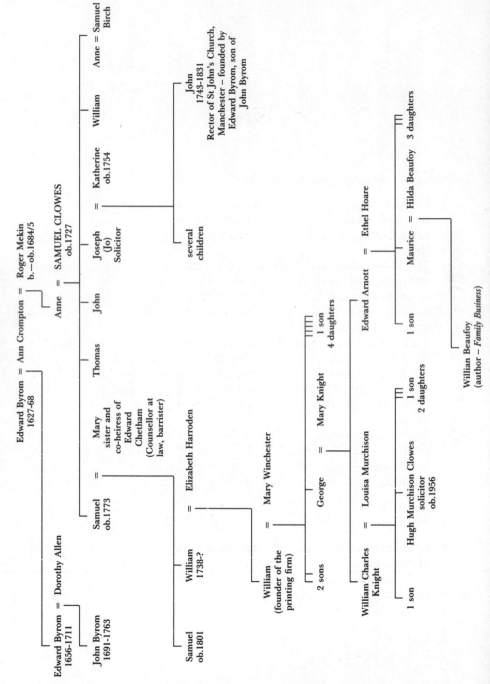

Notes

PREFACE   Unexpected Beginnings

1. Beatrice Stott, 'James Dawson and Thomas Syddall', Manchester, Lancashire and Cheshire Antiquarian Society, Vol.XLVI, 1929, p. 14
2. Sarah Bolger, 'Last Will and Testament', 1889
3. Ibid.
4. This sheet, written on both sides, is the only part of Byrom's Journal transcribed by Sarah Bolger for the 1854 edition known to have survived. While much has been left out at various points on both sides, the published diary shows that the birthday entry in the original shorthand continued beyond this sheet.

   In addition to deliberate omissions, some words have been altered in the published transcript to disguise the editing. For example 'Went to the Royal Society' in the original shorthand becomes 'Thence to the Royal Society'. The use of the word 'thence' indicates that Byrom has been somewhere else beforehand, and that fact has been deliberately left out.
5. *Palatine Note-book*, Manchester, Vol. 3, 1883, pp. 262-3
6. John Houghton, Preface to *Miscellaneous Poems* by John Byrom, Manchester, J. Harrop, Vol. 1, 1773, p.i
7. Eleanora Atherton, 'Last Will and Testament', 1870

CHAPTER ONE   Early Years

1. John Byrom, *The Private Journal and Literary Remains*, Vol. 1, Part 1, Manchester, Chetham Society, 1854, p. 20 – 4 October
2. Ibid., p. 18 – 24 June 1712
3. Ibid., p. 27 – 26 August 1714
4. Ibid., p. 24 – 7 March 1714
5. Ibid., p. 26
6. Ibid., p. 31 – 3 May 1715
7. Ibid., p. 32 – 14 July
8. Ibid., p. 33
9. Ibid., p. 34 – 19 March 1717

10. Ibid., p. 34 – 17 August 1717
11. Ibid., p. 36 – 3 January 1718
12. Ibid., Vol.2, Part 1, p. 259 – 1 August
13. F.A. Bruton, *A Short History of Manchester and Salford*, Manchester, 1924, p. 88
14. *The Remains*, Vol. 1, Part 1, p. 41 – 3 May
15. A.W. Ward, note to 'A Pastoral' in *The Poems of John Byrom*, Vol. 1, Part 1, Manchester, Chetham Society, 1894, p. 1
16. *The Remains*, Vol. 1, Part 1, p. 113 – 10 April

CHAPTER TWO   A Chance Encounter, etc.

1. Daniel Defoe, *A Tour through the Whole Island of Great Britain*, 1724, quoted by B.W. Downs, *Cambridge Past and Present*, London, Methuen, 1926, pp. 21-5
2. Wrongly attributed to John Taylor, referred to by Byrom as 'my shorthand disciple'. See Appendix 1, p. 240.
3. John Byrom, 'Letters to Stansfield', Appendix 1, *The Poems*, Vol. III, Manchester, Chetham Society, 1894, pp. 171-2
4. *The Remains*, Vol. 2, Part 1, pp. 211-12 – 2 February 1739
5. Ibid., Vol. 1, Part 2, p. 356, *circa* 15 May
6. Juvenal, 'Third Satire', translated by N. Rudd, O.U.P., 1991, lines 38-40
7. *The Remains*, Vol. 2, Part 1, p. 133
8. John Michell, *The Dimensions of Paradise*, San Francisco, 1988, p. 37
9. John Yarker, 'Notes on the Temple and Hospital of St John', Masonic paper, Manchester, 1869, p. 12
10. Charles K. Francis, 'Facts regarding Masonic Knighthood', Masonic paper, 1906, p. 1
11. John Nichols, *Rise and Progress of The Gentleman's Magazine*, London, 1821, p. *iii*

CHAPTER THREE   First Years in London

1. Henry Sadler, *Thomas Dunckerley*, London, 1891
2. Appendix 1 to Byrom's poems (1894 edition), Vol. 3
3. Royal Archives Windsor Geo 28, 56
4. E.H.Butler, *The Story of British Shorthand*, London, Pitman, 1951, p. 44.
5. *The Remains*, Vol. 1, Part 1, p. 85 – 15 February
6. Royal Archives Windsor, Add Geo 28, 60
7. Ibid.
8. *The Remains*, Vol. 1, Part 2, p. 436 – 23 March 1730
9. Ibid., Vol. 1, Part 1, p. 43 – 18 February 1720
10. W.H. Thomson, *Byromiana*, Vol. 2 (privately printed), p. 63
11. Elijah Hoole D.D., *Byrom and the Wesleys*, 1864, p. 22

12. Attributed to S.T. Lewis in an unpublished MS note by W.H. Thomson
13. *The Remains*, Vol. 1, Part 1, p. 209 – 24 February 1726
14. New Round Court Rate Books, Westminster City Reference Library, 1721 – p. 26. 1723 – p. 39, 1725 – p. 30
15. *The Remains*, Vol. 1, Part 1, p. 52 – 25 July 1723
16. Ibid., p. 55 – 15 August 1723
17. 'Tunbridgiale', lines 73-80
18. The shorthand symbols are: ⟨symbols⟩ . These stand for C_L_N. The name 'Kitty' (as in 'Upon a Bee Stinging a Lady's Cheek') Byrom writes as ⟨symbol⟩. Kelly would be ⟨symbol⟩ . However, Byrom has added the symbol ⟨symbol⟩ (for the letter 'n') at the end. This can be seen despite an ink-smudge on the MS.
19. *The Remains*, Vol. 1, Part 1, p. 64 – 30 January 1724
20. Ibid., Vol. 1, Part 2, p. 419 – 30 January
21. Ibid., Vol. 2, Part 1, p. 87
22. Ibid., Vol. 1, Part 1, pp. 67-8
23. Ibid., Vol. 1, Part 1, pp. 69-70
24. Reprinted in *The Poems*, Vol. 1, Part 2, 1894, pp. 592 and 601
25. *The Remains*, Vol. 1, Part 1, p. 98
26. Ibid, p. 114
27. Appendix V, *The Poems*, Vol. 2, Part 2, 1895, p. 607
28. *The Remains*, Vol. 1, Part 1, p. 157 – 17 June 1725
29. Ibid., Vol. 2, Part 1, p. 227 – 14 February, 1739

CHAPTER FOUR   Societies and Clubs

1. Royal Society Journal Book, 12 March 1723 (O.S.)
2. *The Remains*, Vol. 1, Part 1, p. 120 – 18 April
3. Ibid., p. 136 – 17 May
4. Ibid., p. 150 – 4 June
5. Ibid., p. 133 – 13 May 1725
6. Ibid., p. 103 – 30 March 1725
7. Bryant Lilywhite, *London Coffee Houses*, Allen and Unwin, 1963, pp. 163-4
8. *The Remains*, Vol. 1, Part 1, p. 90
9. Ibid., Vol. I, Part 2, p. 600 – 30 April
10. Appendix V, *The Poems*, Vol. 2, Part 2, 1895, p. 600
11. *The Remains*, Vol. 1, Part 1, pp. 155-6 – 9 June 1725
12. Nathaniel St Andre, once a dancing master, became anatomist to George I
13. *The Remains*, Vol. 1, Part 1, p. 254
14. Ibid., p. 253 – 18 May 1727
15. Ibid., p. 255 – 18 May 1727
16. Ibid., p. 259 – 20 May 1727
17. Ibid., p. 264

18. Ibid., p. 260
19. A typical code which held Byrom's interest is set out in the Journal on Sunday 27 March 1737 (Vol. 2, Part 1, p. 92)

1	15	4	9		Our	will	art	thy
3	8	14	6		which	be	thy	heaven
2	12	7	10		father	kingdom	hallowed	name
11	5	13	&		thy	in	come	&

The code is based on the Lord's Prayer, each word is given a number, the first word of the prayer being number 1.

20. *The Remains*, Vol. 1, Part 1, p. 252
21. Ibid., p. 261 – *circa* 11 May
22. C.R. Hudleston and R. Boumphrey, *Cumberland Families and Heraldry*, Titus Wilson & Son, Kendal, 1978, p. 292
23. *The Remains*, Vol. 2, Part 1, p. 6 – 9 March
24. Public Record Office, Kew, Adm. 39/352
25. *The Remains*, Vol. 1, Part 1, p. 264 – 12 June 1727
26. Ibid., p. 265
27. Lady Sundon, *Memoirs of the Court and Times of King George II*, Vol. I, London, 1850, p. 30
28. Ibid., p. 14
29. *The Remains*, Vol. 1, Part 1, p. 268 – 2 July 1727
30. Ibid., p. 275 – 30 November 1727
31. Lord John Hervey, *Memoirs of the Court of George II*, ed. J.W. Croker, Vol. 1, London, 1884, p. 60
32. *The Remains*, Vol. 1, Part 1. p. 283 – 21 December 1727

CHAPTER FIVE   Blue Nuns and Jacobites

1. *The Remains*, Vol. 1, Part 1, p. 294 – 13 February 1728
2. Ibid., p. 296 – 29 February 1728
3. Ibid., p. 295 – 22 February 1728
4. Ibid., p. 292 – 27 January 1728
5. Ibid., p. 313 – 4 July 1728
6. 'A Full and True Account of an Horrid and Barbarous Robbery, Committed in Epping Forest upon the Body of the Cambridge Coach. In a letter to M.F. Esq.', *The Poems*, Vol. 1, Part 1, 1894, pp. 62-73
7. *The Remains*, Vol. 1, Part 2, p. 383 – 1 July 1729
8. Ibid., p. 356 – 20 May 1729
9. Ibid., p. 423 – 5 February 1730
10. C.P. Hampson, *The Book of the Radclyffes*, privately printed, Edinburgh, 1940, p. 250
11. In 1725 a bookseller, Whitworth, told Byrom that 'the Duchess of Grafton would subscribe for five books, and Mr Somebody for five more, that she might recommend it, it was because she liked Mr

Byrom's character, he said, not that she had any curiosity for shorthand.' (*The Remains*, Vol. 1, Part 1, p. 105.) Later that year Whitworth
reported to Byrom: 'the Duchess of Grafton had my Tunbridge verses
and liked them very well'. (*The Remains*, Vol. 1, Part 1, p. 122.)

12. *The Remains*, Vol. 1, Part 2, p. 363 – 3 June 1729
13. Ibid., p. 369
14. Ibid., p. 370
15. Information from Librarian of The United Grand Lodge of England
16. *The Palatine Note-book for 1884*, Manchester, p. 77
17. *The Remains*, Vol. 1, Part 2, p. 555
18. Ibid., p. 380 – 28 June 1729
19. Henry Broxap, *A Biography of Thomas Deacon*, Manchester Univer-
    sity Press, 1911, p. 99

CHAPTER SIX   Critical Times

1. *The Remains*, Vol. 1, Part 2, p. 428
2. From Charles Chenevix-Trench, *George II*, Allan Lane, 1973, p. 185
3. *The Remains*, Vol. 1, Part 2, p. 335 – 27 February 1729
4. R. Halsband, *Lord Hervey, Eighteenth Century Courtier*, OUP, 1973,
   p. 222
5. *The Remains*, Vol. 1, Part 1, pp. 112-13 – 10 April 1725
6. Ibid., Vol. 1, Part 2, p. 490 – 13 April 1731
7. Ibid., p. 493
8. 'Lines to Stephen Duck', *Poems*, 1894, p. 218
9. Lord Hervey, *Memoirs*, Vol. 2, 1884, p. 223
10. Ibid., p. 223
11. *The Remains*, Vol. 1, Part 2, p. 518
12. Published as 'Appendix V' to *The Poems*, Vol. 2, Part 2, 1895,
    pp. 582-648
13. *The Remains*, Vol. 1, Part 2, p. 521
14. Ibid., p. 523 – 27 October 1733
15. Ibid., p. 524 – 9 November 1733
16. In 1755, his daughter, Margaret Georgiana, married John Spencer, first
    Earl Spencer, ancestor of the present Princess of Wales
17. Ibid., p. 541 – 28 December 1734
18. Ibid., Vol. 1, Part 1, p. 229 – 4 April 1726
19. Ibid., Vol. 1, Part 2, p. 552

CHAPTER SEVEN   Ward's Drop and Pill

1. *The Remains*, Vol. 1, Part 2, p. 543 – 31 December 1734
2. 'The Drop and Pill of Mr Ward considered by Daniel Turner in an
   Epistle to Dr James Jurin', London, 1735
3. Ibid., p. 13
4. Ibid., p. 32

5. *The Remains*, Vol. 1, Part 2, p. 573
6. Joseph Clutton, 'A True and Candid Relation of the Good and Bad Effects of Joshua Ward's Pill and Drop', London, 1736, p. 24
7. Ibid., pp. 112-13
8. *The Remains*, Vol. 2, Part 1, p. 26
9. Ibid., p. 46 – 20 May
10. Ibid., Vol. 1, Part 2, pp. 328-9 – 18 February
11. Ibid., p. 599 – 29 April 1735
12. Ibid., p. 602 – 3 May 1735
13. Ibid., p. 604 – 4 May 1735
14. Ibid., p. 607 – 10 May
15. Ibid., p. 620
16. Ibid., p. 617
17. Ibid., p. 618
18. Ibid., p. 628 – 15 June 1735
19. Ibid., p. 630 – 19 June 1735
20. Ibid., p. 637 – 1 July 1735

CHAPTER EIGHT   Shorthand and Prince William

1. *The Remains*, Vol. 2, Part 1, p. 5 – 7 March 1736
2. Ibid., pp. 32-3
3. Ibid., p. 23 – 26 March 1736
4. Ibid., p. 45
5. Ibid., Vol. 1, Part 2, p. 605 – 5 May 1735
6. Ibid., Vol. 2, Part 1, pp. 55-6
7. Ibid., p. 57 – 10 July 1736
8. Ibid., p. 84
9. John Campbell, *Lives of the Lord Chancellors*, Vol. IV, 3rd edition, London, 1847, p. 597
10. Lord John Hervey, *Memoirs of the Court of George II*, ed. J.W. Croker, Vol. III, London, 1884, p. 219
11. Ibid., p. 222
12. Ibid., p. 169
13. Ibid., p. 174
14. P.C. Yorke, *Life and Correspondence of Philip Yorke, Earl of Hard-wicke*, p. 178 et seq.
15. *The Remains*, Vol. 2, Part 1, pp. 106-7
16. Ibid., p. 96 – 28 March 1737
17. Ibid., p. 115 – 19 April 1737
18. Ibid., p. 133
19. Ibid., p. 96 – 28 March 1737
20. Ibid., p. 144
21. Ibid., pp. 152-3
22. Ibid., p. 153 – 9 May 1737
23. Ibid., Vol. 1, Part 2, p. 555 – 21 January 1735

24. Ibid., p. 556 – 22 January 1735
25. Moray McLaren, *Bonnie Prince Charlie*, Panther, 1974, p. 122
26. *The Remains*, Vol. 2, Part 1, p. 176 – 17 June 1737
27. Ibid., p. 222 – 13 February 1739

CHAPTER NINE   Caroline – the Power Game Ends

 1. *The Remains*, Vol. 2, Part 1, p. 172 – 11 June 1737
 2. Ibid., pp. 184-6 – 2 September 1737
 3. W. H. Wilkins, *Caroline the Illustrious*, Vol. 1, London, Longmans, 1901, p. 174
 4. Alexander Pope, *The Dunciad*, book 2, line 110
 5. 'To Master Pencenot at Cambridge', lines 5-8
 6. Lord John Hervey, *Memoirs of the Court of George II*, ed. J.W. Croker, Vol. 1, London, 1884, p. 92
 7. Elizabeth Charlotte, Duchess of Orleans, to the Raugravine Louise, quoted in W. H. Wilkins, op. cit.
 8. Lord John Hervey, *Memoirs*, Vol. 1, 1884, pp. 93-4
 9. *The Remains*, Vol. 2, Part 1, p. 52 – 29 May 1736
10. 'To Master Pencenot at Cambridge', lines 22-5
11. *The Remains*, Vol. 2, Part 1, p. 122
12. R. Halsband, *Lord Hervey, Eighteenth Century Courtier*, O.U.P., 1973, p. 215
13. The following account is based on the *Memoirs* of Lord John Hervey, Vol. 3, Chs 38-40
14. Egmont Papers, British Library, Department of Manuscripts, Add. Ms. 47029, Vol. CX
15. *The Remains*, Vol. 2, Part 1, p. 208 – 22 June 1738

CHAPTER TEN   The Stage Empties

 1. *The Remains*, Vol. 2, Part 2, p. 541 – 14 April 1752
 2. Ibid., p. 332 – 22 August
 3. R. Halsband, *Lord Hervey, Eighteenth Century Courtier*, O.U.P., 1973, p. 293
 4. *The Remains*, Vol. 1 Part 2, p. 624 – 14 June 1735
 5. John Ranby, *A Narrative of the Last Illness of the Right Honourable Earl of Orford*, 1745, p. 1
 6. Ibid.
 7. Ibid., p. 11
 8. *The Yale Edition of Horace Walpole's Correspondence*, ed. by W. S. Lewis, W. H. Smith and G. L. Lam, Vol. 19, O.U.P., 1955, p. 24
 9. *The Remains*, Vol. 2, Part 1, p. 244
10. John Rutty, 'An Account of Some New Observations on Joanna Stephens's Medicine for the Stone', 1741/2
11. Ibid.

12. Ibid.
13. James Jurin, Appendix to John Rutty, 'An Account of Some New Observations on Joanna Stephens's Medicine for the Stone', 1741/2
14. John Rutty, op. cit
15. 'The Charge to the Jury or The Sum of the Evidence on The Trial of A.B.C.D. and E.F. All M.D. For the Death of one Robert at Orfud', London, 1745.
16. Ibid.
17. Ibid.
18. *The Remains*, Vol. 1, Part 1, p. 275 – 30 November 1727
19. Horace Walpole, *Memoirs*, Vol. 1, p. 52
20. W. Coxe, *Memoirs of the Life and Administration of Sir Robert Walpole*, Vol. 1, London, 1798, p. 687
21. Ibid.
22. John Rutty, op. cit.

CHAPTER ELEVEN The '45

1. Duke of Cumberland, *Historical Memoirs*, London, 1767, p. 268
2. Sir Oswald Mosley, *Family Memoirs*, privately printed, 1849, pp. 42-3
3. Ibid., p. 45
4. Ibid.
5. This diary is included in full in Byrom's *Remains*, Vol. 2, Part 2
6. *The Remains*, Vol 2, Part 2, p. 389
7. Ibid., p. 393 – 30 November 1745
8. Ibid., p. 394
9. Rupert C. Jarvis, *Collected Papers on the Jacobite Risings*, Manchester University Press, 1972, p. 73
10. Ibid., p. 77
11. Ibid., p. 85
12. Ibid., p. 84
13. *The Remains*, Vol. 2, Part 2, p. 398
14. Ibid. p. 413 – 1 March 1746
15. *The Remains*, Vol. 2, Part 2, pp. 406-7 – 3 January 1746
16. Ibid. p. 413 – 1 March 1746
17. Ibid. pp. 410-11
18. Ibid. pp. 411-14
19. John Harland, 'The Executed Syddalls, Father and Son', *Manchester Collectanea*, Chetham Society, Vol. 68, 1866, p. 220
20. *The Remains*, Vol. 2, Part 2, p. 422 – 17 March 1747/8
21. Ibid., p. 434 – 7 April 1748
22. Ibid., p. 435 – 7 April 1748
23. Ibid., p. 438 – 28 April 1748
24. Ibid., p. 455 – 23 July 1748
25. Ibid., p. 504 – 3 August 1749

26. Ibid., p. 444 – 18 June 1748
27. Ibid., p. 455 – 4 August 1748
28. Ibid., p. 456, included as Editor's Note
29. Beatrice Stott, 'Charles Clement Deacon and William Brettargh', Lancashire and Cheshire Antiquarian Society, Vol. XLI 1924, p. 23
30. *The Remains*, Vol. 2, Part 2, p. 441 – 17 May 1748
31. Ibid., pp. 466-9. This letter from Paris was in Byrom's shorthand.
32. Ibid., p. 486
33. Ibid., p. 487 – 28 February 1748/9
34. Ibid., p. 503 – 31 July 1749

CHAPTER TWELVE   Final Years

1. *The Remains*, Vol. 2, Part 2, p. 510 – 16 August 1750
 2. Ibid., p. 512 – 16 August 1750
 3. 'Warriner's Folly', *The Poems*, Vol. III, 1912, p. 29
 4. *The Remains*, Vol. 2, Part 1, p. 271 – 27 August 1739
 5. Ibid., p. 275 – 28 August 1739
 6. Ibid., p. 279 – 5 September 1739
 7. Ibid., Vol. 1, Part 2, p. 328 – 18 February 1729
 8. Ibid., Vol. 2, Part 2, p. 615 – 25 March 1760
 9. Ibid., Vol. 2, Part 1, p. 196 – 3 March 1737/8
10. Ibid., p. 97 – 28 March 1737
11. Ibid., p. 137 – 2 April 1737
12. Ibid., Vol. 1, Part 2, p. 594 – 26 April 1735
13. Ibid., p. 578
14. Sarah Brearcliffe, unpublished diary, p. 1
15. Ibid., p. 3
16. *The Remains*, Vol. 2, Part 2, p. 654

EPILOGUE   The Enigma Persists

1. Joy Hancox, *The Byrom Collection*, London, Cape, 1992, p. 229
 2. Ibid, pp. 232-5
 3. James Chetham, 'Bill of Complaint', filed in Chancery, 1869
 4. Richard Foster, *Patterns of Thought*, London, Cape, 1991, p. 3
 5. M. Baigent, R. Leigh and H. Lincoln, *The Holy Blood and the Holy Grail*, London, Cape, 1982, pp. 101-2
 6. A leading figure in the dissemination of these ideas was Theodore de Bry (1528-98), goldsmith, engraver and publisher. His publishing enterprise provided the inspiration for many writers and artists, including the Le Blons.
 7. M. Baigent, R. Leigh and H. Lincoln, *The Messianic Legacy*, London, Cape, 1986, p. 219
 8. The Minutes of the Masons' Company, London, June 1853
 9. B.E. Jones, *Freemasons' Guide and Compendium*, London, Harrap, 1956, p. 100
10. See Clowes genealogy, Appendix II

Bibliography

ARTICLES AND ESSAYS

Bailey, J.E., 'John Byrom's Journal, Letters etc. 1730-1731', *Palatine Note-book*, Manchester, 1882

Crofton, Henry T., 'Broughton Topography and Manor Court', Manchester, *Chetham Miscellanies*, New Series, Vol. 2, 1909

Earwaker, J.P., 'Local Gleanings', Manchester, Vol. 1, 1876

Francis, Charles K., 'Facts Regarding Masonic Knighthood', London, 1906

Harland, John, 'The Executed Syddalls, Father and Son', *Manchester Collectanea*, Manchester, Chetham Society, Vol. 68, 1866

Letts, E.F., 'A Palimpsest Brass in Manchester Cathedral', *Palatine Note-book*, Manchester, 1884

Nixon, John A., 'Thomas Dover – Physician and Adventurer', reprinted from *The Bristol Medico-Chirurgical Journal*, March 1909, Bristol, J. Arrowsmith, 1909

Stott, Beatrice, 'Charles Clement Deacon and William Brettargh', Lancashire and Cheshire Antiquarian Society, Manchester, Vol. XLI, 1924

Stott, Beatrice, 'James Dawson and Thomas Syddall', Lancashire and Cheshire Antiquarian Society, Manchester, Vol. XLVI, 1929

Yarker, John, 'Notes on the Temple and Hospital of St John', Masonic paper, Manchester, 1869

BOOKS: PRIMARY SOURCES

Andreae, J. Valentin, *Mathematicum Memoriale*, Tübingen, 1614

Anon., *The Charge to the Jury or The Sum of the Evidence of the Trial of A.B.C.D. and E.F. All M.D. For The Death of one Robert at Orfud*, London, 1745

Anon., *The Session of the Critics*, London, 1737

Anon., *A Treatise Upon The Use and Properties of Quicksilver, By a Gentleman of Trinity College, Cambridge*, London, 1733

Byrom, John, *The Poems*, ed. J. Houghton, Manchester, 1773

Byrom, John, *The Poems*, ed. A.W. Ward, Manchester, Chetham Society, 1894/5 and 1912
—— *The Private Journal and Literary Remains*, Chetham Society, 1854
—— *The Universal Shorthand*, Manchester, Joseph Harrop, 1767
—— *Unpublished MS Notebook of Poems*
—— *A Catalogue of the Library*, Manchester, privately printed, 1848
Clowes, William, *Family Business*, London, Clowes, 1953
Clutton, Joseph, *A True and Candid Relation of the Good and Bad Effects of Joshua Ward's Pill and Drop*, London, 1736
Coxe, W., *Memoirs of the Life and Administration of Sir Robert Walpole*, London, 1798
Cumberland, Duke of, William Augustus, *Historical Memoirs*, London, 1767
—— *Diary of The Blue Nuns*, London, Catholic Record Society Publications, Vol. 8, 1910
Hervey, Lord John, *Memoirs of the Court of George II*, ed. J.W. Croker, 3 vols., London, 1884
Johnstone, Chevalier de, *Memoir of the Forty-Five*, London, Folio Society, 1958
Mosley, Sir Oswald, *Family Memoirs*, privately printed, 1849
Ranby, John, *Narrative of the Last Illness of the Earl of Orford*, London, 1745
Royal Society, *Journal Book* 1723-4
—— *Index to Philosophical Transactions*
Rutty, John, *An Account of Some New Observations on Joanna Stephens's Medicine for the Stone*, London, 1741/2
Sundon, Lady Charlotte, *Memoirs of the Court and Times of King George II*, London, 1850
Turner, Daniel, *The Drop and Pill of Mr Ward considered in an Epistle to Dr James Jurin*, London, 1735
Walpole, Horace, *Correspondence, The Yale Edition*, Vol. 19, O.U.P., 1955
—— *Memoirs of the Reign of King George II*, ed. by Lord Holland, London, 1847

BOOKS: SECONDARY SOURCES

Ashley, Maurice, *England in the Seventeenth Century*, London, Pelican, 1967
Baigent, M., Leigh, R., and Lincoln, H., *The Holy Blood and the Holy Grail*, London, Jonathan Cape, 1982
Baigent, M., Leigh, R., and Lincoln, H., *The Messianic Legacy*, London, Jonathan Cape, 1986
Baigent, M., Leigh, R., and Lincoln, H., *The Temple and the Lodge*, London, Cape, 1989
Baldwin, A.W., *The Macdonald Sisters*, London, Peter Davies, 1960

Broxap, Henry, *A Biography of Thomas Deacon*, Manchester University Press, 1911

Bruton, F.A., *A Short History of Salford*, Manchester, Sherratt and Hughes, 1924

Butler, E.H., *The Story of British Shorthand*, London, Pitman, 1957

Campbell, John, *The Lives of the Lord Chancellors and Keepers of the Great Seal of England from the Earliest Times till the Reign of George IV*, Vol. IV, 3rd edition, London 1847

Carleton, J.D., *Westminster School – A History*, London, Rupert Hart-Davis, 1965

Charteris, Sir Evan, *William Augustus, Duke of Cumberland, His Early Life and Times (1721-1748)*, London, Edward Arnold, 1913

Chevenix-Trench, Charles, *George II*, London, Allan Lane, 1973

Dictionary of National Biography, Oxford, 1917

Doran, John, *Princes of Wales*, London, 1860

Downs, Brian W., *Cambridge Past and Present*, London, Methuen, 1926

Duke, Winifred, *In The Steps of Bonnie Prince Charlie*, London, Rich & Cowan, 1953

Falk, Bernard, *The Royal Fitz Roys*, London, Hutchinson, 1950

Field, John, *The King's Nurseries: The Story of Westminster School*, London, James and James, 1987

Foster, Richard, *Patterns of Thought*, London, Jonathan Cape, 1991

Gould, William (ed), *Lives of the Georgian Age, 1714-1787*, London, Osprey, 1978

Halevi, Z'ev ben Shimon, *kabbalah, Tradition of hidden knowledge*, London, Thames and Hudson, 1979

Halsband, Robert, *Lord Hervey, Eighteenth Century Courtier*, O.U.P., 1973

Hampson, C.P., *The Book of The Radclyffes*, privately printed, Edinburgh University Press, 1940

Hancox, Joy, *The Byrom Collection*, London, Jonathan Cape, 1992

Hatton, Ragnild, *George I, Elector and King*, London, Thames and Hudson, 1978

Huddleston, C.R. and Boumphrey, R., *Cumberland Families and Heraldry*, Kendal, Titus Wilson & Son, 1978

Jarvis, R. C., *Collected Papers on the Jacobite Risings*, Manchester University Press, 1972

Joelson, Annette, *Heirs to the Throne*, London, Heinemann, 1966

Jones, B.E., *Freemasons' Guide and Compendium*, London, Harrap, 1956

Juvenal, *Satires*, translated N. Rudd, O.U.P., 1991

King, Sir Edwin and Luke, Sir Harry, *The Knights of St John in the British Realm*, London, St John's Gate, 1967

Lillien, Otto, *Jacob Christoph Le Blon*, Stuttgart, Hiersemann, 1985

Lilywhite, Bryant, *London Coffee Houses*, London, Allen and Unwin, 1963

Lincoln, Henry, *The Holy Place*, London, Jonathan Cape, 1991

Marple, Morris, *Poor Fred and The Butcher*, London, Michael Joseph, 1970

McLaren, Moray, *Bonnie Prince Charlie*, London, Panther, 1974
Michell, John, *The Dimensions of Paradise*, San Francisco, 1988
Nichols, John, *The Rise and Progress of The Gentleman's Magazine*, London, 1821
Petrie, Sir Charles, *The Jacobite Movement*, London, Eyre and Spottiswoode, 1959
Papus, *The Qabalah*, Wellingborough, The Aquarian Press, 1983
Pine, L.G., *Princes of Wales*, London, Herbert Jenkins, 1959
Ronan, Colin, *Sir Isaac Newton*, London International Profiles, 1969
Sadler, Henry, *Thomas Dunckerley*, London, 1891
Shaw, William A. ed., *Bury Classis Part 2*, Manchester Chetham Society, New Series, Vol. 41, 1898
Shaw, William A. ed., *Manchester Classis Part 3*, Manchester Chetham Society, New Series, Vol. 24, 1891
Talon, Henri, ed., *Selections from the Journals and Papers of John Byrom*, London, Rockliff, 1950
Thomson, W.H., *The Byroms of Manchester*, Vols 1-3, Manchester, privately printed, 1959-1968
Tomasson, Katherine, *The Jacobite General*, London, Blackwood, 1958
White, R.J., *Dr. Bentley – A Study in Academic Scarlet*, London, Eyre and Spottiswoode, 1965
Williams, Penry, *Chetham's Old and New in Harmony*, Manchester University Press, 1986
Yorke, P.C., *Life and Correspondence of Philip Yorke, Earl of Hardwicke*, Cambridge University Press, 1913

MISCELLANEOUS PAPERS

Atherton, Eleanora, Last Will and Testament, 1870
Act of Parliament 1742, concerning Byrom's shorthand
Bolger, Sarah, Last Will and Testament, 1889
Brearcliffe, Sarah, Unpublished diary for 1763
Byrom, John, Unpublished notebooks
Caroline of Anspach, Miscellaneous Letters, Royal Archives, Windsor, Geo. 28
Chetham, James, Bill of Complaint in Chancery, 1869
The Gentleman's Magazine 1731-1745
P.R.O. Kew, Naval Records
Royal Naval Museum Library, Greenwich, Naval Records
Thomson, W.H., Unpublished notes on John Byrom

Index